Samia Khatun is a writer, filmmaker and cultural historian whose documentaries have screened on SBS-TV and ABC-TV. She was born in Dhaka, educated in Sydney, and has held research fellowships in Berlin, Dunedin, New York and Melbourne. She is the Chair of the Centre for Gender Studies at the School of Oriental and African Studies at the University of London. *Australianama* was the winner of the Scholarly Non-Fiction Book of the Year in the 2020 Educational Publishing Awards Australia, and was shortlisted for the Douglas Stewart Prize for Non-Fiction and the NSW Multicultural Award in the 2020 NSW Premier's Literary Awards.

PRAISE FOR *AUSTRALIANAMA*

'By tracking stories from Muslim and Aboriginal sources, by illuminating the lives, literature and mythologies of women, Samia Khatun has created interdisciplinary bridges between Aboriginal history and South Asian history. The result is an original contribution to Australian history writing that recalls the groundbreaking work of Greg Dening.'
Hilary McPhee AO

'By delving deep into the Australian interior, Khatun has brought forth a brilliant postcolonial history for our times. *Australianama* eschews the conventional migrant narrative in favour of a startlingly original perspective on settler colonialism.'
Marilyn Lake, Professorial Fellow in History
University of Melbourne

'A tour de force. Khatun weaves together an extraordinary range of powerful South Asian and Aboriginal narratives from across Australia, showing how stories in colonised tongues can transform our understandings of past and present, and point the way to a more hopeful future.'
Catherine Hall, Emeritus Professor of History
University College London

'A riveting and timely intervention in global feminist and migration histories, *Australianama* is a pioneering excavation of an Australian Aboriginal archive of memory.'
Indrani Chatterjee, Professor of History
University of Texas at Austin

'Every page of this iridescent books shimmers with insight. Exquisitely written and ingeniously crafted by a superb scholar-storyteller, *Australianama* will become a classic.'
Isabel Hofmeyr, Global Distinguished Professor, NYU and Professor of African Literature, University of the Witwatersrand

SAMIA KHATUN

Australianama

The South Asian Odyssey in Australia

UQP

University of Queensland Press
PO Box 6042, St Lucia, Queensland 4067 Australia

uqp.com.au
uqp@uqp.com.au

First published in the United Kingdom in 2018 by C. Hurst & Co. (Publishers) Ltd.
This edition published 2019 by University of Queensland Press
Reprinted 2020

Original design by Rob Pinney; cover photograph of Arabunna Sandhills in South Australia © Richard Wilson, 2010
This edition adapted by Stan Lamond
Author photograph by Jannatul Mawa
Typeset in Perpetua Std
Printed in Australia by McPherson's Printing Group

Epigraph from *Kami*, Ali Cobby Eckermann, © 2010. Used with permission from Ali Cobby Eckermann.

A catalogue record for this book is available from the National Library of Australia.

ISBN 978 0 7022 6262 3 (pbk)
ISBN 978 0 7022 6378 1 (pdf)
ISBN 978 0 7022 6379 8 (epub)
ISBN 978 0 7022 6380 4 (kindle)

University of Queensland Press uses papers that are natural, renewable and recyclable products made from wood grown in well-managed forests and other controlled sources. The logging and manufacturing processes conform to the environmental regulations of the country of origin.

FSC www.fsc.org MIX Paper from responsible sources FSC® C001695

Wild Flowers

Mallets pound fence posts
in tune with the rifles
to mask massacre sites
Cattle will graze
sheep hooves will scatter
children's bones
Wildflowers will not grow
where the bone powder
lies

Ali Cobby Eckermann
Kami, 2010

CONTENTS

NOTE ON TRANSLATIONS AND TRANSLITERATIONS

The primary sources used in this book include texts in South Asian languages and Australian Aboriginal languages, making it difficult to adopt a specific transliteration schema. For the sake of simplicity, diacritical marks have been kept to a minimum. Where a word in another language has entered English usage (for example lascar, Sufi etc.), it is not italicised.

I have reproduced names as they appear in Australian settler sources without 'correcting' the spelling.

Unless otherwise stated, all translations are mine.

LIST OF ILLUSTRATIONS

PROLOGUE

THE MELTING QURAN

In 2008, a story I had lived inside for many years collapsed. That year, I stopped being able to inhabit the contradictions of Western multiculturalism. It was spring. At Liverpool Hospital in Sydney's southwest, in a walled garden at the end of a long corridor, the jacaranda trees were in full, purple bloom. Inside the building, my mother Eshrat was trying to decipher her Quran at a small, white table in her room.

A few weeks earlier, my mother had undergone major surgery for ovarian cancer. Here, with chemotherapy looming, Eshrat was far away from her sisters, cousins and aunts, and was no longer able to create meaning from what was happening to her. She began to see things. During visiting hours, we often walked the perimeters of the garden attached to the mental health ward, arms linked if we weren't bickering. There was a pergola in the centre. As we rested on its benches, she would tell me what she was seeing. Terrifying yet exquisite, her visions were truths amplified.

Inside the ward, when psychiatrists asked my mother questions, her responses in English were cheerfully bland. Everything was fine. She was coping with it all very well, she told them. She insisted that she was remarkably strong. But her visions are only in Bengali, I pleaded with doctors and nurses. Yet hospital staff would not engage an interpreter. She is perfectly capable of speaking English, they informed me. Day after day, I translated Eshrat's escalating delusions to psychiatrists in windowless interview rooms.

PROLOGUE

At first, Eshrat found solace in her Quran. Hers was an edition printed in Dhaka, Bangladesh. The Arabic was accompanied by literal Bengali translations, with an explanatory gloss in Bengali in the margins. It was from these pages that my brother and I had learnt to read *surahs* years ago, fidgeting on the living room carpet of a first-storey apartment in Dhaka. On those evenings, dimly aware of General Ershad's military dictatorship outside, we first imagined ourselves in a different story – one we saw on television, in our schoolbooks, everywhere. 'Will we move to New York, or Sydney?' was the question. Regardless of the answer, the destination point was always the West. We were going to travel from one of the poorest parts of the world to one of the wealthiest. We would be migrants, citizens of the West. As this tale came to structure our entire lives, for over a decade, Eshrat's Quran kept her company at some of the most difficult junctures between Dhaka and Sydney. But that spring, in Liverpool Hospital, she could find neither peace nor meaning in her Quran. When she tried to read, the text melted from the page. Dripping to the ground, the words took the form of the images they named.

After nightfall, when visiting hours had ended and I had driven home, the nurses would lock Eshrat into her shared room. It was a 'safe room' where glass and electrical cords were not allowed. Her roommate was a soldier from the nearby army barracks and artillery range in Holsworthy. She had just returned from Afghanistan. It can't have been an easy time for the white woman confined with my mother. Soldier-woman wore her military uniform all day, every day. It was part of her condition. In her mind, she was perpetually trapped at the battlefront in Afghanistan. During visiting hours, soldier-woman sat inside with her always-uniformed visitors from Holsworthy Barracks. In the garden, Eshrat would tell me that her roommate killed Muslims. It was true. Outside, Australian troops were involved in a war that has killed over one million people in Muslim-majority countries to date.[1] Every day, sometimes sitting in the pergola, at other times circling the perimeter of the garden, my mother insisted to me that soldier-woman was trying to murder her in her sleep. And so, refusing to sleep, Eshrat slipped deeper into another world.

Eshrat and her melting Quran cannot be imprisoned overnight with the soldier killing Afghans at the battlefront, I begged the doctors and nurses. But I could not get anyone at the hospital to see why. On a cloudless afternoon, as the jacarandas shed purple refuse over the footpath that I treaded with my mother, it suddenly became clear: Western states cannot bomb, exploit, drone, invade and kill South Asians *and* have us as part of their citizenry at the same time. The migrant story I had inhabited for much of my life buckled, and eventually collapsed. I had abandoned the commitment to 'Destination: West' that structures how the settler imagines their motion from past to present to future.

Writing that same year from Glasgow, Jamaican-born poet Kei Miller observed that the many people living somewhere on the margins of the West 'become blessed with a kind of double vision.'[2] He wrote, 'you see your life from the inside, and also from the outside … conscious always of the reality of what you are living and the strange narrative of it.' For too many diasporic people – navigating distance from loved ones, the various forms of racism that structure white man's countries, and the everyday stresses of life – this double vision is too much. As Miller points out, the highest incidence of patients suffering from schizophrenia in the United Kingdom has for many years been among migrants from places once colonised by the British Empire.[3] Just as white soldiers are forever imprisoned at the imperial battlefront, the fluorescent halls and walled gardens of Australian mental health units are likewise haunted by non-white people, some once colonised, many still colonised.

Arriving at the institutions of Western nation-states by different trajectories, all their lives veer from scripts of progress from East to West, from the Third World to the First, Aboriginal country to settler nation. What they have in common is that they no longer have narratives to inhabit: no tales that can hold together their experiences of the world, carrying them smoothly from yesterday to today to tomorrow. In that garden where I abandoned the migrant narrative, and where Eshrat and I both lost the stories that we had long used to make sense of the world, there was only one thing that could bring either of us any peace. It was a song. Sitting in the pergola each day as the end of visiting hours drew close, I would sing my mother's favourite song from the handful of Hindustani classical *ragas* I knew – *Vrindavani Sarang*. Its lyrics and melody together tell the tale of Radha relentlessly searching the forest for her lover Krishna, wondering why his flute has fallen silent.

It was during that terrible spring that an image inside an Australian history book caught my attention. The photograph was of a worn, tattered book that remained in one of the nineteenth-century desert mosques in the Australian interior. The image's caption stated that it was a Quran.[4] The words on the book's distant pages were barely perceptible from the picture. Yet, the text looked like it might be in Bengali. Could there be a nineteenth-century Bengali translation of the Quran in desert Australia? In winter 2009, I travelled to the old mosque to find out. What I was seeking was another story to inhabit, another future to look toward. *Australianama* tells the story of that search.

1

THE BOOK OF BOOKS

Some 1,000 kilometres inland from Sydney, over the Blue Mountains, past the trees that drink the tributaries of the Darling River, there stands a little red mosque. It marks where the desert begins. The mosque was built from corrugated iron in around 1887 in the town of Broken Hill. Its green interiors feature simple arabesque and its shelves house stories once precious to people from across the Indian Ocean. Today it is a peaceful place of retreat from the gritty dust storms and brilliant sunlight that assault travellers at this gateway to Australia's deserts.

By a rocky hill that winds had 'polished black', the town of Broken Hill was founded on the country of Wiljakali people.[1] In June 1885, an Aboriginal man whom prospectors called 'Harry' led them to a silver-streaked boulder of ironstone and Europeans declared the discovery of a 'jeweller's shop'.[2] Soon, leading strings of camels, South Asian merchants and drivers began arriving in greater numbers at the silver mines, camel transportation operating as a crucial adjunct to colonial industries throughout Australian deserts. The town grew with the fortunes of the nascent firm Broken Hill Propriety Limited (BHP) – a parent company of the largest mining conglomerate in the world today, BHP-Billiton. As mining firms funnelled lead, iron ore and silver from Wiljakali lands to Indian Ocean ports and British markets, Broken Hill became a busy industrial node in the geography of the British Empire. The numbers of camel merchants and drivers fluctuated with the arrival and departure of goods, and by the turn of the twentieth century an estimated 400 South Asians were living in Broken Hill.[3] They built two mosques. Only one remains.

In the 1960s, long after the end of the era of camel transportation, when members of the Broken Hill Historical Society were restoring the mosque on the corner of William Street and Buck Street, they found a book in the yard, its 'pages blowing in the red dust' in the words of historian Christine Stevens.[4] Dusting the book free of sand, they placed it inside the mosque, labelling it as 'The Holy Koran'. In 1989, Stevens reproduced a photo of the book in her history of the 'Afghan cameldrivers'.

I travelled to Broken Hill in July 2009. As I searched the shelves of the mosque for the book, a winter dust storm was underway outside. Among letters, a peacock feather fan and bottles of scent from Delhi, the large book lay, bearing a handwritten English label: 'The Holy Koran'. Turning the first few pages revealed it was not a Quran, but a 500-page volume of Bengali Sufi poetry. Sitting on the floor, I set out to decipher Bengali characters I had not read for years. The book was titled *Kasasol Ambia* (Stories of the Prophets). Printed in Calcutta, it was a compendium of eight volumes published separately between 1861 and 1895. It was a book of books. Every story began by naming the tempo at which it should be performed, for these poems were written to be sung out loud to audiences.

As I strained to parse unfamiliar Persian, Hindi and Arabic words, woven into a tapestry of nineteenth-century Bengali grammar, I started to visualise Chitpur Road in Calcutta, the main artery of the cheap Bengali print industry where the book was published. There, poets, publishers and compositors were engaged in the process of yoking stories to these eight books, each available for the price of 8 annas.[5] Further into the book, beyond the din of the publishing industry, awaited the imaginative world of the poetry itself.

The first of the book's three poets, Munshi Rezaulla, wrote that his poetry was a translation from Persian and Hindi poetry. The creative process of translation, Rezaulla wrote, was like stepping into a sea of stories, in which he found gem after gem, with which he began to thread together a string of pearls. Over the 500 pages of verse that follow, Adam meets Purusha, Alexander the Great searches for immortal Khidr, and married Zulekha falls hopelessly in love with Yusuf. Its pages stringing together motif after motif from narratives that have long circulated the Indian Ocean, *Kasasol Ambia* described events spanning thousands of years, ending in the sixth year of the Muslim Hijri calendar. Cocooned from the winds raging outside, I realised I was reading a Bengali book of popular history (Fig. 1).

In the time since Broken Hill locals dusted *Kasasol Ambia* of sand in the 1960s, why had four Australian historians mislabelled the book? Why did the history books accompanying South Asian travellers to the West play no role in the histories that are written about them? Moreover, as Christine Stevens writes, the people who built the mosque in North Broken Hill came from 'Afghanistan and North-Western India'.[6] How, then, did a book published in Bengal find its way to an inland Australian mining town?

Captivated by this last enigma, I began looking for clues. First, I turned to the records of the Broken Hill Historical Society. Looking for fragments of Bengali words in archival collections across Australia, I sought glimpses of a traveller who might be able to connect nineteenth-century Calcutta to Broken Hill. As I searched for South Asian characters through a constellation of desert towns and Australian ports once linked by camels, I encountered a vast wealth of non-English-language sources that Australian historians systematically sidestep. A seafarer's travelogue narrated in Urdu in Lahore continues to circulate today in South Asia and in Australia, while Urdu, Persian and Arabic dream texts from across the Indian Ocean left ample traces in Australian newspapers. One of the most surprising discoveries was that the richest accounts of South Asians were in some of the Aboriginal languages spoken in Australian desert parts. In histories that Aboriginal people told in Wangkangurru, Kuyani, Arabunna and Dhirari about the upheaval, violence and new encounters that occurred in the wake of British colonisation, there appear startlingly detailed accounts of South Asians.

Central to the history of encounter between South Asians and Aboriginal people in the era of British colonisation were a number of industries in which non-white labour was central: steam shipping industries, sugar farming, railway construction, pastoral industries, and camel transportation. Camels, in particular, loom large in the history of South Asians in Australia. From the 1860s, camel lines became central to long-distance transportation in Australian desert interiors, colonising many of the long-distance Indigenous trade routes that crisscross Aboriginal land. The animals arrived from British Indian ports accompanied by South Asian camel owners and drivers, who came to be known by the umbrella term of 'Afghans' in settler nomenclature (Fig. 2). The so-called Afghans were so ubiquitous through Australian deserts that when the two ends of the transcontinental north-south railway met in Central Australia in 1929, settlers rejoiced in the arrival of the 'Afghan Express'.[7] Camels remained central to interior transportation until they were replaced by motor transportation from the 1920s. Today the transcontinental railway is still known as 'the Ghan'.

As a circuitry of camel tracks interlocking with shipping lines and railways threaded together Aboriginal lives and families with those of Indian Ocean travellers, people moving through these networks storied their experiences in their own tongues. Foregrounding these fragments in languages other then English, this book tells a history of South Asian diaspora in Australia. I start by reading the copy of *Kasasol Ambia* that remains in Broken Hill, and interpret the many South Asian- and Aboriginal-language stories I encountered during my search for the reader who brought the Bengali book to the Australian interior. Entry points into rich imaginative landscapes, these are stories that ask us to take seriously the epistemologies of people colonised by the British Empire.

This book challenges the suffocating monolingualism of the field of Australian history.[8] I do not argue for the simple inclusion of non-English-language texts into existing Australian national history books, perhaps with updated or extended captions. Instead, I show that non-English-language texts render visible historical storytelling strategies and larger architectures of knowledge that we can use to structure accounts of the past. These have the capacity to radically change the routes readers use to imaginatively travel to the past. Stories in colonised tongues can transform the very grounds from which we view the past, present and future.

Colonial Epistemes and Knowledge Relations

Underlying Australian historians' inattention to sources in non-European languages is an assumption that these texts do not change the larger thrust of history. This is an idea that can be traced to the interconnected rise of nineteenth-century British imperial historiography and Anglicists' views in British India that there was nothing to be learnt from subject peoples.[9] Today, most appearances that non-English-language texts make in Australian history books remain organised around a myth at the foundation of modern Western thought: the claim that the knowledge systems of Europeans are more advanced than the epistemic traditions of the peoples they colonised.

The first writers in English to make this claim about the Australian region were those who navigated the seas on the HMS *Endeavour* to witness the transit of Venus across the southern skies. When this vessel rounded an inhabited coast on 19 April 1770, Captain James Cook wrote in his journal that the British were 'the first who discover'd this Land'.[10] This was a lie. These were lands peopled by many distinct groups, who today are known collectively as the Eora people. By renaming the shore 'New Holland', Cook implied the irrelevance of Eora people's knowledge of coasts they had long cultivated, storied, named, inhabited and built trade networks from. As another correspondent wrote to London, on board the *Endeavour* was a 'fine library of natural history'.[11] It was the tables and classification systems contained in those books rather than Aboriginal knowledge that mediated how colonists viewed the shore they eventually named Botany Bay. To a growing library of European knowledge, they added not just seeds, leaves and the creatures they shot, but also fragments of Aboriginal people's stories, which they categorised as 'customs'.[12] As botanist Joseph Banks wrote, they had not 'understood a word' uttered by the Eora people, whom he described as 'Indians' who were 'black but not negroes'.[13]

While European scientists and anthropologists systematically converted colonised people's knowledges into artefacts, Western historians played a key role in the invention of progress narratives that ordered not just peoples in a racial hierarchy, but also their knowledges. In 1817, when James Mill published the hugely influential *History of British India*, he drew on Scottish Enlightenment theories of stadial progress from barbarism to civilisation to order his account of South Asians. Mill's claim was that there was a single route of progress that all societies must travel, leading to the highest pinnacle of human achievement: Western civilisation. Narrating this drama of progress toward a teleological destination point, he partitioned South Asian pasts into three successive stages: a golden period of ancient Hindu rule, a dark age of medieval Muslim rule, and the enlightened, civilised rule of modern Britain.[14] Significantly, Mill's *History* relied exclusively on European-language accounts of South Asia. 'Required reading' for colonial officials in British India for decades, it set a powerful precedent for subsequent historians' approaches to texts in the languages of colonised peoples across the British Empire.

In the context of competing colonial ideologies in British India, Mill's *History* was written as an Anglicist/utilitarian challenge to the orientalist/Romantic viewpoint of Sir William Jones, an East India Company scholar-administrator who founded the Asiatic Society of Bengal in Calcutta in 1784. In Jones' vision, literacy in South Asian languages was not only imperative for effective strategies of imperial rule, but even further, he saw in the 'wildness and sweetness' of Persian poetry a source of inspiration for the revitalisation of European literature itself.[15] In the Persian-language training manual that Jones wrote to instruct young East India Company officials, he translated an excerpt from the poetry of Hafez Shirazi (d. 1390). Focusing on the poet's metaphor for writing itself, Jones rendered a verse as, 'O Hafiz! when thou composest verses, thou seemest to make a string of pearls.'[16] In an infamous translation in which he likened Hafiz's verse to 'orient pearls at random strung', Jones was celebrating the unfamiliar order of things that structured Persian poetry.[17] Yet, his reading served to lay the template for a long-influential hegemonic story about the incoherence of Perso-Arabic poetic traditions, as Julie Meisami shows. Ultimately, Mill's *History*, stringing together a tale of ancient Hindus, medieval Muslims and enlightened Britons, became the principal text for training colonial officials, replacing the language instruction that eighteenth-century Britons had been inducted into.

Despite differences, what Anglicists and orientalists shared with each other and with the various colonial ideologies across Australasia was their conviction of the superiority of Enlightenment epistemes in producing 'true' statements about the world, however imaginative the knowledges of the colonised might be. It is a belief that still profoundly shapes historians' strategies for narrating the past today. While in Australia the continuing strangulation of non-European-language stories is facilitated by the pervasive linguistic Anglocentrism of historians, the problem cannot be entirely attributed to a lack of language competency. This becomes abundantly clear through an examination of the earliest analysis of *Kasasol Ambia* by a historian writing in English.[18]

In 1864, Rajendralal Mitra reproduced an excerpt from *Kasasol Ambia* in an article published in Calcutta in the *Journal of the Asiatic Society*. The librarian of the Asiatic Society of Bengal, Mitra was a historian of early India and trained as an orientalist scholar of Hindi-Urdu, Bengali, Sanskrit, Arabic, Persian, French, Greek, and Latin, not to mention English (Fig. 3).[19] Tabulating an excerpt of poetry from *Kasasol Ambia*, Mitra categorised each word as either 'Bengali (B)' or 'Foreign (F)'.[20] In classifying words with Sanskrit roots as 'Bengali' and words with Persian and Arabic roots as 'foreign', Mitra partitioned the poetry into 'Hindu' and 'Muslim' elements, inserting the excerpt of *Kasasol Ambia* into a progress narrative about ancient Hindus conquered by Muslim 'foreigners' that can be traced to Mill's *History*.

Mitra's analysis of *Kasasol Ambia* in 1860s Calcutta has a crucial element in common with Australian historians' lack of engagement with the book discovered in Broken Hill – all rob the poetry of the ability to perform its purpose: to imaginatively transport people to the past. These readings, though from different contexts and historical moments, all share the problem of using interpretive techniques born of colonial rule, which operate by transforming the knowledges of the colonised into dead, inert artefacts that have no place in an imagined future.

Central to these problematic reading strategies is what I describe in this book as a 'knowledge relation' – a particular relationship between readers and books, scientists and specimens, historians and archives, and scholars and scholarship. Enlightenment knowledge relations were most spectacularly dramatised by Michel Foucault. In a laboratory lit by a 'glass sun', in Foucault's writing, the modern scientist dissects dead specimens on a 'nickel-plated, rubbery table swathed in white', classifying and naming things in countless workshops, entering data into textual tables to meticulously tabulate disorder into order.[21] By stepping into this knowledge relation to produce modernist truths about Sufi texts, as historian Aditya Behl lamented, too many scholars to this day produce 'yet another object of Indological study analysed into its component parts, in T.S. Eliot's phrase, "like a patient etherised on a table".'[22]

The result is that Mitra's tabulation of *Kasasol Ambia* conveys little about the stories that the poetry itself tells, or about how Sufi discourse worked. Instead it gives us a glimpse of the operating table on which a tale from a British imperial history book met a story from a Bengali history book in 1864, the former enacting a conquest over the latter. Today, Mitra's analysis offers a useful warning. Firstly, despite extensive language skills, interpreting non-English-language stories on the epistemological grounds born of colonial rule can reduce them to dead artefacts. Secondly, by disciplining the stories that South Asians and Aboriginal people told about the past into the overarching historical narratives taken to be true today, we risk obscuring the pathways that colonised peoples from different parts of the British Empire understood themselves to be travelling through time, concealing the 'futures past' that shaped their horizons.[23] If Mitra's reading lays bare the operating tables on which non-English-language history texts die, on what alternative epistemological grounds can we read South Asian- and Aboriginal-language histories circulating across oceans and deserts?

Critiques of colonial epistemes are not new in the field of South Asian historiography. Particularly since the publication of Edward Said's *Orientalism* in 1978, historians have contended with the problem of how else to read texts in South Asian languages without disciplining them into tales of progress, without endlessly reproducing 'transition narratives' plotting the movement through time from tradition to modernity.[24] In dialogue with Hayden White's influential critiques of the genre of modernist history writing, many South Asianists have grappled with the question of the 'truth value' of South Asian historiographical traditions.[25] Most recently, some innovative writers in this voluminous field have highlighted the workings of non-Enlightenment knowledge relations, drawing attention to the ongoing resilience of South Asian epsitemes.[26] This book offers a methodological contribution to these debates through a reading of a particular 1895 edition of *Kasasol Ambia* that remains in an old mosque in arid Australia. I propose that texts belonging to South Asian historiographical traditions are underpinned by, and sometimes theorise, knowledge relations that we can step into today to create true narratives about the past.

Enigmatic Reading

In an exhilarating piece about his translation of a sixteenth-century Sufi text, Aditya Behl describes a methodology of 'reading enigmatically', reflecting on the process of decoding *Mrigavati* (The Magic Doe).[27] *Mrigavati* is a Hindavi story about a prince who sees the fleeting apparition in a forest of a woman disguised as a seven-coloured doe. Falling in love, he follows the spectre deeper into the woods. Behl suggests that rather than approaching stories as dead artefacts, a better hermeneutic method is to treat narratives as if they are sentient beings with the capacity to move from the written page and through audiences, imprinting people's consciousness with images, metaphors and motifs. As he shows, in the context of sixteenth-century Jaunpur, the performance of *Mrigavati* by seasoned, skilled performers pulled audiences into a highly structured knowledge relation to the text, the spectre of the seven-coloured doe sparking interior journeys in the most attentive listeners. Intriguingly, writing from Philadelphia in 2008, he hints that *Mrigavati* continues to have the capacity to 'imprint' contemporary audiences, casting readers within the knowledge relations theorised by the metaphors in the poetry.[28]

From the moment that the image of a Bengali book compelled me to travel to interior Australia, the poetry in *Kasasol Ambia* began scripting me into a knowledge relation that would take me years to understand. Even so, from the very beginning it was clear that succumbing to the text's strange yet familiar logic was an incredibly productive method of doing historical research. The same question that led me to the various South Asian- and Aboriginal-language stories that I read in this book also illuminated the approach I use to interpret their meaning: Who brought the compendium of eight Bengali books to Broken Hill?

The search for that traveller, literate in the difficult language and elusive meanings of the *Kasasol Ambia*'s poetry, saw me go to Kolkata in 2010 hoping to catch glimpses of readers buying books from the Battala neighbourhood, home to cheap print production. The first page of *Kasasol Ambia* features the seal of the book's publisher, Kazi Sofiuddin. In the preface to the volume, the publisher details the addresses where this 1895 edition of the text began its journey to interior Australia, writing that *Kasasol Ambia* was available for sale at Hanifia Press on

'Nimogombhir Lane off Chitpur Road' in the Battala locality. It was also sold on 'no. 1 lane Chandni' where Sofiuddin's family had a bookshop. Over the course of my search for these addresses in Kolkata, it became increasingly clear to me not just how best to read Bengali stories, but also how to approach other non-English-language sources.

On the way to Kolkata, I stopped briefly in Bangladesh. In Dhaka, at her reading/writing/dining table covered in clear laminex, my great-aunt Sanjida Khatun re-taught me the order of Bengali letters, carefully explaining the logic of the alphabet table. While I still knew how to read, I had forgotten the sequence of the letters. A retired professor of Bengali literature and linguistics, my octogenarian great-aunt was thrilled to hear about the book discovered in Broken Hill. She picked up her mobile to make a call. 'Yes, in Australia,' she confirmed. 'Yes, in a desert mosque!' A fan overhead made the papers on her table dance under glass paperweights, as she said into the phone, 'We will need a copy of Hilali's *Perso-Arabic Elements in Bengali* before she leaves for Kolkata.' The next day, my great-aunt's former students Ovee and Jhumur Chowdhury arrived with the requested book. Jhumur was a singer and Ovee, a poet. They insisted we exchange phone numbers in case I should need any more books from Dhaka.

A few weeks later, I was in Kolkata and filling in a membership form at the library of Jadavpur University, tightly clutching my *Samsad Bengali-English Dictionary* under my arm. I had carefully pasted the alphabet table into its inside cover in anticipation of the difficult books I would encounter. The order of the letters, my great-aunt had impressed on me, is key – the relationships between Bengali characters underpins the logic behind the spelling of words and can unlock book indices, library catalogues and dictionaries. Despite all best-laid plans, the library staff confiscated my dictionary at the entrance. With no intended irony, a sign on the bench informed patrons that 'books are not allowed in the library'.

Finding the wooden card catalogue of Bengali books, I stood paralysed for a while, straining to remember the alphabet. Pulling out a drawer of cards marked 'ব' for 'Battala', I wondered how I would locate the next letter, 'ট'. Suddenly the answer was glaringly obvious. The façade of the card catalogue itself was an alphabet table; the matrix of Bengali characters is in fact hard to 'lose'. I ordered the first book with

'Battala' in its title, and before long the linguist Sukumar Sen's history of the nineteenth-century Bengali book industry arrived in my hands.[29] I thumbed through its pages with little hope of understanding the formal prose, enjoying the exhilaration of reading without a dictionary, when suddenly the name 'Kazi Sofiuddin' jumped out from the book.

Page 109. According to Sen, publisher Kazi Sofiuddin was one of the most successful entrepreneurs in the Battala book industry, and *Kasasol Ambia* was his magnum opus. Sofiuddin had commissioned poets to translate the Persian stories of the prophets, publishing book after book over many years. When he died after the publication of the fifth book of *Kasasol Ambia*, his son Kazi Shahabhik continued where Sofiuddin had left off.

Surely, reading in the privacy of my apartment accompanied by many dictionaries, I could come to know much more about Kazi Sofiuddin's *Kasasol Ambia*, perhaps even catch sight of the readers purchasing copies of it from Nimogombhir Lane in Battala. Hoping to buy a copy of the latest 2008 edition of Sen's book, I followed a friend's directions to Lokenath's Paper House nearby – a bookshop behind the 8B bus station in Jadavpur. There, hearing me order a history book on Battala, a man loitering on the steps cryptically said to me, '*Robbar Pratidin*.' I ignored him. He kept repeating in Bengali, louder each time, 'Sunday everyday (*Robbar Pratidin*), that's where you need to go,' obscurely insisting, 'there you will find whatever it is you are looking for.' Again, I pretended not to hear him. The bookseller behind the counter was carefully writing down the details of my requested title. Occupying myself with the order of the Bengali alphabet, I wondered if his name was Lokenath, beginning with 'ল'.

Three days later the book arrived at Lokenath's. I was on an autorickshaw on my way to pick it up when my phone rang. It was Ovee Chowdhury calling from Dhaka. His first book of poetry had just been published in Kolkata. It would take a long time to ship copies across the border to Bangladesh and the first-time author was aching to hold his book sooner. 'Could you please get some copies from the publisher and bring them to Dhaka on your next visit?' he asked. I agreed.

The books would need to be picked up from an address in Chandni Chowk, beginning with 'চ'. I scrawled the name on my palm. Changing autos, I set off to collect fifty copies of Ovee's book. Yes, it was a diversion from my search for nineteenth-century Bengali poetry, but this was his first book, after all. Following Ovee's directions, I caught the metro to the northern part of the city. The stairs out of Chandni Chowk metro station led me up to one of the busiest commercial districts of Kolkata.

The address Ovee had given me was for the offices of the daily Bengali newspaper *Pratidin*. From there a newspaper editor ran a small press publishing Bengali poetry. Ordering me a cup of tea, Ovee's publisher dispatched an assistant to get the books headed to Dhaka. While I waited, I chatted with Anindya Chatterjee, editor of the weekend magazine issued with the Sunday edition of *Pratidin*. I was flicking through the latest issue of *Robbar*, the slim, glossy magazine that Anindya had handed me, when suddenly, 'Kazi Sofiuddin' again jumped out from the text.

Page 13. According to an article printed the previous Sunday, Kazi Sofiuddin was from the village of Bandpur in the district of Hugli – long a centre of cultural production in Bengal.[30] Engaging poets to translate not just Persian and Urdu books into Bengali verse, Sofiuddin had commissioned Bengali translations of the *Mahabharata*, *Ramayana* and various other titles that trace a genealogy to Sanskrit literature. The article reproduced an excerpt of a poem Sofiuddin had written over 150 years ago, in which he told readers about his father Kazi Jeleruddin, who followed the *bhakti* movement, and his grandfather Kazi Amirulla, a judge presiding over twelve districts in Hugli. While Sofiuddin's forefathers had lived in a village in Hugli, the publishing business had seen him move to Calcutta. In 1855, he wrote, 'my address is at Chandni Chowk'. I was at that moment discovering his story at the very same address in 2010.

The author of the article, which appeared in the Sunday (*Robbar*) supplement to the daily newspaper *Pratidin*, was historian Gautam Bhadra, a charismatic teacher well known to generations of students in Kolkata. When I tracked down his phone number, barely audible over a crackling phone line, Gautam Bhadra told me to meet him in the foyer of the National Library of India at 3.00 p.m. the following Tuesday.[31] There was no direct bus route from the 8B bus depot in Jadavpur to the National Library, so I caught a bus heading in the direction of Belvedere Estate, Alipore Road – an estate whose grand 30-acre grounds, built during the British colonial era, housed not only the National Library but also what was once Government House.

It was there that Thomas Macaulay, liberal reformer and later popular historian, drafted and delivered his 'Minute of Education' in February 1835 to the governor-general of India, marking an Anglicist turning point in British colonial ideology. In his minute, Macaulay vehemently opposed the use of British revenue to train British colonial officials and 'natives' alike in South Asian languages. He infamously declared that 'a single shelf of a good European library was worth the whole native literature of India and Arabia'.[32] English, he prophesied, was not only 'likely to become the language of commerce throughout the seas of the East', but its influence would also grow alongside British power across the Indian Ocean, as it was 'the language of two great European communities which are rising, the one in the south of Africa, the other in Australia.'[33] Exposure to English-language books, Macaulay proposed, was central to the project of cultivating 'a class who may be interpreters between us and the millions whom we govern, a class of persons Indian in blood and colour, but English in tastes, in opinions, in morals and intellect.'[34]

Within three months of Macaulay's minute, English was made the official language of education funded by colonial resources, displacing an earlier orientalist ideology that had cultivated Persian as the language of British colonial administration. It marked a key moment in the institution of English as a South Asian language, and a shift in colonial ideology that left profound legacies. Explicitly yoking English literacy to a project of cultural assimilation, the education reforms that followed created the infrastructure of schools and universities that inducted generations of the most powerful South Asians into progress narratives mapping routes to Western civilisation.

Many years later, trying to find Belvedere Estate, I alighted at a bus stop from where I hoped to walk to the National Library, once known as the colonial library. Hopelessly lost, I tried to read unknown streets for recognisable signs, as 3.00 p.m. came and went. Eventually defeated, I caught another bus to Esplanade metro station, relieved that at least I would be able to find my way back to my apartment.

It was weeks before I summoned up the courage to call on Gautam Bhadra again. This time I made it to the National Library by taxi. When

I told him the tale of the Broken Hill book, it calmed his irritation at me – at first. 'That book you found is likely a Bengali translation of the Persian and Urdu *qissa* literary genre,' he informed me. 'Have you read the whole book?,' he asked. I had not. 'Why not? Why haven't you read it?' I did not want to admit that the language was very difficult for me to understand. I kept quiet as his voice grew louder with each question. 'Is it because you think you know more then the writers of the book?' Raising one arm in the air, he switched from Bengali to English to ensure that I would understand him, bellowing, 'Do you even know what a *qissa* is?' I did not. 'You seculars …' he boomed, his voice echoing across the library foyer, 'are ruining history!'

I left the National Library with a list of books that he had ordered I read before returning to see him. Recovering under the fan at home, I looked up '*qissa*' in my many dictionaries. It was a Persian word with an Arabic root that had entered not only Bengali, but many South Asian languages. A word beginning with 'ক', the first letter of the alphabet, a *qissa*, at its simplest, is a 'story'.[35]

The story is the deceptively simple common entity that underpins all the non-English-language sources I read in this book. It was while navigating the streets and archives of Kolkata, searching for glimpses of the premises where *Kasasol Ambia* was sold, that I first happened upon a reading strategy that can animate stories embedded within non-European epistemes. As I became aware in Kolkata, stories can, and frequently do, behave according to logics quite apart from Western reason. As the spectre of nineteenth-century publisher Kazi Sofiuddin led me from card catalogues to books to magazines, from library to library to newspaper offices, it was as if sentient Bengali characters were signposting a research pathway 'beyond the sterile contrasting of "rational" and "irrational"', as historian Carlo Ginzburg put it.[36]

Like *Kasasol Ambia*, all the South Asian- and Aboriginal-language stories I read in this book have encoded within them an order of things – a conceptual grid that we can use to interpret them, a narrative logic according to which they unfold. I do not discipline accounts of South Asians into larger English-language historical narratives of colony, empire and nation. Instead, while drawing on a wide range of archival materials, including settler records in English, I use the storytelling strategies and interpretive keys contained in non-English-language texts to order and organise a history of South Asian diaspora.

Ginzburg uses that 'tricky word, intuition' to reflect on 'the instantaneous running through of the thought processes' in his extraordinary history of reading clues.[37] As he points out, 'the capacity to leap from the known to the unknown by inference (on the basis of clues)' was a science densely theorised in Arabic and Persian physiognomy using the vocabulary of Sufi philosophy.[38] Suggesting that these were modes of thought that were part of the heritage of late-nineteenth-century Bengal, Ginzburg gestures at the various other interpretive methodologies circulating the Indian Ocean world alongside British colonial knowledges.[39] In this book, I take the cue from Ginzburg's use of non-European reading techniques to construct historical methodologies. What he calls intuition, I approach as 'subjugated knowledges' – the set of knowledges disqualified from the late eighteenth century by modern European institutions as 'beneath the required level of cognition or scientificity'.[40] Situating colonised people's texts within architectures of 'subjugated knowledges' reveals the epistemological terrains on which past South Asians stood across the Indian Ocean rim.

Connecting Histories

In following South Asians across a vast ocean and into Australian deserts densely storied by Aboriginal people, this book invites readers to travel across disciplinary boundaries, connecting debates in South Asian historiography and Indigenous history. In doing so, I contribute to a new scholarship on migration that has emerged in the last two decades in 'a post-9/11 environment of increased surveillance, detention and deportation'.[41] These writers have observed that in the era since the attacks of 11 September 2001, working-class South Asians or those of Muslim heritage have been demonised in the US precisely while elite South Asians, particularly those belonging to wealthy business communities, have been held up as 'model citizens.' As historian Vivek Bald has pointed out, this binary of the 'model minority' versus the 'undesirable other' has long structured 'American Orientalism,' profoundly shaping histories of South Asian migrants.[42]

In the Australian context, as the imprisonment and torture of the refugees known as 'boat people' in settler discourse have established the Australian nation-state as the architect of one of the most racist border regimes in the contemporary world, histories of South Asian migrants have increasingly been structured around the question: 'Are they Pioneers or Aliens?'[43] As historian Hsu-Ming Teo has pointed out, the 'problem' is that insisting that past Asian travellers were 'pioneers' who helped build the Australian nation inserts non-white migrants into settler narratives celebrating the usurpation of Aboriginal land.[44] The deeper architecture of colonial thought that belies this problem becomes apparent if we examine the distinct 'imaginative geographies', to use Edward Said's phrase, which framed British settlers' accounts of South Asians and Aboriginal peoples – colonised peoples from different parts of Anglo imperial terrain. Settlers' knowledge production about South Asians was underpinned by the imaginative geography of 'the orient' versus 'the occident' and the ongoing process of enacting a border between these mutually constituted categories. In addition, imagining a cluster of British colonies at the southwestern rim of the Indian Ocean as part of 'the occident' or 'the West' relied on the ongoing active production of Aboriginal lands as 'blank spaces'.

By the close of the nineteenth century, Australian governments introduced 'state-based instruments of surveillance, the census, the passport and the literacy test' in response to the increasing arrival of non-white populations.[45] The drawing of a 'global colour line' through the Australian region culminated on 1 January 1901 in the federation of six separate British colonies into Australia, creating a white nation that excluded from citizenship both 'Asiatics' and 'Aborigines'. As tightening race-based border regimes inaugurated the era of 'White Australia', the oceanic traffic in camels and drivers from South Asia was brought to a halt, but the camel industry continued to flourish in Australian desert parts. In comparison to the various measures of racial exclusion that South Asians were subjected to in 'White Australia', settler persecution of Aboriginal people was far more violent. In the twentieth century, one particularly brutal set of settler regimes that sought to realise the settler fantasies of empty lands was the systematic removal of Aboriginal children from their families, for their intended 'absorption' into white working-class Australia. The legacies of the violent rupture of the intimate relationships so central to knowledge transmission – between grandmothers and grandsons, mothers and daughters – profoundly shape Aboriginal lives today.[46]

Despite comprising two very different regimes of British rule, what the imaginative geographies of 'blank space' and 'the orient' shared was that both were structured by progress narratives destined toward Western civilisation. As historians have shown, by the late nineteenth century, the racial hierarchies of stadial thinking that plotted schemas of movement from savage to civilised, east to west, came to be reconfigured as questions of inclusion/exclusion at the national boundary: Were the 'Asiatics' savage or civilised? Could 'Aborigines' be inside the nation or should they be outside the nation? Would non-white peoples be part of the future, or should they be relegated to the past?

A focus on the knowledge traditions of the colonised offers a productive starting point for generating new research questions. In contributing to a new scholarship that examines 'migration through larger histories of imperialism and neoliberalism',[47] I argue for a closer focus on the texts, stories and knowledges that moved with people – the narratives which 'cannot be accommodated within the stern pages of History', as Shahid Amin put it.[48] For the repeated careless mislabelling of *Kasasol Ambia* by Australian historians offers us an invaluable clue: insertions of South Asians into the interlocking narratives of Anglo imperialism and nationalism are premised on the erasure of non-European knowledges.

While South Asian elites were (unequal) co-producers of orientalist knowledges and racial hierarchies in British India and beyond, Aboriginal people in the Australian context were not incorporated into colonial bureaucracies to a comparable extent.[49] Just as the Wiljakali man, Harry, led Europeans to the silver in Broken Hill, Aboriginal people and their knowledges were always central to colonial projects as evidenced by the enigmatic figure of 'the tracker' in Australian cultural production.[50] Yet, settlers in colonial Australia did not construct the institutional infrastructures for training in colonised languages that were established in South Asia. Nor was the university in colonial Australia central to Anglicist strategies for cultural assimilation, unlike in British India. While the establishment of the first university in the Australian colonies in 1857 was undoubtedly an important moment in the epistemic invasion of Aboriginal lands, it was not until 1966 that the first Aboriginal student graduated with a degree from an Australian university – Charles Perkins, an Arrernte man born in Alice Springs.

In the decades that followed, a new generation of Australian history students influenced by the methodologies of 'history from below' began encountering Aboriginal activists, sometimes in university classrooms, more often within union and land rights movements.[51] It is from these encounters that the field of Aboriginal history emerged in the early 1980s. The crucial interventions that writers of Aboriginal history made into Australian historiography were underpinned by the research methodology that Marx called praxis: knowledge produced in the process of settlers and Aboriginal people articulating joint political projects and imagining shared futures. One of the central insights about knowledge-power generated by the first generation of writers in this field was that clear, accessible prose was pivotal to the practice of Aboriginal history. For it is essential that Aboriginal people, now and in the future, are able to access material that is written about their families and pasts – without having a university degree. Another insight from the field of Aboriginal history that I draw upon in this book is that non-Aboriginal historians, always complicit in the ongoing settler occupation of Aboriginal lands, must make visible the dynamics of research encounters between university-based scholars and Aboriginal people, as part of a process of interrogating the conditions of knowledge production.

A decade after Aboriginal history was established as a field in Australian universities, the 1992 Mabo judgement in the High Court of Australia inaugurated legal recognition of Aboriginal relationships with land prior to British colonisation, challenging the fiction of 'blank spaces'. With legal professionals formulating 'native title' as a framework for viewing these stakes and claims to country as a kind of property relations, there emerged an entire scholarly apparatus involving historians, linguists and anthropologists for determining precisely which Aboriginal families were the 'traditional owners' of which lands. It inaugurated a new era of fraught relationships between many Aboriginal families and university-accredited researchers.

Within this context, the Aboriginal English term 'country' is a dense place word that has itself become a site of epistemic struggle. As anti-nuclear activist and Arabunna poet Kevin Buzzacott wrote in 1998 in response to scholarly attempts to define 'country', 'anthropologists and all that mob – they're trying to tell us who we are, and what we are and what we think. I'm saying, "No you can't tell us that." ... we *know* the country.'[52] As Deborah Bird Rose pointed out, the ongoing epistemic struggle between university researchers and Aboriginal people is shaped by the reality that 'anything that is written in Australia today that says anything about Aboriginal people has the potential to end up in court as part of a native title case'.[53]

The Dhirari, Dieri, Wangkangurru, Kuyani and Arabunna texts that I use in this book are deeply implicated in these complex politics. I speak none of these Aboriginal languages. Nor do Aboriginal knowledges form part of the repertoire of inherited knowledges that I draw on in my reading of South Asian-language texts. Instead, my entry point into reading Aboriginal texts comprised the invaluable political education I received in Aboriginal communities throughout New South Wales during the anti-racism activism so formative to my history education.[54] At a practical level, it was through these student activist networks that I began contacting the families of some of the storytellers whose Aboriginal-language narratives I encountered in print form as I trawled archives in search of glimpses of a copy of *Kasasol Ambia*. So, knowing very little about Aboriginal languages, I wrote to poet and activist Kevin Buzzacott: Could I come and talk to his family about the Arabunna-language stories about South Asians?[55]

Over the last decades, through engagement with Aboriginal articulations of and political struggles for 'country', a body of place-oriented writing has emerged as one of the methodological innovations in the field of Aboriginal history.[56] 'Place-oriented research', as Deborah Bird Rose describes it, is a call 'for writing that seeks to do justice, ethically and methodologically, to the richness of time, human endeavour, and the multiplicities of living things whose tracks cross a given place.'[57]

Using these strategies to narrate encounters between South Asians and Aboriginal peoples throughout this book, I develop techniques for writing histories of migration that refuse to participate in the ongoing discursive erasure of Aboriginal peoples and their geographical imaginations – an erasure that is foundational to settler mentality. I show that travellers who arrived from across the Indian Ocean on Aboriginal geography always stood at the conjuncture of many knowledge traditions; whether those South Asians really saw Aboriginal peoples and histories or not is of course another question. Drawing on the conventions and insights in the field of Aboriginal history, this book adds to the much longer history of Aboriginal encounters with peoples from across the Indian Ocean.

Australia in the Indian Ocean

Arriving each year with sailing craft propelled by monsoon winds, stories about the prophets of Islam travelled to the Australian mainland long before European colonisers did. With Aboriginal seafarers threading the northern coasts of Australia into vast trading networks, stories, goods and words from across the Indian Ocean today remain embedded in Aboriginal geographies throughout Australia. Today, in north-eastern Australia, *rupiah* remains the word for 'money' in Aboriginal languages spoken around Arnhem Land. That a word in Yolngu-Matha languages can be traced to the '*rupiah*' in circulation in the islands of Indonesia, to South Asia where the '*rupiya*' was introduced as currency during the rule of Afghan sovereign Sher Shah Suri (d. 1545) hints at the larger histories of ongoing connections across an ocean densely storied in non-European languages.[58]

The Indian Ocean is increasingly imagined as a 'liquid continent' in English-language scholarship. With fiction writers such as Amitav Ghosh illuminating the human dramas that have long unfolded here, a body of lyrical writing has been produced by a growing number of humanities scholars who have imaged the Indian Ocean as 'a theoretical terrain, a geographical space and a historical network of human connectedness'.[59] This recent focus in English-language public spheres on non-white mobility across this region has flourished precisely as the 'Five Eyes' intergovernmental surveillance alliance between the US, Britain, Canada, New Zealand and Australia has transformed the Indian Ocean into 'the new cartography of imperial power'.[60] In narrating histories of the Australia–South Asia axis of oceanic circulation, my intervention into Indian Ocean studies puts debates about knowledge-power into direct conversation with a burgeoning field.

Following the establishment of Botany Bay, the Indian Ocean began to be mapped from Australian colonial settlements as a terrain of competing European empires. Sketching the region from British India to the Australian colonies in 1845, Thomas Mitchell, the surveyor general of the British colony of New South Wales, mapped this slice of the Indian Ocean as 'The Indian Archipelago' (Fig. 4). A phrase at the time describing the chain of over 12,000 islands under Dutch imperial control, Mitchell's reimagining of the 'Indian Archipelago' was a strategic statement about the role of the Australian colonies in British imperial penetration into Dutch territory.[61]

With Australia long operating as a strategic base for Anglo empires in the Indian Ocean region, today there are over fifteen joint Australia–US military bases on Australian soil and waters.[62] Following the dissolution of the USSR, the gaze of imperial surveillance has shifted away from Russia and toward 'Muslim-majority' countries. Today, intelligence infrastructure in Australia is key to imperial surveillance of the Indian Ocean world, driving covert US drone strikes in South Asia and elsewhere.[63] Alongside Australian government support for US-led military operations in Yemen, Syria, Afghanistan, Iraq, Somalia and Pakistan, a global Islamophobia industry has produced 'Islam versus the West' as a new binary replacing the Cold War dichotomy in the English-speaking world. These were the larger geopolitics that played out so grotesquely night after night in a hospital ward in South Western Sydney, in the encounter between my mother and the returned soldier from Afghanistan, making visible the paradoxes of liberal multiculturalism.

Keeping in view the infrastructure of successive Anglo imperial regimes that have imaged this vast water body, I treat the Indian Ocean as a site of epistemic struggle. Seeking an out from the progress narratives oriented to 'Destination: West' that failed both those women imprisoned at Liverpool Hospital in spring 2008, I approach the Indian Ocean as something akin to an immense reservoir of knowledges. As Said wrote many years ago, 'perhaps the most important task of all is to ask how one can study other cultures and peoples' from a 'nonrepressive and nonmanipulative' perspective[64] – an undertaking that has only grown in urgency as war after war has been launched across the realm of the Indian Ocean. However, as Said warned, such a task would require us to 'rethink the whole complex problem of knowledge and power'.[65] I demonstrate that the stories long circulating the Indian

Ocean according to the logics of non-Enlightenment philosophies offer us powerful tools with which to rethink precisely this problem. After all, as a certain song about Radha's search for Krishna's flute suggested during the terrible Sydney spring of 2008, at the junctures where colonial modernist narratives fail us, stories belonging to other epistemes can help make sense of the world.

History and Subjectivity

With triumphant tales of the superiority of Western civilisation long buttressing Anglo imperial aggression and colonial regimes across the Indian Ocean, since the nineteenth century historians have been key architects of the narrative that the Western nation comprises the most advanced form of human community. This is a story inextricable from tales of the superiority of Western man, as the writings of Thomas Macaulay highlight. Having set in motion education reforms in British India that refashioned elite South Asians in the image of Englishmen, Macaulay returned from Calcutta to London to write his five-volume *History of England* – one of the most popular texts to shape British historical imagination at a critical moment of nation building. As Catherine Hall writes, Macaulay's *History* narrated a drama of past actors marching through time from barbarism to civilisation toward 'the multiethnic nation named England, an example of the route to modernity, laying out a path which others could follow'.[66] Inviting English-reading publics to script themselves into a particular template of progress through time that leads to the Western nation, as Hall argues, 'Macaulay was engaged in the making of a liberal subject – more especially a white liberal subject'.

Historical storytelling has of course long oriented readers toward imagined futures across the left–right political spectrum. It is precisely this insight that gave rise to various forms of 'history from below' – a series of 'historiographical rebellions' first inspired by Marxist critiques of liberal progress.[67] The hope that history books can induct readers into revolutionary subjectivities was most memorably dramatised in the work of historian of the Caribbean Cyril Lionel Robert James. Narrating a history of the Haitian Revolution, James' *The Black Jacobins* is a foundational text in both anti-colonial and Marxist historiography.

The protagonist is the slave Toussaint L'Ouverture (d. 1803). Early in the narrative, enslaved L'Ouverture encounters a history book in the library of his master – a French colonist who owns a sugar plantation on the Caribbean island of San Domingo, today known as Haiti. L'Ouverture pores over the French Enlightenment text, returning again and again to a particular passage that claims, 'Only a courageous chief is wanted. Where is he?'[68] Ultimately scripting himself into this role, L'Ouverture leads rebelling slaves to revolution in James' account, dramatising the role that history books can play in altering pathways to the future. However, is it only history books encountered in colonisers' libraries that can illuminate strategies for challenging imperial regimes? Were there really no other knowledge traditions outside Enlightenment epistemes in which people critiqued power?

As David Scott wrote, *The Black Jacobins* was first penned in the context of twentieth-century anticipation of African and Caribbean emancipation from European colonialism. In narrating the history of black anti-colonial movements, James sought to orient readers toward new revolutionary post-colonial nations.[69] However as Scott points out, unlike the political context that James was writing from, in the twenty-first century 'nation and socialism do not name visionary horizons of new beginnings any of us can look toward as though they were fresh thresholds of aspiration'.[70] Many writers grappling with the failures of post-colonial nation building share Scott's lament for the loss of 'utopian hopes for a possible alternative future'.[71]

Aboriginal writers producing scholarship from sites that are unambiguously still colonised offer another outlook. As Amangu historian Crystal McKinnon wrote from Australia in 2010, 'the struggle for Indigenous rights is unrelenting within the structures and spaces of settler colonialism'.[72] McKinnon's work anticipates the future as perpetual struggle, subtly shifting the focus to the route forward rather than a concrete, utopian destination point. From this standpoint, her history of Aboriginal music, echoing one purpose of the music itself, is produced to ensure that communities can keep 'fighting not to win, but to fight again'.[73]

Turning toward futures of perpetual struggle, history books from the libraries of the colonised raise important questions at our contemporary moment of escalating racism. It is a juncture where coherent alternatives to global capitalism are not yet apparent, where models challenging the modern nation-state remain elusive. But while visionary horizons of new beginnings are not yet visible, nor are they foreclosed. Might it be possible to situate new critiques of power in non-European epistemes? Is progress really the only narrative that can offer us hope for more just futures? Given that reducing vast libraries of non-European knowledges to dead objects was central to European imperial projects, I propose that books in those libraries contain valuable strategies for connecting past, present and future that render visible alternative axes along which we might glimpse new beginnings.

Structure of the Book

Over four centuries after Hafez Shirazi compared writing poetry to threading pearls in his poem '*Turk e Shirazi*', Munshi Rezaulla drew on this recurring motif in Arabic and Persian poetry in his description of the process of writing the *Kasasol Ambia*. Stepping into a sea and 'searching for pearls', Rezaulla wrote, 'I began threading a chain.' Reading Rezaulla's metaphor closely in Chapter 2, I argue that it theorised a knowledge relation that is quite different to Enlightenment strategies of reading texts, one that historians today can use as a research methodology to investigate the past.

Reading a seafarer's travelogue, in Chapter 3 I narrate seven of Khawajah Muhammad Bux's voyages. Beginning his life as a lascar at the bottom of the racial hierarchy of a British ship, Bux was a wealthy merchant by the end of his days in 1920s Lahore. He recounted a lengthy family history to his scribe that continues to circulate between South Asia and Australia, published most recently in Urdu as *Lahore Ka Sindbad* (Sindbad of Lahore), and as 'Memoirs of Khawajah Muhammad Bux' in English. I examine the path the text lays out for future generations of Indian Ocean travellers.

Turning from oceans to deserts, in Chapter 4 I follow the trail that the very first South Asian camel drivers traced inland to Beltana – a hilly region in Kuyani lands where the first Australian camel depot was established. Telling the history of the settlers and the Aboriginal groups who gathered in Beltana in the evening in 1885 when the very first steam train was due, I piece together the contours of the contested epistemic terrain onto which South Asians led the earliest camels.

Moving from the 'Dreaming' stories that structure Aboriginal geographies to Muslim practices of dream interpretation in Beltana, in Chapter 5 I examine the Ahmadi variety of Islam that flowered along Australian camel tracks, leaving in the town of Bourke today a Persian-language doctrinal treatise that lays out some of its main principles. Established in Punjab in the 1880s, the Ahmadiyya movement grew as its founder issued prophecy after prophecy following vivid dream after dream in Urdu, Persian, Arabic and occasionally English. Piecing together the traces Ahmadi dreams left in Australian newspapers, I plot a practice of dream interpretation that circulated across the Indian Ocean during the era of camel transportation.

In Chapter 6, I read an Arabunna story of encounter at a lonely railway siding in around 1895. The tale of what happened when two South Asian men met two Aboriginal women in South Australian deserts continues to circulate in Arabunna families today. I undertake a camping trip through South Australian deserts with Reg Dodd, the Chairman of the Arabunna People's Committee, and show that these Arabunna histories of South Asians can offer glimpses of the terrain on which Arabunna historiographical traditions are inscribed.

Following the figure of the Muslim woman between South Asia and Australia, in Chapter 7 I challenge one of the masculinist assumptions that too often belies the field of Indian Ocean studies: the claim that women do not move. Reading marriage contracts that saw some women traverse vast distances, sometimes for love, I draw on storytelling strategies in Muslim knowledge systems to propose a new framework to house feminist histories of women across the Indian Ocean.

Returning to *Kasasol Ambia*, in the eighth and final chapter I revisit the central question that underpins this book: Who brought the compendium of Bengali poetry to Broken Hill?

Over two centuries ago, when the HMS *Endeavour* departed from Eora shores in 1770, British colonisers left behind not just a site they eventually named Botany Bay, but an epistemological ground from which to view lands, waters, people and stories. Since then countless people have navigated vast oceans and travelled through Aboriginal lands with the conviction of the superiority of European epistemes. The following chapters show that just because they did, we don't have to.

2

STORIES OF THE PROPHETS

The first book of *Kasasol Ambia* was published in 1861.[1] Over the decades that this title became a bestseller, a steam shipping revolution saw Calcutta emerge as a major crossroads for shipping companies. By the time an eighth edition of the book was published, a thriving Australia–India trade was threading Bengal closer to the Australian colonies. By then Australian governments were frontrunners in racial border drawing, immigration restriction against 'Asiatics' emerging as a 'quintessential expression of the masculine sovereignty' of British settler colonies.[2] Accompanying one South Asian traveller who would have negotiated various Australian border regimes, a copy of an 1895 edition of *Kasasol Ambia* reached a mosque in Broken Hill, over 500 kilometres inland from the nearest Australian seaport. Since then, *Kasasol Ambia* has repeatedly been treated as a dead object in Australian history books, obscuring the strategies it contains for thinking about, seeing and narrating the past.

Creation began with a pen, wrote Munshi Rezaulla, the first of the three poets of *Kasasol Ambia*.[3] As a concealed pen inscribed words onto a tablet, he narrates, seven heavens and seven lands came into being, and 'Adam Sufi' was sculpted from clay.[4] The pages that follow tell stories about a chain of prophets from Adam to Muhammad, threading together events spanning across thousands of years, ending in the sixth year of the Muslim Hijri calender (H), or 628 CE.

As its presence in Broken Hill confirms, the stories in *Kasasol Ambia* not only imaginatively transported many people to the past, but accompanied people navigating vast physical distances. It offers a window into how late-nineteenth-century South Asians made sense of where they had come from and where they were going at a moment of escalating racism. Animating the narrative motifs of the poetry and thinking through its metaphors reveals histories of South Asians who have been systematically obscured and omitted from English-language historiography.

As Indologist Ronald Inden pointed out in an influential critique of orientalist knowledge production about South Asia, historians writing in European languages, despite being situated across a wide political spectrum, often share the common presumptions of colonialist epistemes.[5] Drawing on Foucault's insights, Inden showed that the central problem was Enlightenment theories of knowledge that operate within the assumption that 'true knowledge merely represents or mirrors a separate reality which the knower somehow transcends'.[6] Arguing that this is a position that allows 'the scholar to claim that his (rarely her) knowledge is natural and objective and not a matter for political debate', Inden charts how modern epistemes operate by producing a hierarchical power binary between the knower and known – an asymmetrical knowledge relation between scientists and their specimens, psychiatrists and their patients, historians and their archives, or readers and their texts.[7] When non-Europeans and their knowledges are analysed through interpretive methods born of Enlightenment thought, the resulting scholarship itself systematically works to establish the 'positional superiority of Western knowledge' as Maori writer Linda Tuhiwai Smith put it, writing from within the field of Indigenous history.[8]

The poetic imagery in *Kasasol Ambia* shows us an alternative theory of knowledge we can use to produce accounts of the past. The first few pages of the book detail a constellation of knowledge relations binding together humans and stories in different ways to the knower/known hierarchy that underpins Enlightenment epistemes. In a narrative titled the 'Story of the Poet and an Account of Translating Books' Munshi Rezaulla constructs an elaborate metaphor for translation, reflecting on his own relationship to knowledge.[9] He tells us that his spiritual guide (pir Shaikh Chand Dada) and his friend (publisher Kazi Sofiuddin) both urged him to translate stories of the prophets from Persian and Hindi to Bengali verse. Overwhelmed by the task, Rezaulla replied, 'I am so ignorant, in what form (*rupa*) will I write poetry?'[10] Submitting to a higher power, he realised that 'whatever, whomever you search, the protector grants'.[11] Placing his faith in this logic, the poet wrote, 'I leapt into the sea. Searching for pearls, I began threading a chain.'[12] The imagery of his body immersed in the sea evoked a pen dipped in ink stringing together lines of poetry, and Rezaulla wrote, 'Stories of the Prophets (*Kasasol Ambia*) I name (*nama*) this chain.'[13]

This is a dense metaphor that rewards slow, repeated readings. In it Rezaulla shows us the particular knowledge relation that he stepped into when writing *Kasasol Ambia*. In various South Asian philosophical traditions, authors have long used the pair of terms '*rupa* (form)' and '*nama* (name)' to signpost theorisations of knowledge itself, at least since the *Upanishad* corpus of Sanskrit texts from around 400 BCE. As cultural historian Aditya Behl writes, '*nama* and *rupa* are widely used in Indian traditions to articulate quite different modes of the relation between mind, body and consciousness, as well as to reflect on the shape and form of the cosmos itself and its relationship to the embodied human being.'[14] However, as Behl warns, 'in a Borges-like twist' Sufi texts in particular often resist their own reading and 'only if one enters into the virtual universe of the text do the purposes and outlines of the text become clear.'[15]

Rezaulla's metaphor for translation offers clues for how to relate to the poetry. In describing his own relation to knowledge, Rezaulla invites us to follow in his steps. Signalling that audiences are entering an episteme that operates by revealing 'whatever, whomever you search', Rezaulla also summons us to step into a sea of stories while engaged in a search or a quest. Appearing on page 6 of *Kasasol Ambia*, it is an image hinting that the pages of poetry that follow are best interpreted if we read/recite/listen to them while asking questions.

In July 2009, when I first encountered *Kasasol Ambia*, the Bengali book long mislabelled as a Quran made front-page news in Broken Hill. With touching enthusiasm, the journalist announced that I would 'begin work on a full translation shortly.'[16] Overwhelmed by such a task, I began trawling mosque records held by the Broken Hill Historical Society. I did not know how to decipher the difficult book, and so in these archival materials I hoped to glimpse, however fleetingly, the skilled nineteenth-century reader who had once performed its poetry. Slowly, it dawned on me that I was following the narrative logic that Rezaulla outlines in his schema for translation. For I had stepped into the imaginative world of the poetry grappling with a series of hard questions: How do we write histories of South Asian diaspora which pay attention to the history books that travelled with them? Who was the unnamed traveller who brought Bengali stories of the prophets to Broken Hill? What form of historical storytelling in English can do more than simply inducting readers into white subjectivities? Threading together seven narrative motifs that appear in *Kasasol Ambia*, I began to piece together a history of South Asians in Australia.

I. Adam

Kasasol Ambia became a popular title in the decades following the upheaval of the Sepoy Rebellion that swept across northern parts of British India in 1857–9. In its aftermath, the era of East India Company rule in alliance with the Mughal court came to an end with the establishment of the British Raj. With an entire colonial surveillance infrastructure emerging around 'seditious literature' one British administrator reported in 1879 that in Calcutta, 'frequently … natives collected around a Tailor or native grocer's shop to hear a man … reading a Tale in the Musalmani-Bengali.'[17] He observed that performers had a 'fluency of reading, which is always rapid, sonorous, and musical … accompanied with rapid motions of the head and body.'[18] As the increasing colonial tabulation of Bengali books after 1857 confirms, when agents of empire surveilled these performances from their margins, they saw people who were either Hindu or Muslim.[19] From within these gatherings, what did listeners hear and see?

The first book of *Kasasol Ambia* opens with a two-page preview of the drama of creation, narrated in the *payar* beat of Bengali poetry. Following the creation of seven heavens and seven lands, a statue of Adam is sculpted from clay.[20] Adam's form (*surat*) falls from the heavens to earth and his children are as different to each other as the 'body and two eyes, arms, legs, nose, ears' of a shattered statue.[21] Distinct in 'colour and shape', some were black, some fair, some shimmered like moonlight, while others were as striking as darkness itself.[22]

Continuing in the *payar* metre, 'The Story of Abdullah's Questions' sets the stage for a lengthier history of Adam. Narrating a dialogue between Muhammad and his younger cousin Abdullah Ibn Abbas (d. 687), the poem explicitly situates itself within Muslim historiography – the *ta'rikh* genre of storytelling about the past. Abdullah was one of the earliest Muslim scholars, and his writings comprise an important source in works of *ta'rikh* and other bodies of Muslim knowledge. In *Kasasol Ambia*, Abdullah asks, 'From where did that water come?' When Muhammad answers, 'From one drop of sweat,' young Abdullah asks, 'How was sweat created? Tell me, prophet.'[23] The remainder of the stories in the first book proceeds within the frame-tale.

A detailed story of Adam begins when angels arrive from heaven to earth seeking a fistful of dust. Trembling with fear, the earth protests. It pleads that any creature created from earth will only inflict destruction and ruin. Despite these protests, one angel returns to the heavens with a fistful of earth, sculpting a clay statue.[24] Switching to *tripadi* metre, the pace of the story slows when detailing the transformation of the statue into a sentient being. The four angels mix musk and perfume with moist clay. They smear this paste on the forehead of the statue, and wait. Forty days later a spirit (*ruh*) is created. Unimpressed with the inanimate statue that it must inhabit, the *ruh* explores the earthen form, entering and leaving again seven times. When the *ruh* enters the statue an eighth time, it does so through its nose. As it travels through the four parts of the intellect, Adam's eyes open. Gathered around a performer reciting *Kasasol Ambia* in shrines, streets and verandahs across Bengal, audiences heard that only when the eyes of the clay figure opened did life finally course through the statue, transforming it from an inanimate form into a Muslim being (*jan pak*).[25]

This is an account of Adam that drew on many stories familiar to audiences in nineteenth-century Bengal. On hearing these opening verses of *Kasasol Ambia*, some listeners would have heard the tale of Purusha falling from the skies and splintering into Adam's children. In a story recounted in the *Rigveda* corpus of Sanskrit poetry dating to 1500 BCE, Purusha is a being with 1,000 heads, 1,000 eyes and 1,000 feet, who falls from the heavens to earth, shattering on impact.[26] The destruction of Purusha creates animals, trees, poetry and people, in addition to an order of things that Europeans began calling 'caste'.[27]

The narrative of Purusha is another creation story that has long circulated the Indian Ocean alongside tales of Adam. As the most recent English translation of the *Rigveda* narrates, after Purusha shattered, 'The Brahmin was his mouth. The ruler was made his two arms. As to his thighs – that is what the freeman was. From his two feet the servant was born.'[28]

On hearing the account of the earth's pleas with the angels, some listeners would have recalled the tale of earth's quarrels with Shiva. It is a dialogue recounted in the *Mahabharata*, one of the Sanskrit texts codified as 'Hindu law' during the British colonial era.[29] When the creator god Brahma descends from heaven to earth, the earth complains bitterly about the destruction wreaked upon it by warring gods. Negotiating with the gods for the earth's kinder treatment, Brahma creates an avatar of Vishnu: Krishna, who perpetually moves between the heavens and earth through cycles of death and rebirth.[30]

Unlike British officials, at performances of Battala books, audiences saw characters moving along different timelines. The story of Adam contained inflections of the story of Purusha and Bhrama. Narrated together, these figures trained listeners to imaginatively travel through time along multiple indices, on narrative pathways connecting past, present and future. With the eyes of 'Adam Sufi' opening at a conjuncture of knowledge traditions, the poet theorises a form of human becoming that has access to numerous temporalities. Some would have left performances of *Kasasol Ambia* having seen and heard many intersecting stories, inducted into a particular schema of Muslim being.

As Rajendralal Mitra's 1864 orientalist reading of *Kasasol Ambia* at the Asiatic Society of Bengal confirms, British historical narratives circulating alongside South Asian historiographical traditions were moulding the way people related to non-European epistemes. While the colonial tale of 'Muslim foreigners' and 'ancient Hindus' that Mitra inserted Rezaulla's poetry into can be traced to James Mills' *History*, by the late nineteenth century many colonial institutions were reproducing this story by partitioning complex textual communities into distinct, separate 'religions'. It was a schema of categorisation central to the rule of the British Raj.[31] Enacting European ownership of South Asian knowledges, during the Royal Tour of British India in 1875–6, the Prince of Wales presented Indian princes with an orientalist translation of the *Rigveda*.[32] It was a symbolic act that harnessed stories of Purusha and others to buttress new pacts of colonial rule between South Asian sovereigns and the British Crown.

It was in response to this new political order that a range of Islamic reform movements emerged during the British Raj, arbitrating between 'pure' and 'impure' strands of Islam. As the semi-autobiographical fiction of Syed Mustafa Siraj (d. 2012) suggests, Sufi texts increasingly came under attack from these movements in the late nineteenth century. In his novel *Aleek Manush* (Mythical Man), an elderly man is sitting on a verandah reciting poetry when Islamic reformers arrive in his village in North Bengal.[33] Sighting the approaching newcomers, the man quickly discards the book – a copy of *Kasasol Ambia*. While many readers were discarding Sufi stories at this historical juncture, an 1895 edition of *Kasasol Ambia* captivated one traveller to the Australian colonies. With whom did a 500-page compendium of Bengali poetry cross the Indian Ocean, and what route did its stories travel to Broken Hill?

II. Nuh

The second book of *Kasasol Ambia* begins with the voyage of Nuh – the spiritual guide who wept when no one listened to his stories.[34] In a land of unbelievers, a sapling grew 600 yards high and 400 yards wide, watered by Nuh's tears for forty years. When he breaks a branch from this tree to build a ship, its many birds shape the wood into beams, inscribing the names of prophets on each plank. From these Nuh crafts a mighty vessel. When salty waters begin to flood lands far and wide, Nuh gathers pairs of every animal, not realising that the disgraced angel Azazel boards the ship concealed as an ass. With two tigers, two pigeons, two elephants and two ducks arriving on a new land, so too disembarks cloaked Azazel with his lantern of darkness – a lamp casting a black light obscuring truth. To counter the work Azazel does with his lantern, Allah commands Nuh, 'from the planks of your ship, build a mosque.'[35] Out of the fragments of stories of the prophets inscribed on the wood, Nuh builds a house of prayer in the mountains.

Could *Kasasol Ambia* have arrived in Broken Hill with a spiritual guide? With the earliest shipload of camels departing from British

India, spiritual guides travelled to the Australian colonies. In 1865, the *Blackwell* set sail from Karachi with thirty-one South Asian camel drivers on board, as well as '124 camels, 31 donkeys, one quagga, black and grey partridges, 2 deer, 80 sheep, 1 cow and 2 bullocks'.[36] On arrival at the colony of South Australia, Haji Mulla Meheraban, 'a pious and very popular priest and poet', was among the South Asians who led the camels to peaks today known as the Flinders Ranges.[37] There the first Australian camel-breeding yard was established in Beltana in mountainous Kuyani country.

From the 1880s, many South Asians in Beltana entered the Australian camel trade themselves, shipping animals on speculation. The most powerful South Asian merchants operating in the Australian colonies described themselves as 'Afghans'. While some sourced their animals from Afghanistan, others purchased their stock from the deserts of British India.[38] As a close inspection of camel-trading routes reveals, many traders shipped animals through Bengal; advertisements in late-nineteenth-century Australian newspapers sometimes distinguished between 'Calcutta camels' and 'hill breeds' from Afghanistan and Balochistan.[39]

In 1887, when Haji Mulla Meheraban arrived at the colony of Western Australia with a shipment of Calcutta camels, accompanying him was 22-year-old Mirza Khan. A man from a family of spiritual leaders, Mirza Khan soon left the camel business, pursuing a trade in books. By 1888, he had a bookbinding business on Hay Street, Perth.[40] He advertised book repairs, 'cheaply and neatly executed', while also selling 'Indian goods' from the same address. When he was twenty-four years old he married a white actress by the name of Julia Thorne.[41] Whether he left the colony because his marriage fell apart or did so for other reasons, by 1894 Mirza Khan was operating a store in Redfern, Sydney in the colony of New South Wales. At the age of twenty-eight, Mirza Khan departed from Australia, travelling to British India.[42]

A few months later he received an order from Abdul Rahman Khan – the king of Afghanistan. The court chronicler in Kabul recorded that on '1 October His Majesty sent a farman to Mirza Khan of the Kharuti Afghan tribe who resided in Australia but was (currently) in India.'[43] The document instructed Mirza Khan to collect '15,000 rupees' from the ambassador of Afghanistan in Calcutta to purchase a flock of

Australian sheep 'and send them to Kabul'. Deploying his Australian networks, Mirza Khan purchased 600 head of sheep from the colony of South Australia. In February 1895, the animals were dispatched from Adelaide 'to be sent to Afghanistan by railway from Calcutta'.[44]

As this order shows, the state of Afghanistan maintained connections to the Afghan diaspora in both British India and the Australian colonies, the Calcutta embassy operating as a node in renewing these relationships. Mirza Khan's family, like some of the self-described 'Afghan' merchants in the Australian colonies, might have been based in Bengal for generations. Families claiming a genealogy to Afghanistan have been present in Bengal for centuries. However, from the 1890s, the camel merchants operating between Calcutta and the Australian colonies increasingly started to assert their direct connections to the nation-state of Afghanistan, often effacing Bengal from the histories they told about themselves. Gunny Khan, for example, despite his trading and political links centring on Calcutta, insisted in a Broken Hill newspaper that 'by Afghans I mean subjects of the Ameer of Afghanistan'.[45]

When the 600 sheep finally arrived in Kabul they would not breed. The court chronicler in Kabul described the venture as a 'disaster'.[46] However, for Mirza Khan, completing a transaction connecting Adelaide, Calcutta and Kabul built a connection to the sovereign of Afghanistan that ensured his future success as a spiritual guide. When he returned to the Australian colonies in late 1895, Mirza Khan attracted the public support of Gunny Khan – proprietor of Gunny Khan & Company (GKCo), a carrying company based in Broken Hill and with camel camps throughout the Australian interior. In step with developments in wider imperial politics, Gunny Khan was an increasingly vocal Afghan nationalist. After the Durand Line was drawn in 1893, demarcating the imperial–national boundary between British India and Afghanistan, Gunny Khan began writing to Australian presses drawing distinctions between 'Indians' and 'Afghans'.[47]

Accompanied by Gunny Khan, Mirza Khan undertook a tour of Australian mosques in December 1895 (Fig. 5). While nationalists such as Gunny Khan were fanning sharpening divisions between Australian camel camps, Mirza Khan was one of the well-known mullahs mediating differences across class and regional distinctions. He was reputed for his fluency in 'five different languages' and one Perth newspaper reported that he was contemplating 'founding a free Mohamedan library'.[48] Many spiritual guides were travelling Australian camel routes patronised by competing merchants, but Gunny Khan insisted that the 'true and only priest here is Mirza Khan'.[49] He pointed out that Mirza Khan was the 'author and possessor of two books' bearing Arabic titles, though he did not mention whether this mullah's travelling library included a copy of *Kasasol Ambia*.

'Mirga Khan' continues to be remembered by Broken Hill locals today as a man who travelled from city mosques to desert towns, completing many circuits through Australian camel camps over the course of a decade.[50] If a copy of *Kasasol Ambia* accompanied Mirza Khan to Broken Hill, it travelled alongside another story that obscured the routes connecting Australian camel camps to Bengal: the nationalist story mapping 'Afghans' directly to the state of Afghanistan. With Australian historians replicating this tale today, the trajectory of the camel trade through Calcutta continues to be systematically omitted from history books.

III. Khidr

A third tale in *Kasasol Ambia* is the story of Khidr's patronage of sailors.[51] In a dark jungle Khidr drinks from the fountain of life and becomes immortal, his heart illuminated by the entirety of the world's knowledge. For an eternity he wanders the world, his only known address 'by the edge of the water'.[52] When Musa meets him by a riverbank and asks to glimpse the workings of his knowledge, Khidr leads him to a new boat.[53] It belongs to a poor sailor who feeds ten mouths with the meagre earnings of his oar. Khidr boards the craft and breaks two or three of its planks with great force. The vessel fills with water. Astonished, Musa asks what the logic of this destruction could be. Khidr answers by revealing stories about the future only visible to him. Further down the river, there is a cruel and powerful king called 'Manju'. He seizes the belongings of poor sailors. If the boat had remained on course, Khidr explains, the sailor and his ten dependents would have all died in the grip of Manju's power. An immortal figure possessing knowledge of every possible path to the future, Khidr has long been understood as a guide for sailors and lost people, able to intervene to change their routes.

Could *Kasasol Ambia* have arrived in Broken Hill with a sailor headed into the grip of power? As its preface confirms, the book was particularly popular in Khidirpur, a dockside neighbourhood of Calcutta.[54] A locality known for its many shrines where Sufi texts were performed, Khidirpur was also one of the neighbourhoods where shipping companies recruited Bengali sailors for ships to Australia and elsewhere.[55]

As the latest edition of *Kasasol Ambia* was circulating through a labyrinth of lanes, shrines and bazaars in Calcutta, 38-year-old Anno Khan contracted as a sailor on the SS *Darius*.[56] He was part of a crew of eighty 'lascars' – a racial category first invented in negotiations between the British government and British colonists in the early nineteenth century. The lascar regime enabled British shipping companies to employ South Asian sailors legally, while restricting their ability to remain at British ports. By the time Anno Khan contracted as a fireman, lascars were remunerated at one-fifth to one-third the wages of European sailors.[57]

With Anno Khan working in the furnace, the *Darius* departed from Calcutta on 31 March 1895.[58] The vessel was owned by Archibald Currie & Company (ACCo) – a Melbourne-based shipping firm engaged in the Australia–India trade.[59] The ship's log written by the captain recorded the movement of commodities, and only rarely mentioned lascars explicitly. While we know the vessel was carrying 1,123 bales of jute bags, 2,300 bags of rice and twenty-one cases of nutmeg, the captain's log omits any mention of the stories that might have been travelling with lascars.[60]

As a wider range of seafaring narratives beyond official logs suggests, the non-European stories that boarded European vessels circulated most noticeably outside of hours of duty. As Herman Melville recalled in his autobiographical novel *Redburn*, white 'Officers lived astern in the cabin, where every Sunday they read the church of England's prayers, while the heathen at the other end of the ship were left to their false gods and idols.'[61] After decades in British merchant shipping, another naval officer wrote that 'when several Asian manned ships are in port together ... a crowd of Moslems will foregather in a mess room or [deck] to make that weird, though rather intriguing, cacophony of sound, Eastern music. They will sit cross-legged on the deck and chant their songs to a musical accompaniment.'[62] Australian newspapers also confirm that songs were sung at the most crucial junctures of lascars' voyages. When the SS *Maloja* sank in 1916, for example, the *Argus* reported that 'some of the gallant natives could be heard singing as they went to their death.'[63]

Docking at Penang, and then in Singapore, the captain recorded 'very fine weather to Cheribon'.[64] As the *Darius* rounded the southwestern tip of the Australian mainland, the captain did not detail where, why and how tensions began to mount among the lascar crew. By the time the vessel approached Adelaide, assaulted by 'strong gales from west to W.N.W.', plans to protest against ACCo might already have been circulating.[65] As historian Gopalan Balachandran writes, with class tensions 'simmering for weeks at sea', countless clashes between white employers and lascars 'came to a head at key moments, usually upon arrival at a foreign port.'[66]

On 30 April 1895, at Port Adelaide, Anno Khan was one of the fourteen lascars who left the ship to protest their working conditions. A delegation of six workers took their complaints to the marine superintendent. They reported they had received insufficient rations during the voyage. Declaring that the lascars' 'allegations were unjustified', police forced them back onto the ship.[67] Along with another sailor, Anno Khan escaped, making a run for Jervois Bridge. Spanning the mouth of the Murray River, which emptied into the sea, the bridge was the only route connecting Port Adelaide to the city.

At the bridge, 'two policemen and a Customs officer' arrested the two runaways, settler newspapers scripting them into another story about 'Asiatic immigrants'.[68] In 1895, the Immigration Act in the Colony of South Australia only explicitly barred Chinese arrivals from landing. That port authorities made the two protestors each pay 10s 6d for a medical examination illustrates how settlers used medical narratives to enforce borders around white man's countries. As one newspaper reported, 'having passed muster and paid the money' they 'triumphantly left the vessel and the Port, carrying their personal effects.'[69]

It is not clear whether a copy of *Kasasol Ambia* crossed Jervois Bridge in Anno Khan's bundle of belongings. My search of dockside records – where racist regimes targeting 'lascars' and 'Asiatics' overlapped at the water's edge, precisely where one might expect to find stories of Khidr – revealed many striking Bengali lascars stepping onto Australian shores. In 1888, 120 'lascars on strike' refused to serve on the *Carthage* at Newcastle, while 'forty lascar seamen' went on strike at Williamstown Pier in Melbourne the same year.[70] Bengali crew on ACCo vessels were striking with increasing frequency at the turn of the century, and in 1904 protestors took the company to court in Melbourne.[71] In the same court seven years later, twenty-nine lascars protested that they were 'being ill treated and knocked about' by the captain.[72] Insufficient rations were a frequent cause for strike – in 1922, eight lascars submitted samples to a court in Sydney of the 'old fishbones and rice' they were expected to eat.[73]

'Jumping ship and skirting empire' at Australian ports, many former lascars found their way to Broken Hill as camel drivers, one of the few industries where South Asians continued to find employment despite the increasing controls placed on 'Asiatics'.[74] As the recollections of one Balochi camel-owner confirms, many people from Calcutta worked along Australian camel tracks. Ossman complained that his Bengali drivers were not 'good' camel men. 'Him – hawkers from Calcutta,' he said. 'One man drive'm cab in Calcutta, the others – fools. White men think because him got black skin him camel man.'[75]

The records at Australian docks reveal histories of lascars negotiating the various power regimes interlocking at the water's edge. As labour historians have shown, docksides were cosmopolitan sites of confluence where Aboriginal workers met not only South Asian sailors, but also Garveyite activists from Caribbean and American ports, giving rise to some of the strongest anti-colonial movements over the next century.[76] If a copy of *Kasasol Ambia* arrived with a sailor, it was travelling alongside not just stories of 'lascars' and 'Asiatics' enforced by colonial institutions, but also a powerful story of collective action.

IV. Yusuf and Zelekha

The fourth book of *Kasasol Ambia* tells the tale of Yusuf and Zelekha, one of the most popular love stories circulating the Indian Ocean.[77] In a dream, Yusuf foresees that he will be a future king. His ten older brothers cannot accept the prophecy and throw him in a well deep in the jungle. When a traveller finds Yusuf at the bottom of this dark pit, he rescues him and takes him to Egypt.

Elsewhere, Zelekha, the daughter of a king, sees Yusuf in a dream. Though she has never met him, Zelekha's vision ignites in her heart a burning desire for Yusuf. Seeking the spectre she glimpsed too briefly, and guided only by the flame of love (*ashk*), she travels to Cairo. There she marries Aziz, a senior court administrator. But her husband is not whom she desires, and by a divine command he is made impotent.

One day Zelekha chances upon Yusuf at the slave market – he is in chains, and for sale. When she introduces her husband to her enslaved beloved, Aziz purchases Yusuf for their household, unaware of Zelekha's passion. By day, Zelekha and Yusuf are painfully close within domestic quarters; by night she is tortured by forbidden desire. Before long Zelekha is carrying Yusuf's child. Most famously written as a popular epic by Persian poet Jami (d. 1492), tales of Yusuf and Zelekha's impossible love have been translated into Bengali poetry for centuries.

Could *Kasasol Ambia* have arrived in Broken Hill with a lover caught in the plot of an impossible love story? When romances such as Yusuf and Zelekha were performed by spiritual guides, they were used as teaching texts for inducting novices into Sufi epistemes. In the narrative grammer of this genre, an elusive being embodied as a beloved (Yusuf) ignites desire in a lover (Zelekha), sparking a quest. Within Sufi romances, the lover's search for the beloved operates an overarching frame organising smaller tales. These stories lead audiences step-by-step through a series of successive realisations – truths illuminated by the flames of *ashk*. Designed to spark interior journeys in listeners, the story of Zelekha and Yusuf had particular appeal for the broken-hearted. For, according to the logic of Sufi romances, the only balm that can soothe the burning pain of impossible love is stories about the burning pain of impossible love.[78]

Along Australian camel tracks, many people fell in and out of love. Some men married the women they were intimate with. Balochi camel-owner Bejah Dervish did not. Whether or not their encounters were tender or violent, or both, in 1891 Bejah Dervish had a child with Anne Murray, an Aboriginal woman living near the railway town of Marree in the colony of South Australia. Over eight decades later, their son Ben Murray recalled, 'We didn't go by his name because he wasn't interested in looking after us. Mother had to carry on herself.'[79]

As colonists increasingly drew sharper distinctions between 'Asiatics', 'Aborigines' and 'whites' from the 1890s, at times restricting intimate relationships across these boundaries, these categories came to signpost the racial order of civilisational hierarchy. As one Christian missionary wrote in South Australia, Aboriginal people could be categorised into two groups in desert towns: 'first were the camel boys employed by Afghan teamsters [who] were used to the ways of civilisation [and] understood English ... the second type were harder to deal with ... the nomadic blacks.'[80] In response to British imperial narratives of racial hierarchies, some of the most powerful South Asian 'camel kings' insisted that they occupied a similar stage to white colonists in a schema of civilisational progress, asserting their distance from the 'savages being conquered and civilised by England'.[81]

While Bejah Dervish lived with his white wife at the camel camp in Marree, his son Ben Murray lived with his Aboriginal mother at Frome Creek, a riverbed locally known as 'the Frome', a few miles outside of town.[82] From watching both settler society and the Marree camel camp from the Frome, Ben Murray collected many stories about South Asians, which he told in English, as well as Wangkangurru, Dieri and Dhirari. Linguists began to record these Aboriginal-language narratives from the 1960s. One of the tales Ben Murray told and retold for decades concerned the failed love of Sher Khan, a camel driver 'living in Broken Hill'.[83]

Born in Kabul in 1869, Sher Khan was one of the '*Kabuliwallahs*' peddling wares in Calcutta at the turn of the twentieth century.[84] In 1900, he entered into a contract with camel merchant Abdul Wade, and departed for the port of Sydney as a camel driver.[85] Two years after he arrived in the Broken Hill region with a shipment of Calcutta camels, Sher Khan fell in love with a girl living at the Marree camel camp.[86] Her name was Adelaide. Unfortunately for Sher Khan, in February 1904 Adelaide became engaged to Moosha Balooch, a wealthy merchant with powerful connections to white authorities in the government of South Australia.[87]

Three months later, Sher Khan caught a train to Marree, disguised in a three-piece tweed suit and with a felt hat pulled over his eyes.[88] On 24 May 1904, Sher Khan alighted from the train at Marree railhead at 8.45 p.m., and shot Adelaide's fiancé. After firing five bullets at Moosha

Balooch, he disappeared into the shadows cast by the 'peculiarly bright moon' that night.[89]

At dawn, Charley, an Aboriginal man who described himself as 'from the Charlotte Waters tribe', was engaged by settler police at Marree to follow Sher Khan across the desert.[90] Charley traced Sher Khan's steps from sunrise to sundown for over 35 miles, pursuing him to Farina, where he was arrested. With Charley, Sher Khan's story of impossible love travelled to Frome Creek, where it was told and retold in many Aboriginal languages.

In November 1975, Ben Murray recounted this story in Dhirari to Peter Austin, a linguistics student camping by the creek at Farina.[91] The names of the people in the story had changed from Murray's Wangkangurru telling in the 1960s, and changed again in his English narration in the 1980s. What is consistent is that in each telling the focus is on the tracker's pursuit and an Aboriginal character always remains at the centre of the story. After shooting his rival at Marree, Ben Murray recounted that 'Shirkhan then went that way to the creek,' resituating the action at the Frome Creek bed. He continued, 'From there he went along the creek this way here coming back to Farina.'[92] Sher Khan 'put his boots on again and took them off again. That's how he went along. Then a *karna* (Aboriginal man), he followed the tracks.'[93] In the lengthy Dhirari drama of pursuit and escape, while Sher Khan tries repeatedly to obscure his tracks, the Aboriginal tracker outwits him each time.

Murray emphasised that Sher Khan 'didn't leave the creek', steering the chase toward 'Paradise Creek'.[94] This waterway did not feature in Charley's account of the chase in 1904. It was a site where Murray worked for many years as a drover. Not only did he tell many stories about it, Murray also told stories at Paradise Creek, taking Peter Austin there in May 1974. The tale of Sher Khan's escape threaded together places of significance for both the storyteller and his audience. As Murray eventually told Austin, 'then he came barefoot here to the creek where you are camped now,' thereby scripting the listener into the story.[95] Like in Charley's testimony of tracking Sher Khan for the police in 1904, in Murray's accounts the start and end points of the chase remain Marree and Farina railheads respectively.

Sher Khan was sentenced to Yatala labour prison.[96] When he was released he worked for a while in Western Australia, eventually returning to Broken Hill. If a copy of *Kasasol Ambia* arrived in Broken Hill with someone who fell in love, its stories had circulated alongside another tale about the racial order that was taking hold along Australian camel tracks, shaping intimacies.

Some children, like Ben Murray, were born of encounters between South Asian men and Aboriginal women, and were never publicly acknowledged by their fathers. Murray was never privy to the knowledge forms that arrived in Australia with his father. He was, however, well versed in the many dynamic epistemes that continued to flourish at the Frome, where he lived with his mother. Just as the quest for the beloved is a narrative trope in Sufi epistemes, Ben Murray's account deployed the drama of pursuit and escape that is a recurring motif in many Aboriginal epistemes. Both operate as frame-tales, housing stories that continue to change, live and transform from telling to telling. With his Dhirari history of Sher Khan illuminating an inland water system that shaped Aboriginal livelihoods and imaginations, Ben Murray's story offers a glimpse of one index, quite distinct to progress narratives, shaping Aboriginal historiographical traditions.

V. Yunus

Yunus crossed dangerous waters many times, says *Kasasol Ambia*, in the tale of how he traversed the grip of powers far larger then him.[97] Yunus foresaw that his future lay in the distant city of Ninu. Seeking to escape this destiny, he departs instead for his own village with his wife and their two sons. Upon reaching a river, they cannot find a boat. Yunus crosses the water carrying his two boys on his shoulders. Leaving them on the dry shore, he swims back to his wife. They enter the water holding hands. Yet the might of the tide loosens her fingers from his, and they lose each other. The wave washes Yunus ashore, where he finds that a tiger has taken his children. Alone and devastated, Yunus heads to Ninu, 'now known as Damascus city'.[98] There he spends many years. When he leaves, before his work in Ninu is complete, he again reaches a river. The waters are calm and he boards a boat. But soon a storm awakens the power of the river, and he is thrown overboard. A giant fish appears and swallows him. Travelling into the depths of the water with Yunus in its belly, the fish talks to him. Assuring him that 'I will not harm you,' it instructs him on how to endure the darkest moments of distress.[99] After forty days, the fish returns Yunus to the edge of the water. A doe appears by the riverside, nursing him back to health with its sweet milk.

Could *Kasasol Ambia* have arrived in Broken Hill with traders crossing perilous inland Australian rivers? From the eastern ports of Brisbane, Melbourne, Sydney and Adelaide, many Bengali textile traders from Hugli built livelihoods along the Murray-Darling – a circuit shaping the topography of eastern Australia.[100] In addition to Indian Ocean ports, Hugli traders travelled to New York, Mississippi and Caribbean ports, selling 'clothing and domestic goods embroidered in the intricate decorative style known as chikan'.[101] At Australian ports they were known as '*chikanwallahs*'. They gathered in the largest numbers at Sydney, where vessels from Calcutta ended their voyages. With *chikanwallahs* navigating 'lascar' regimes across oceans and 'hawker' regimes inland, one Melbourne newspaper confirmed that the distribution of textiles to 'interior towns' was 'to a large extent carried on by the Lascars from the boats'.[102]

Abdul Sattar was seventeen years old when he first worked his passage to Australian ports as a lascar, leaving his family behind in the village of 'Nabasan Sinhet' in Hugli.[103] During the 1890s he spent four years trading textiles from Sydney, and four years from Melbourne.[104] Despite pressure from Australian colonial governments to place greater restrictions on South Asians, British colonial officials in Calcutta continued to grant landing certificates to 'Chikenwallas' departing for Australian ports, categorising them as 'traders' and not 'labourers'.[105] Along with Bengali lascars who also traded in textiles slipping past Australian customs, Abdul Sattar disembarked at Sydney in December 1897 with cloth products for sale.[106]

From about '50 shops' on Elizabeth Street in Redfern, South Asian merchants importing 'drapery, Indian silks, jewellery and goods' distributed their wares through an extensive inland network of hawkers.[107] From 1895, the Redfern magistrates' court stopped issuing new hawker's licenses.[108] As regulations tightened, 'an animated business in licenses' emerged at Redfern. One reporter claimed, 'Should a man leave the colony he hands his license to the storekeeper ... the latter sells it to a late arrival who duly presents it at the court for renewal, and represents himself as the original holder.'[109] *Chikanwallahs* sometimes took advantage of settlers' inability to distinguish between South Asians. Those who were most successful in evading settler regimes 'disappear' from colonial records, trading under multiple names that obscure their trajectories.

By the turn of the century, South Asian hawkers were a common sight along Australian rivers, 'gaudy hawker's boats' conveying wares along the arteries of the Murray-Darling to 'spots where you would never think it possible that a boat could reach'.[110] Traders on foot navigating smaller tributaries appear in settler presses coinciding with the sudden flooding of inland waterways. At Kotupna, for example, two South Asian hawkers engaged a young and inexperienced settler boatman to row them across an overflowing tributary of the Murray. The vessel capsized. One newspaper detailed that the 'growth of aqueous plants ... became entangled with the legs of the three men.'[111] One of the South Asian men 'came to the surface and cried piteously for help before he drowned.'[112]

For travellers who were well versed in negotiating the grip of the various power regimes they were beholden to, hawking proved a profitable livelihood. As one journalist reported in 1898, at Narrandera on the Murrumbidgee River 'nearly thirty' hawkers gathered at their camp to 'do honour to two of their number who were about to return to India with savings amounting to £200 each.'[113] This was an assembly that offers a glimpse into the occasions when stories of Yunus may have captivated listeners on their way to Broken Hill.

Abdul Sattar saved his earnings over many years. With an investment of £200, he opened a drapery business in Fremantle on the eve of the federation of seven Australian colonies into the new nation of 'White Australia' in 1901. Abdul Sattar married a woman in Hugli in India and built a family across the Indian Ocean, at the height of racially exclusive immigration restrictions. In March 1909, he received an urgent letter from his mother. In Hugli, his son had died and his mother had suddenly fallen ill. Abdul Sattar departed on the next available vessel, without completing the extensive paperwork that would ensure he could return to the Commonwealth of Australia. As he wrote in a letter from Hugli to Fremantle, 'Before I arrived home my mother was dead. I was very ill for months.'[114] When Australian officials refused to let him re-enter 'White Australia' two years later, Abdul Sattar mobilised his network of friends to petition immigration administrators. He eventually returned to Fremantle another two years later (Fig. 6).[115]

If a copy of *Kasasol Ambia* reached Broken Hill with a Hugli *chikanwallah*, it did so with a traveller who knew how to endure the grip of power. Alternatively scripting themselves into the roles of 'lascar', 'hawker' and 'trader', South Asians also navigated the demarcations between 'illegal alien' and 'legal' travellers by obscuring their trajectories from settler view. While the strategies they used to negotiate power remain in the family records of some of their descendants in Australia, contemporary Australian hysteria about 'boat people' and 'illegals' crossing the Indian Ocean does significant work to hide these stories. For some of the descendants of nineteenth-century South Asians, histories that do not unfold according to the script of 'pioneers of the inland' remain a source of shame.[116]

VI. Ayesha

The last two pages of *Kasasol Ambia* tell a story about a chain once lost by Ayesha (d. 678) – Muhammad's wife.[117] Accompanying Muhammad and a regiment of soldiers to a battlefield, Ayesha leaves her necklace by a lake while washing. She returns to the cloaked litter on her camel within which she practises seclusion from men. It is only in the dead of night that she realises her precious chain is missing. Leaving the door ajar, she traces her footsteps back to the lake. Reminding listeners that 'what you search [for] is what will be revealed', the eighth book of *Kasasol Ambia* tells us that despite the darkness Ayesha finds her shell necklace precisely where it had broken and slipped from her throat, at the edge of the water.[118] When she returns to the camp, she finds that her camel is gone, her litter having departed with the regiment. Ayesha re-joins them the next day, accompanying another traveller on a camel – a man. It is an episode that Muhammad's political opponents use to accuse her of adultery, one incident among many in the long history of power regimes exploiting stories about Muslim women.[119]

Could the *Kasosol Ambia* have arrived in Broken Hill with a woman? Not according to the narrative logic of English-language historians in a number of fields. As Christine Stevens asserts, 'no women, wives or children accompanied the Afghans who came to Australia.'[120] More recently, Margaret Allen stops short of examining the South Asian women who departed for Australia in feminist analyses of transnational movements, noting only that 'it was very difficult for British Indians to bring their families to Australia.'[121] Within histories of Indian Ocean mobility, while foregrounding non-European travellers, Engseng Ho prefaces his account with the claim that 'most were men ... a diaspora in the etymological sense of a scattering of seed.'[122] Yet, as Ayesha's story in the final pages of *Kasasol Ambia* hints, for those who know what they are looking for, searching for women's chains reveals them with ease.

Reading passenger lists of ships arriving at Australian ports with some knowledge of how to recognise South Asian women's names reveals that many women travelled from Bengal to the Australian colonies. From the 1860s, while Australian governments implemented assisted migration schemes to actively recruit white working-class women from Britain as domestic servants, settler legislation remained ambivalent about non-white domestic servants from across the British Empire.[123] In that context, many Bengali women arrived as domestic servants – ayahs accompanying white employers from British India to Australian ports and inland towns. A worker called Begum Ayah even 'summoned her mistress for unlawful assault' in Melbourne in 1870.[124] While her employer Mrs Moss admitted assaulting her, 'the magistrates ... dismissed the case', and 40-year-old Begum Ayah returned to Calcutta on board the *Loch Lomond*.[125]

In addition to ayahs contracted for employment, some women travelled to Australian shores upon marriage to South Asian merchants. Departing from Calcutta, 19-year-old Kewsee Beebe travelled to Sydney with her husband in 1892, while 46-year-old Mrs Daytum crossed the Indian Ocean in 1895, and 31-year-old Jumnah arrived in Sydney in 1893, travelling with her two children and husband.[126] Throughout the era of the British Raj, government officials in British India continued to issue landing certificates at Australian ports for South Asian women on the basis of their marriage contracts to merchants trading in Australia. With Australian immigration officials implementing a class-based system of certificates that sometimes exempted merchants from racial exclusion, the wives of many South Asian traders continued to arrive at Australian shores.

The Urdu memoirs of Muhammad Bux from Lahore highlight that, in addition to tightening settler borders, wives also negotiated the partitions structuring gender relations in their families. In around 1891, when his wife Fatima Ghulam and their youngest daughter approached the port of Fremantle, it was still daytime. Bux recounted, 'I thought that if we leave for the city straight away, it will be a strange thing for the locals to see a lady with a veil, because they do not know anything about the veil and they have no such concept.'[127] Fatima Ghulam and her daughter spent their first afternoon in Fremantle on board the ship, only coming ashore when dusk had fallen. As Bux's recollections confirm, the institution of *purdah*, or seclusion, played a role in cloaking the travels of South Asian women from settler view.

While the written accounts of Bengali women confirm that gendered partitions profoundly shaped the architecture of South Asian knowledges in the decades that *Kasasol Ambia* was circulating, they tend to omit the omnipresence of ayahs in domestic spaces.[128] The relationships between gender, class and knowledge are not at all simple, the ayah often featuring in Sufi narratives as the seasoned storyteller guiding her young charge at key junctures.[129] By the time British missionaries began to arrive in late-nineteenth-century Bengal to 'educate' women observing seclusion, in the district of Khulna, for example, Moslema Khatun already knew how to write, rejecting a suitor by means of a Bengali letter she left lying on her father's bed.[130] By the time Moslema's only daughter, Sajeda Khatun, was sewing the English alphabet into a quilt under the tutelage of Christian missionaries in Hugli, she had already published Urdu translations of excerpts of two Bengali novels. Years later, in 1960s Dhaka, it was an ayah by the name of Bubu who first introduced Sajeda Khatun's granddaughters to the songs circulating in Sufi shrines in the dockside neighbourhoods of Bengal.

As the 1895 edition of *Kasasol Ambia* was circulating through Bengal, an ayah described as 'One Native Adult (Servant) (Female)' and 23-year-old 'Dowlah' were two of the women who departed from Calcutta for the Australian colonies.[131] Dowlah was the only woman among the sixteen South Asian passengers on the *Lalpoora*. She crossed the Indian Ocean in steerage with her 5-year-old son. Shipping records do not tell us whether she observed seclusion; some South Asian women travelling to Australian ports did not.[132] She arrived in Sydney in spring 1896.[133] On landing, it is likely that Dowlah, her son Boolbahar Shah and her husband Nasseralla Shah made their way to Redfern, where the draperies on Elizabeth Street operated as important nodes in South Asian migration. Whether or not Kewsee Beebe, Mrs Daytum or Jumnah lived on Elizabeth Street in Redfern during Dowlah's first few days, other women who had recently arrived from the port of Calcutta were 30-year-old Shubhadra from 'Nepaul' and 30-year-old Nanki from 'Benaras', the latter travelling with her 8-year-old daughter Ramrutty.[134] Many South Asian women also arrived in Sydney from British Indian ports other than Calcutta.

White hysteria about the 'darkest colony of Redfern' frequently erupted in newspapers during the 1890s. The week that Dowlah's family arrived, a debate was underway about the granting of hawkers' licenses to 'female hawkers' in Redfern, confirming that some women were working peddling goods.[135] As the memoirs of Aboriginal writer Ruby Langford Ginibi confirm, South Asian women were travelling the routes connecting Redfern importers to Australian interior towns. Reminiscing about her childhood spent along the Richmond River in inland New South Wales, she recalls that 'we used to row across here to buy lollies from an old Indian woman called Mrs Singh who had a caravan with wheels that was pulled along by a draughthorse.'[136]

We do not know when Dowlah departed from Australian shores. While some women stayed in the Australian colonies for years, crossing the Indian Ocean many times, Fatima Ghulam left in January 1895 and flatly refused to return.[137] Dowlah's departure from Australia likely left a trace in shipping records, a graveyard inscription, or family archives – a record that may one day confirm that the Bengali book of stories of the prophets accompanied her as she travelled back and forth across the sea, negotiating a series of borders. If a copy of *Kasasol Ambia* arrived in Broken Hill with a woman, it travelled along a route that has been obscured by a bewildering multiplicity of historical narratives that assume that women do not cross the Indian Ocean and have no relationship to knowledge.

VII. The Pen

Creation began with a pen, wrote Munshi Rezaulla, the first of the three poets of *Kasasol Ambia*. The first book claims that a concealed pen was one of the first things created, and the motif of the pen reoccurs throughout all eight books. In Rezaulla's metaphor for translation, the pen appears fleetingly to articulate a relationship between people and stories – a knowledge relation. As the poet's name tells us, writing was central to the livelihood of his family. 'Munshi' was a professional title for scribes – state secretaries in the Persian-language administrative apparatus of successive imperial regimes across South Asia.[138] The word *munshi* remains in use in many South Asian languages today. It is rendered most simply as 'writer' in English, but a more thorough translation describes a relation between people and texts. In Arabic, *munshi* is derived from the root *insha'* – creative works of prose composition. According to the rules of Arabic grammar, *munshi* (writer) is the creator of *insha'* (writing). While Rezaulla wrote that he was the son of Munshi Nozhatulla of Hugli, he did not specify whether his father served the British administration or South Asian courts.

When Rezaulla lamented his ignorance and asked 'in what form (*rupa*) will I write poetry?' his question had a double meaning. He was searching for the form of two entities: 'poetry' and 'I'. Articulating a twin search for narrative and self, Rezaulla realised he would find 'whatever, whomever' he sought, writing, 'I jumped into the sea.' His body immersed in an ocean of stories and his hands grasping pearls, when Razaulla narrates himself 'threading a chain' his words evoke a pen immersed in ink, threading lines of poetry. On careful reading, it is a metaphor that shows Rezaulla becoming a *munshi* (writer), the creator of *insha'* (writing). Concluding with 'Stories of the Prophets I name (*nama*) this chain', Rezaulla dramatises how he came to embody his name (*nama*) Munshi, and takes his place within a chain of scribes.

The pen, fleetingly visible at the heart of Rezaulla's account of translating books, theorises a knowledge relation that is quite distinct from the asymmetrical knower/known binary that underpins historiographical traditions born of European colonial rule. Michel Foucault characterised the power relation between knower and known in Enlightenment epistemes by evoking the striking image of the scientist gazing at specimens splayed on a white, rubbery table.[139] Munshi Rezaulla's metaphor invites audiences to inhabit another relation to knowledge. It entices audiences to immerse themselves in South Asian epistemes, even to grasp a pen that embodies another mode of knowledge production.

Its intricate imagery shimmering with many possible interpretations, the popularity of Rezaulla's poetry established the success of *Kasasol Ambia*. When he died, a second poet, Amiruddin, continued where Rezaulla had left off. On Amiruddin's death, Mohammad Ashraf became the third in a chain of writers to translate stories of the prophets into Bengali. As an 1897 edition of the book at the library of the University of Dhaka confirms, *Kasasol Ambia* was a title that continued to grow, as writer after writer picked up the pen.[140]

The stories they published under this title claimed genealogies to a number of non-European historiographical traditions. The claim that creation began with a pen, for example, can be traced to Muslim historiography (*ta'rikh*). Abbasid-era historian Al-Tabari (d. 923) narrated a lengthy account of the first pen in *The History of the Prophets and the Kings* – one of the foundational works of the *ta'rikh* genre. By Tabari's account Muhammad said that 'the first (thing) created by God is the Pen. God said to it: Write!, and it proceeded at that very hour to (write) whatever is going to be.'[141] To back up this claim, Tabari records that Yunus heard it from Abdallah, who heard it from Muawiyah, who heard it from Ayyub, who heard it from Ubadah, who heard it from his father Walid, who heard it from his father Ubadah, who heard it from Muhammad.[142] Recounting this chain of transmission, Tabari constructs what is known as an *isnad* – a footnoting strategy that underpins truth-claims in Muslim historiography. Using slightly different phrasing, Tabari then writes, 'The first thing created by God is the Pen. God commanded it to write everything', supporting this statement with another *isnad*.[143] In his history of the first pen, Tabari lays out ten different chains of transmission, several of which cite the dialogue between Muhammad and Abdullah.

Not all Muslim writers agreed that the pen was the first object; some claimed that a throne was created first. Others claimed it was 'light and dark'. With an *isnad* supporting each claim, Tabari's history collates the debates surrounding the first object. Each *isnad* highlights a route along which a history of the first object travelled from

Muhammad's lifetime to tenth-century Baghdad. Narrated together, they detail a circuitry of knowledge that comprises a far richer history of Muslims than any definitive 'truth' about the first object. While the first volumes of his work tell stories of the prophets, in the later volumes Tabari uses the *isnad* methodology to corroborate the histories of kings.

Tabari's *History* profoundly shaped the contours of the *ta'rikh* genre of historical storytelling. A few decades after the publication of *History* in Arabic, Abu Ali Balami (d. 997) wrote a Persian abridgement that circulated widely in the Indian Ocean region.[144] With the rise of European maritime power, when Enlightenment modes of historical storytelling arrived in South Asia with European colonisers, stories of the prophets were already travelling around Bengal, within works of *ta'rikh* and as standalone volumes. While there were significant innovations in citation strategies used by authors of *ta'rikh*, 'the truth' within Muslim historiography remained 'only as good as the *isnad* (chain) of its "construction,"'[145] as Janet Abu-Lughod writes. A corollary of this is that the possibility, even the necessity, of accommodating multiple truth claims about the past is built into the architecture of the *ta'rikh* discourse. As one Mamluk-era historian in Cairo wrote in around 1516, 'O you who say there exist perfect works on history, you are related to camels which do not know what they are carrying.'[146]

When the three poets of *Kasasol Ambia* put pen to paper in nineteenth-century Bengal, they drew on some of the strategies in Persian and Arabic history books to order stories from South Asian knowledge systems. The tale of Khidr explicitly cites *Iskandarnama* (The Book of Alexander) – a genre of books narrating the travels of Alexander the Great in South Asia. The evil king 'Manju' from whom Khidr shelters the poor boatman is a character from Buddhist texts. The account of Zelekha's love for Yusuf draws on Persian Sufi romances, citing the many Bengali translations already in circulation. The fish's words of advice to Yunus echo dialogues from the *Panchatantra* genre of Sanskrit texts in which animals speak and offer counsel.

We can trace figures like Manju and Purusha, Shiva and Brahma, advice-giving birds and fish to Sanskrit texts. However, in nineteenth-century Bengal, these were characters who became popular through performances of Bengali-language books belonging to the *itihasa-*

puranas historiographical tradition. In South Asian languages today, some of the meanings of '*itihasa*' and '*purana*' approximately correspond to the English word 'history'. As historian Kumkum Chatterjee writes, works of *itihasa-puranas* 'constituted a very important seed bed from which various literary and narrative traditions in different South Asian languages drew sustenance for many centuries.'[147]

Importantly, when 'Indic' characters from the *itihasa-puranas* genre appear in *Kasasol Ambia*, they are not simply inserted into 'Islamic' epistemes. Their stories retain something of the architecture of knowledge that the characters were orginally embedded in. For example, the fish only speaks to Yunus in a 'second narration', when the poet returns to the story in greater detail. This storytelling method of interlocking frame-tales – stories within stories within stories – organises the *Panchatantra* genre of animal fables, which originated in around 300 CE. It is a strategy that appears throughout *Kasasol Ambia*, Muhammad and Abdullah's dialogue providing one of the many frames within which stories unfold. When the three poets of *Kasasol Ambia* put pen to paper in nineteenth-century Bengal, we can also say that they drew on Bengali storytelling strategies to order stories from Muslim knowledge systems.

When a traveller departed from Calcutta with an 1895 edition of *Kasasol Ambia*, they were accompanied by a text that showed them how to inhabit a knowledge relation quite different from Enlightenment epistemes, inducting attentive listeners and readers into a multiplicity of narratives that move between past, present and future. Whether it was Dowlah or Abdul Sattar, Sher Khan, Anno Khan, Mirza Khan or an unnamed ayah who brought these Bengali stories of the prophets to Broken Hill, each highlights a route along which many South Asian stories travelled to Australian interiors, if not a copy of *Kasasol Ambia*. Narrated together, they detail a circuitry of knowledge that comprises a far richer history of South Asian diaspora than any definitive truth about who brought this particular book to Broken Hill.

Confirming that South Asians travelled with methods of historical storytelling, the presence of the copy of *Kasasol Ambia* at Broken Hill offers a glimpse into the vast libraries of knowledge that arrived in the Australian interior with colonised people from other parts of the British Empire. In contrast to the singular narratives of progress leading to the modern nation-state that British historians have told from the late nineteenth century, *Kasasol Ambia* could accommodate multiple traditions without arranging them in racist hierarchies. Whether or not they viewed the world through the metaphors contained in *Kasasol Ambia*, these were meaning-making techniques available to South Asians at a moment of escalating racism. As I have shown in this chapter, these are also emplotment strategies that we can use today to narrate the past.

Critiques of colonial relations between knower and known have now long shaped analyses of imperial power. The many alternative knowledge relations articulated in colonised peoples' epistemes belongs in the palette of tools that writers today use to critique power. When writing histories of class, race and gender relations, we can claim continuity to, extend, argue with and innovate historiographical traditions belonging to non-European epistemes.

3

SEVEN VOYAGES OF KHAWAJAH MUHAMMAD BUX

Sindbad the Sailor is the most infamous teller of Indian Ocean tales. He departed seven times from the port of Basra, returning each time with a heavier purse and an extraordinary story. After a lifetime of voyaging, having retired to his gardens in Baghdad where warbling birds praised Allah 'in various voices and tongues', Sindbad invited into his grand home a poorer man – a porter.[1] The prosperous merchant spun the tale of his very first sea voyage, beginning, 'Porter my story is astonishing ... how much toil and trouble I have endured at the beginning!'[2]

Within the frame-tale of a dialogue between a richer and a poorer man, Sindbad's seven voyages string together narrative motifs from various genres of merchant storytelling long circulating the Indian Ocean. With the earliest extant reference to his voyages appearing in a tenth-century book catalogue compiled in Baghdad, listing the title 'Sindbad the Wise', the fabled Sindbad has left his trace on many seafarers' narratives in turn.[3] In the early 2000s, a family of traders circulating between Australia and South Asia for over a century compiled two more such travelogues: an Urdu manuscript titled *Lahore Ka Sindbad* (Sindbad of Lahore) and an unpublished English translation called 'Memoirs of Khawajah Muhammad Bux, Australian Businessman'.[4]

The narrator of these travelogues, Muhammad Bux, embarked on his first Indian Ocean voyage in around 1875, when he was eighteen years old. By then a steam shipping revolution had consolidated European dominance over sea-lanes. When Bux retired as a prosperous merchant in the city of Lahore in the 1920s, after a lifetime of navigating waters transformed by steam shipping, his wealthy family were known as the *Australiawallahs*. While some non-European traders flourished under European regimes of colonial rule, very few amassed great wealth through Australian trade, as racially exclusive border regimes had culminated in 'White Australia' placing tight restrictions on both Asian capital and labour.[5] Against the odds, by 1929 the Bux family not only had over £40,000 in capital in Perth, according to settler sources, but also owned more than fifty properties in Lahore.[6] During the last decade of his life, Bux invested his wealth in three monuments in a neighbourhood in Lahore today known as Australia Chowk, or 'Australia bazaar'.[7] In addition to building a mosque and a girls' school at Australia Chowk, Bux employed a *munshi* (scribe) to write an account of his travels.[8] Likely sitting at one of the fifty premises that he owned by 1925 in Australia Chowk, Bux orated to his *munshi* that his early life was full of toil and trouble (Fig. 7).

Since Bux's death in 1929, his family have repeatedly returned to the stories penned during those sittings with his *munshi*. In the 1940s, his son Amir Bux, businessman and the founder of Australasia Bank in Lahore, employed a calligrapher to write the travelogue in Urdu.[9] With the Australasia Bank operating over 100 branches across East and West Pakistan by 1971, theirs was a trading family with significant economic, military and political clout in South Asia by the time multiculturalism was officially adopted in Australia as a new form of nationalism in the aftermath of 'White Australia'.[10]

In the early 2000s, when Muhammad Bux's Australia-based grandson, Khalid Bux, initiated the most recent Urdu and English editions of the travelogue, he did so with the support of senior officials from the Pakistani government and military.[11] Travelling from Sydney to Rawalpindi, he approached General Tareeq Majeed, then the commander of the X Corps military unit, which operates at the India–Pakistan border at Jammu and Kashmir. As Khalid Bux writes, he secured 'the good offices and expertise of Comm. (Rtd.) Tariq Majeed and Mr Syed Haider Hassan, who got the Urdu text translated into English.'[12]

The Bux family enjoyed relations with the founding fathers of the Pakistani nation Muhammad Ali Jinnah and poet Allama Iqbal, and have since 'emerged as informal representatives of Australia in Pakistan', as historian Samina Yasmeen writes.[13] As the preface to the English edition of Bux's travelogue suggests, they are also called upon by the Pakistani state to operate as its representatives in Australia. When the English translation of Bux's memoirs was completed in 2004, it was provisionally titled 'Amazing Migrant'. Its preface was written by the High Commissioner for Pakistan stationed in Canberra and celebrated the 'pioneering zeal' of a seafarer 'defiant in the face of innumerable obstacles'.[14]

As historians of diaspora have pointed out, South Asians in the settler offshoots of the British Empire have long been viewed through the binary of either model minority or undesirable other.[15] In the early 2000s, the Bux family were part of a global tier of some of the most powerful South Asians across the Anglophone West who embraced the roles of the 'pioneer', 'amazing migrant' and 'model minority', precisely as a constellation of Western institutions began imprisoning, deporting and demonising the most vulnerable South Asians in the aftermath of the 11 September attacks.[16] The particular workings of this process in Australia in its Indian Ocean context become clear if we place the translation of Bux's travelogue to English in 2001–2004 within one set of bilateral negotiations that were underway between the Australian and Pakistani governments at the time.

Over the years that Pakistani state officials patronised the English translation of the Bux family history into a tale of the 'amazing migrant', the Australian government spent $3 million imprisoning and deporting another South Asian family: Afghan refugees Roqia and Ali Bakhtiari and their six children.[17] After two years and six months of imprisonment in the remote South Australian desert, 13-year-old Alamdar Bakhtiari and 12-year-old Montazar Bakhtiari escaped from the Woomera Detention Centre in July 2002. Receiving significant media attention, they became the 'face of detention in Australia' when they travelled over 1,000 kilometres to Collins Street, Melbourne to apply for asylum at the British consulate.[18] In retaliation, the Australian government negotiated with the Pakistani government to deport the entire Bakhtiari family to Pakistan, agreeing in exchange to 'liberalise visa policies' for Pakistani 'business communities ... students and academics' travelling to Australia.[19] In addition, Australian authorities committed to resource and train Pakistani military forces operating along the India–Pakistan border.[20]

In this chapter I use the structure of the Sindbad cycle of voyages to construct an alternative narrative to the story of the 'amazing migrant' to house Bux's history. As cultural historians have shown, the Sindbad corpus is a repository of many travel tales, the pages of a recent English edition containing traces of stories from Homer's Greek *Odyssey*, the Sanskrit tales of Sanudasa the Merchant and various Arabic and Persian travelogues belonging to the *aja'ib* (wonders) genre of travel literature.[21] During his second voyage, Sindbad even dramatises how stories circulate through the ages, when he is stranded in a perilous valley of diamonds crawling with snakes. When a slaughtered sheep inexplicably falls from the sky and lands at his feet, as he narrates to the porter, 'I recalled a story I used to hear a long time ago.'[22] He remembers a tale in which merchants baited giant birds with lumps of meat and used them to harvest jewels. Sindbad scripts himself into the older tale, filling his pockets with diamonds and binding himself to the dead sheep with his turban. As he tells the porter, an eagle swoops down to the valley to clutch the slaughtered carcass 'with his talons and flew up into the air with it and with me clinging to it'.[23] As this episode demonstrates, crucial to merchants' ongoing movement across the Indian Ocean world was their ability to inhabit, appropriate and sometime assimilate into the narratives of others.

I read Bux's travelogue as a similar repository of oceanic tales. The various manuscripts detailing Bux's travels, written since the 1920s and more recently printed, bear traces of some narrative motifs circulating the Indian Ocean in the era of steam shipping. From this perspective, the tale of the 'amazing migrant' or 'pioneer' comprises just one of many stories that left a trace on Bux's corpus of tales, as his narratives were harnessed by various storytellers for different purposes. Piecing together some of the stories that left an impression on Bux's journeys as well as his subsequent recollections of them, I retell seven of his many voyages across the Indian Ocean, beginning with a brief account of his childhood.

Early Conditions

Muhammad Bux's father was a trader whose forefathers Bux traced to Kashmir – a region increasingly embroiled in violence through the 1920s as colonial demarcations between Sikhs, Hindus and Muslims were renegotiated in a new era of nationalist movements.[24] Born in 1857, Bux was the eldest son of the eldest son of the eldest son in a household in the walled city of Lahore – the capital of the British Province of Punjab through which five (*panj*) watercourses (*ab*) flow into the Indus River, which in turn eventually empties into the Indian Ocean. Bux's grandfather had served as an administrator for the military regiment of the Sikh kingdom of Ranajit Singh (d. 1839).[25] After Punjab was annexed by the British Empire in 1849, his forefathers began trading in handwoven textiles and camels.

Bux's mother was from Gujranwala, a city some 50 miles away from Lahore, across the Ravi River.[26] Only at the age of eleven did Bux discover that the woman who had suckled him was not his birth mother, but his paternal grandmother. As Bux narrated to his scribe, 'When I was just three years old my mother died.'[27] He does not mention how she died. Listening to his tale of hardship, the *munshi* wrote that Bux was thirteen years old when he first embarked on a solitary journey beyond the gates of Lahore. He ran away from home after being badly beaten. Bux remembered, 'whenever my father was harsh to my stepmother, or abused her, I used to report this immediately to her mother. She would come to our house and take sides with her daughter.'[28] One day, when his tormented stepmother appealed to Bux to fetch her mother, he refused. She responded with anger and 'abused and thrashed' her young stepson.[29]

Leaving the city through Taxali gate, without 'shirt, shoes or headgear' or any money to pay the bridge toll, Bux traversed the Ravi River at a point where poor travellers crossed and headed on foot to his mother's family.[30] When he arrived in Gujranwala, his relatives were deeply aggrieved by his state and took him in to live with them for a while. Eventually, however, Bux's uncle brought him back to Lahore.

Bux's stepmother did not live long. Again, he does not mention how she died. When his father remarried again, Bux's new stepmother was also cruel to him, though covertly so.[31] Seeking escape from the violence endlessly replaying in his father's home, and having learnt at a tender age that there was no return to his mother's home, at the age of eighteen Bux again departed from Lahore. Taking over 200 rupees without telling anyone, this time he headed for Bombay. Decades later, citing Persian poet Sa'adi (d. 1292), he would advise his sons and their sons in turn, 'if you stay home all your life, you will remain immature as a man. Go out and see the world.'[32]

I. Bombay to Basra

Voyaging to the Persian Gulf, Muhammad Bux returned with a story about British capital. When Bux first reached Bombay, he apprenticed himself to a perfume maker. Selling 'scent' by day, he returned each night to a barber's shop in 'Phool Gali' (Flower Alley), owned by Punjabi villager Karam Din.[33] Here at the barber's in Bhindi Bazaar, Bux heard many tales of the sea. While the perfume trade saw Bux make a circuit of 'houses of the rich, the respectable, and the senior officials' in Bombay, it also took him to 'the houses of the prostitutes ... where it was next to impossible to safeguard one's chastity.'[34] Resolving to quit the perfume trade, each night in the Phool Gali den of stories he listened to yarns about 'conditions in Europe'.[35] It was not long before Bux secured a contract on a British steam ship after negotiations with Shadi Khan Pathan – the Punjabi *serang* or boatswain who was in charge of South Asian sailors on board the vessel.

Employed as a fireman shovelling coal into the engine, Bux joined the ranks of the lascars. With fixed-term contracts underpinning their employment, lascars were defined as 'free labour' – one of the key premises of the new era of liberal imperialism that emerged alongside the piecemeal abolition of slavery from the 1830s. The 'lascar' was invented as a category in a series of 'Asiatic Articles' negotiated between the East India Company and the British government, and enabled British firms to legally employ South Asian sailors and pay them one-fifth to one-third of the wages of European sailors, while restricting their ability to remain at ports beyond British India.[36]

There were three first-time sailors on board the steam ship. On the third day the ship encountered a terrible storm that made visible the labour hierarchy, sometimes enforced with beatings, which kept the vessel in motion. Winds were so fierce that it was barely possible to remain upright. As Bux would tell listeners for many years, 'the officer of the ship ordered all the firemen to tie a rope to their bodies and keep shoving coal to the engine furnace ... if one left his place to go to the upper deck, the captain would beat him and send him down.'[37]

It was when the 'nausea' and 'vomiting' started that the three first-time sailors abandoned hope. They 'decided that it would be better to commit suicide by jumping overboard.'[38] Gathering on the pitch dark deck, 'Imam ud Din, a resident of Sialkot, jumped into the sea straightaway.'[39] Bux relayed that he too was about to jump, but that at 'the last second a white guard got hold of my collar and pulled me back. He also caught hold of my companion.'[40] Jumping to their deaths would have put the two lascars in breach of their contract.[41] They were locked up and overnight, 'by the grace of Allah, the adverse winds subsided before dawn, and the sea became calm like a plate.'[42]

At the port of 'Bu-Shehr' where the vessel docked on the Persian Gulf, the two new lascars attempted to desert the ship. They were discovered, and were punished by the captain with imprisonment during off-duty hours. As Bux would tell his sons, when the ship docked at Basra, 'a sweat river falls into the sea' and 'Baghdad, the holy city, was just a day's march from here.'[43]

Under the lascar regime, Shadi Khan Pathan was responsible for the discipline and control of the newly recruited lascar deck hands. Their repeated attempts to 'jump ship' likely played a part in the souring of relations between the British captain and the *serang*. At the time, the port of Basra was under the dominion of the Ottoman Caliphate. With maritime law interlocking with land laws at Indian Ocean ports, at this meeting point of power regimes the *serang* sought to challenge the British captain by mobilising Ottoman law. As Bux recalled, 'Shadi Khan Pathan approached a court in Basra', appealing to the 'rule of the Turkish Caliph'. The *serang* 'petitioned the court that two of his compatriots were locked up in the ship and were not allowed to disembark, although they were innocent.'[44]

In Bux's telling, when Shadi Khan Pathan returned with Ottoman soldiers to the vessel, the captain 'positioned himself on the landing gear of the ship to intercept them.' The captain informed the soldiers 'that these men were employed on the ship and were confined to lock up, to foil their attempt to desert.' He convinced them to turn back, arguing that 'if they were set free, no substitute shall be available to carry on the task on board.'[45]

As soon as the officers of the Ottoman Caliphate disembarked, 'Shadi Khan, the Sarang, was handcuffed and arrested' and imprisoned in the cell along with the two lascars. Bux recounted that 'we were set free on the departure of the ship' and 'when the ship reached "Bu-Shehr," we along with Shadi Khan were locked-up.' His mercantile interests were not thwarted by his imprisonment during off-duty hours, and he saw that 'cotton and rosewater containers were loaded on the ship at that port.'[46]

On return to Bombay, traders crowded at the port to meet the incoming ship. The containers of rosewater and bales of cotton were unloaded and the shipmaster discharged the lascar crew and the *serang*. The two first-time lascars were not awarded salaries or experience certificates. The captain let them off easy 'since we were both raw hands'. The *serang* who had directly challenged British authority received the harshest punishment. Shadi Khan Pathan was discharged with no payment, his 'previous certificates were confiscated and through a publication, he was blacklisted for any further employment.'[47]

Making his way through familiar streets to Karam Din's shop with empty pockets, Bux bore ill tidings for the family of the Punjabi sailor who had jumped to his death. He had earned nothing but had been initiated into the strict rules governing lascars' journeys, having repeatedly witnessed the triumph of British capital. When Bux returned to the den of Punjabi storytelling at Bhindi Bazaar, he had his own extraordinary tales of the sea, describing one of the most powerful stories underwriting South Asians' voyages across the Indian Ocean: contract labour.

When Bux sat with his *munshi* many decades later, the fact he was addressing 'the young in general, and my sons in particular' no doubt shaped how he told this story.[48] The scribe's manuscript dramatised the simultaneous rise of British authority and decline in Ottoman power. While many lascars returned from Indian Ocean voyages with stories of collective action against European shipping companies, the moral weight of Bux's narrative clearly fell on the side of British capital, laying a template for his sons to follow.

II. Bombay to Shanghai

Voyaging to China, Muhammad Bux returned with a story about Asian capital. On this voyage he travelled to ports that feature not only in Arabic and Persian tales, but also in the Sanskrit corpus of stories titled *Kathasaritsagara* (The Ocean of the Rivers of Stories). It was a collection written from the tenth century that claimed to be a retelling of an elusive, even older title composed before the fourth century. During Bux's lifetime tales from the *Kathasaritsagara* were being told throughout Punjab in many spoken South Asian languages.[49] As historians have pointed out, the Arabic tales of Sindbad share many common plots with the adventures of the merchant Sanudasa – the Brahmin hero at the centre of a cycle of voyages in the *Kathasaritsagara*.[50] Reanimating tropes that had recurred over centuries of South Asian narratives about merchant masculinity, on his return from China, Bux told a tale of ports where business acumen could unlock vast riches while duplicitous courtesans lay traps for traders.

When Bux contracted as a lascar headed to Shanghai, he was paid one month's salary of 'fifteen rupees' in advance.[51] Investing more than half this sum, he 'purchased onion baskets worth eight rupees as merchandise'.[52] African and Asian sailors on British ships frequently operated as traders too, and Bux watched as his co-workers sold their onions at markets in the first two ports of Penang and Singapore.[53] When the vessel reached the British colony of Hong Kong, Bux, observing a favourable market, sold his baskets of onions. He recounted, 'I got Rs. 162/- from this sale whereas my cost price was Rs. 8/ only.'[54]

The island of Hong Kong had been ceded to British control by the Qing dynasty following the First Opium War in 1839. Venturing into waters where the rise of steam shipping and the completion of a global telegraph network had dramatically increased the dominance of British merchants, Bux remarked that there were many Punjabi military men in service to the British officials at the port. His travelogue reports the presence of South Asians and, in particular, people from Punjab at every port city, both at mosques and within British garrisons. Leaving Hong Kong with his first profits of 154 rupees, Bux took note of the workings of the tier of trade in which many South Asians began to participate, all the while contracted to British capital.[55]

The vessel next docked at the port of Shanghai for fifteen days. Bux observed women with 'goat-like feet', and commented that Muslims at local mosques looked no different to other residents of Shanghai. He watched with interest when 'the ship officials started procuring merchandise for taking to Bombay.'[56] While the practised traders bought mats and quilts, Bux narrated that, 'being inexperienced and not as knowledgeable', he invested the profits from his onion sale in 'silk handkerchiefs and shawls. Since I had acquired judgment about silk in my early age.'[57]

'Hereditary financial experience', as business historian Rajat Kanta Ray writes, 'was essential to operate with facility through the new circuits created by the communications revolution', and Bux carefully described to his sons how to observe markets, keep accounts and inspect goods.[58] His narration of a chain of exchanges told a story about the economic movement of goods that was quite distinct, but never entirely separate, from the physical processes of circulation across the seas. Bux described the behaviour of merchant capital in oceanic motion, walking readers through his discovery that he could make his earnings grow by transporting onions and silk goods, rather than coins in his purse.

This is an old story. Following the lead of the ship officials to invest his capital in what he knew best – textiles – Bux began telling a tale that has captivated many for centuries. In one didactic story recounted in the *Kathasaritsagara*, for example, a young merchant begins a chain of transactions with the seed capital of a dead mouse, selling it as cat food.[59] He uses the proceeds to buy gram, which he uses to barter with a thirsty woodcutter. In exchange for the gram and a coveted pitcher of water, the shrewd trader receives wood, precisely on the eve of a timber shortage. Beginning with his tale of onions and silks, the long series of exchanges that Bux narrated over the remainder of his travelogue reiterate this narrative of merchant capital, echoing a vast archive of South Asian trading stories. In Bux's narration, while favourable markets and seed capital could stimulate riches, business instinct and knowledge of goods were the keys to profit.

Like in the merchants' tales in the *Kathasaritsagara* corpus, courtesans trading in sex play a recurring role in the city bazaars that Bux describes. On his return voyage – while he praised the port of

Singapore as a city of traders, noting that 'streets were well laid out' and 'the sanitation arrangements were excellent' – Bux cautioned his sons that in such a city, 'one could see every kind of trader.' He elaborated: 'By chance, I visited the quarter of the prostitutes one night.'[60]

Bux described 'beautiful and well made up European prostitutes, sitting there on the chairs, at the end of the bazaar.' He observed that their 'pimps' were 'actively going up and down the bazaar' in search of buyers. While these pimps sometimes accepted lower prices from non-European buyers, Bux warned that they would 'then demand the balance inside the house.' Nearby there were also 'the residences of Japanese prostitutes. In addition there were Malayan and Indian prostitutes.' Observing these streets between dusk and 2.00 a.m., Bux recalled that when rich Europeans arrived in their vehicles, 'the way they were pulled in different directions by the wooing prostitutes was in itself a spectacle worth enjoying. Similarly, the non-Europeans arriving in carriages faced the same ordeal.'[61]

'Houses of ill repute' feature in Bux's accounts of many ports and the appearance of prostitutes always signposts a moral lesson for his sons. For example, it was on turning his back on the 'honour-wrecking surroundings' of the courtesans he encountered as a perfume-seller in Bombay that Bux first began looking for employment as a lascar. As Bux tells his sons, it was at this juncture that he dispatched by money order to his father in Lahore the '217 Rupees' he had 'taken without asking' before embarking on his very first oceanic voyage.[62] Leaving the prostitute's lair behind served to demonstrate Bux's morality, and by employing this trope, his tale was consistent with the British social reform discourse across the British Empire from the mid nineteenth century.

As many writers have shown, prior to the era of the British Raj, courtesans constituted an influential female elite in many South Asian cities, their salons operating as 'finishing schools' educating young elite men in manners, social etiquette, and the ethics of comportment.[63] In the corpus of Sanudasa tales, for example, a courtesan named Ganga entrances rich Sanudasa, inducting him into the art of pleasure. When Ganga drains him of all his wealth, Sandusa embarks on a series of voyages, driven by poverty. In the end, when Sandusa is a rich, celebrated merchant of the sea, his mother, Mitravati, reveals that it was she who enlisted Ganga to apprise her son of the ways of the world.[64]

While the rules dictating how young men should engage with women trading in sex differ between the path that Mitravati laid out for her son and in Bux's tale for his own sons, both storytellers enlisted the courtesan as a character to induct their sons into ethical behaviour. After describing brothel scenes in titillating detail, Bux appeals to his children, 'Readers! At that time, I was at the peak of my youth and had enough money to spend. However, it was the blessing and grace of the Almighty, which kept me safe at such lewd places.'[65]

After a brief stop at a port of exiled South Asian prisoners, likely on the Andaman Islands, Bux's vessel reached Colombo – the port of entry to the island today known as Sri Lanka and referred to 'Sarandip' in centuries of mariners' tales. Consistent with accounts of Sarandip as an island of abundance in both the Sanudasa tales and Sindbad voyages, in Bux's tale it is a place where 'coconut is produced ... in abundance. Tea of many kinds is also grown ... Cardamom and cinnamon are produced in such an abundance that the residents used cinnamon wood as fuel ... every kind of precious stone is also found there.'[66] Colombo had by then undergone a revolution in transportation and been transformed into a major industrial hub. In Bux's words, it was 'a big junction of the major shipping lanes. An electric tram operates in the city.'[67]

British social reform discourse, colonial shipping lines and electric trams shaped the very circuitry that Bux navigated between ports, and it was perhaps over many tellings that his accounts of this voyage came to echo older tales of courtesans and Sarandip. What is certain is that an existing repertoire of Indian Ocean stories found renewed expression in attenuated form in the narratives of Bux's first series of market exchanges penned in Persian in the 1920s by his *munshi*, in Urdu in the 1940s, and in English in the 2000s.

As Bux recounted, when the ship eventually returned to Bombay, 'the traders crowded in immediately' and so continued numerous exchanges of goods and stories. Bux received 'an excellent certificate of performance' – his ticket to future merchant activity while in service to British capital. In addition to receiving his outstanding wages of 15 rupees, he sold the 'silk handkerchiefs on double the profit.'[68] With a full purse, this lascar-turned-merchant once more made his way to Bhindi Bazaar through the streets of Bombay. Like many merchants before him, Bux might have told this tale of onions, silks, coconuts and cinnamon to poorer travellers from Punjab who gathered at a shop in Phool Gali. The physical circulation of a sailor across the Indian Ocean was by no means the same as the economic circulation of the sailor's capital, and as Bux narrated in his old age to those about to inherit his wealth in Lahore and Perth, the key to future prosperity was harnessing each to the service of the other.

III. Bombay to Mecca

Voyaging to the Hejaz, Muhammad Bux returned with a story about being lost in the desert. Growing tired of the working conditions of lascars, at a moment when he didn't know whether to return to Lahore or stay in Bombay, Bux met Fojdar Khan, a very ill man from Amritsar, Punjab who had once worked as a clerk for the colonial government. Khan suggested to Bux that they 'go for Hajj, so that all of our journeys may be blessed.'[69] Together, they went to the ticketing offices of 'Hajji Cassum & Co (HCCo)', one of the major firms in Bombay selling passage to Mecca.[70]

With Bombay at the crossroads of shipping lanes, HCCo operated by connecting poorer groups of *hajjis* on their way to Mecca with richer traders. While 'Hajji Qasim Ji' first informed the two travellers that 'the normal fare for two persons was rupees sixty', Bux haggled the price down to 20 rupees, pleading that they 'were destitute and hence deserved to obtain tickets on concessional rate.'[71] Over the remainder of Bux's account of hajj, negotiations between rich merchants and poor travellers reoccur as a motif propelling the journey.

The hajj pilgrimage to Mecca has long been a dense site of knowledge production in both European and non-European languages.[72] In 1852, for example, former East India Company employee Richard Burton – before he went on to translate *The Seven Voyages of Sinbad* into English – travelled to Mecca, 'disguised as an Afghan doctor'. As he wrote in his *Personal Narrative of a Pilgrimage to El-Medina and Mecca*, 'thoroughly tired of "progress" and of "civilisation" ... longing, if truth be told, to set foot on that mysterious spot which no vacation tourist has yet described, measured, sketched and photographed, I resolved to resume my old character of a Persian wanderer.'[73] The account was an instant bestseller. With a third edition reprinted by the end of the

1870s, the book profoundly shaped British popular approaches to hajj as the 'Moslem pilgrimage'.[74] At the time the rise of steam shipping had dramatically increased the number of South Asians embarking on hajj, and Muhammad Bux's voyage coincided with intensifying production of British surveillance literature about poorer *hajjis* – 'pauper pilgrims' in colonial discourse.[75]

Echoing Burton's narrative, British colonial administrators approached hajj to Mecca through the dichotomy of barbarism versus civilisation, viewing it as a schema of movement that opposed the pathway shaping modern Europe: the march of 'progress' toward 'civilisation'. With the opening of the Suez Canal in 1869 unleashing racialised hysteria about the spread of diseases to Europe from the colonies, the poorer *hajji* was regarded in colonial literature as a dangerous vehicle of sickness.[76] On the basis of the vast corpus of surveillance discourse produced about 'pauper pilgrims', British administrators devised reform schemes targeting South Asian shipping companies, travel agents and Indian Ocean networks of Muslim traders. As legal theorist Wael Hallaq writes, 'the transmutations that were effected in the Muslim world through direct and indirect European domination' and the rhetoric of 'reform' start from the premise that Muslim institutions were 'deficient and in need of correction and modernising revision.'[77] In Hallaq's analysis reform models of 'transition … from uncivilised to civilised' always enacted 'ontological imperialism'.[78] The Raj administrators ultimately appointed the British travel company Thomas Cook & Son as 'the official travel agent of the hajj' in attempts to achieve a government-backed monopoly of hajj traffic.[79]

Khan and Bux departed from Bombay at a time when colonial resources were increasingly being invested in reforming the route to Mecca. They navigated a fierce storm en route to the port of Aden. As they approached the next port of Jeddah, the *hajjis* donned the white robes supplied by HCCo when they 'observed a mountain-like structure rising ahead.'[80] After paying an Ottoman landing tax at Jeddah and with no means to hire camels, Khan and Bux walked for three days to Mecca. There they 'accompanied a trader by the name of Muhammad Hussain to the Indian serail, along with all the other poor Hajjis.'[81] This merchant assigned a guide to his poorer countrymen, who led the *hajjis* in their circumambulation of the Kaaba, which Bux noted was a ceaseless affair: 'You find people going around it at all times.'[82] He recalled that people would steal shoes, even from outside the house of Allah.

With the beginning of the month of Ramadan, more and more *hajjis* arrived from across the world and Bux parted ways with Khan to join a caravan of travellers headed to the city of Medina. While the others rode camels across the distance of nearly 300 miles, Bux kept pace with them on foot despite his wounded, swollen feet, because otherwise 'the route was unknown'. They reached the grave of Muhammad after six days of travelling, where Bux, weary from the journey, fell into a deep sleep. The following morning, he headed to the bazaar 'with the intention to find some means for earning.' There he secured a job with 'an Indian shopkeeper' who was selling *kohl*, or eyeshadow. When the caravan of traders set off on their return to Mecca, Bux remained in Medina. As the *kohl* seller advised him, there existed another shorter route to Mecca for poorer *hajjis* travelling by foot.

A few days later, Bux and an unnamed South Asian man departed from Muhammad's grave following the directions of the *kohl* seller. Many years later, Bux would narrate a lengthy account of his journey through the desert in seven distinct stages. After 'the first stage on this route' the *hajjis* spent the night resting at the home of a hospitable Bedouin family. The following morning they continued on their way toward Mecca. Bux explained that at this 'second stage, we became overtired and lost all hope of making it.'[83] Encountering a girl 'tending to her flock of goats', they found their way to another Bedouin hut, where a couple provided them with a meal and a woven mat to sleep on.[84]

On the third day, for a while following a track their hosts had pointed out, Bux recounted that 'we came to a junction where this path split into three.' There Bux and his travelling companion had a disagreement; 'this was the parting of our ways.' Alone, Bux soon became lost in the desert. Neither trees nor houses marked the horizon. By sunset his 'water container was empty' and he 'prayed to Allah to show me the way.' Soon Bux saw 'a dense black cloud' on the darkening horizon, carried by a 'strong wind-like hurricane'. Caught in the grip of an angry storm, he remembered that 'the stones in the desert started hitting me with full force.' From the storm clouds, instead of rain, hailstones fell from the sky. Remembering that he 'had heard the wise men say that one must keep on running when it is bitterly cold', Bux began to sprint.[85] Reaching some 'wild bushes' he gathered twigs and attempted to start a fire using his shirt. The very last match he had with him ignited not a flame but 'some smoke'. As Bux recounted, 'it rained ceaselessly' all night and 'in my heart I was sure it was going to be my "final call." ... however my hopes revived [when] the flames became strong.'

The rain ceased with daybreak on the fourth day. But when the sun rose, Bux discovered, to his dismay, that 'the rain had obliterated all the paths. I could find not find any beaten path.' Unable to see any way forward, Bux 'started walking in a direction after a lot of reflection.' When he sighted a lone Bedouin with a camel, Bux ran to him, recounting that 'he was quite stunned to see me in this wilderness in such a deplorable condition. I told him my true story in complete detail.' Marvelling at his tale, the hospitable man took Bux to his home and fed him 'meat *pulao*'.[86]

When he awoke on the fifth day, Bux stocked up on dates and bread and continued on the path indicated by his host. He had 'gone about five miles' when he noticed 'two Bedouin ... with loaded double barrel guns.' They robbed Bux, leaving him 'standing stark naked'.[87] With no possessions, no clothes and finding no house to take cover during the night, he slept 'on the bare ground'. Awakening on the sixth day 'at dawn', Bux 'set out again'. At noon he arrived at a village, where he sought out the mosque – many Bedouin soon arrived for noon prayers. Marvelling at Bux's tale, they not only clothed him but also fed him 'with freshly cooked leavened bread, along with meat and dates'. On the seventh day Bux resumed his lone voyage, eventually reaching 'the holy city of Mecca after a journey of five gruelling days'.[88]

Bux's account was part of a vast corpus of hajj narratives that told the story of a solitary spiritual journey within a tale of a collective physical trek.[89] After he leaves the bazaar near Muhammad's grave, Bux traverses the wilderness and soon loses his travelling companion, loses his way, loses all his clothes and money, and almost loses all hope, only to find the way forward again through reflection, recalling the sayings of 'wise men', prayer, and telling his story to those he meets. His organistaion of this arduous twelve-day walk into seven stages signals that Bux was narrating a tale in a register distinct from the story of reform that structured not just British colonial surveillance but also modernist Muslim movements.

While various Muslim, Sikh and Hindu reform movements emerged from Punjab during Bux's lifetime, Muslim reform movements became increasingly yoked to an Urdu public sphere. As historian Farina Mir shows, various other forms of storytelling continued to thrive in Lahore in performance spaces organised around Punjabi-language texts. At the centre of the repertoire of Punjabi narratives disseminating through a network of shrines, tombs, fairs and other popular gatherings were epic romances, in which a (usually) male hero falls in love, retreats within himself and proceeds through seven stages, each step carrying him closer to the divine. Some of the most popular of these Punjabi tales circulating Lahore during Bux's youth were *Layla and Majnun* and *Hir Ranjha*.

In *Layla and Majnun*, when Qais cannot marry his lover Layla, he leaves Mecca and wanders through the Arabian wilderness, losing his way through his own interior landscape and eventually becoming mad (*majnun*) with grief. While *Hir Ranjha* is set in Punjab, one eighteenth-century edition of this story confirms that there has long been a dialogue between hajj narratives and Punjabi romances. Leaving behind his unhappy home in a village of Punjab, Hir falls in love with Ranjha, becoming her cowherd. When they cannot be together, lovesick Hir sings on the banks of the Chenab River, 'the *hajji* goes to Mecca, world by world, my Ranjhu is Mecca for me ... the *hajji* is within, the *ghazi* is within'.[90] These stories, which were transmitted aurally at *qawwali* performances at Sufi shrines throughout Punjab, as Farina Mir writes, sustained highly developed practices of listening, walking audiences through successive stages of the epic.[91]

Whether or not Bux drew on this repertoire of Punjabi tales in around 1880 to make sense of his own wanderings in the wilderness, his story stands apart from hajj accounts published in the 1920s by Muslim reformers who were the contemporaries of his sons and grandsons. For example, writer and reformer Abdul Majid Daryabadi (1892–1977) published an account of hajj in his Urdu-language magazine in 1929. Hailing from a family that had long been in service to the British Empire, Daryabadi undertook hajj about fifty years after Bux. On return to South Asia, the message he brought back from hajj for readers of his Urdu magazine called for them to become 'supporters of religion ... The Prophet does not seek poetry and *qawwali* songs; He seeks support for the religion.'[92] It is well documented that South Asian reform movements seeking to 'purify' and disentangle Hindu, Sikh and Muslim narratives from each other gained traction. Yet, as Mir shows, Punjabi storytelling sustained a discursive terrain that was not resistant to, but rather resilient against, the interconnected British and South Asian narratives of reform that powerfully transformed Islam during Bux's lifetime.

Bux recounts that he stayed in Bedouin households for the remainder of his solitary journey. He re-joined his friend Fojdar Khan in Mecca and completed all the rituals involved in hajj in the company of many others. After the end of 'hajj season', Bux awaited the arrival of a rumoured ship that he heard was 'likely to leave for Bombay soon', earning money by collecting date stones and dying cloth. After some time, a ship arrived whose traders 'accepted all the destitute on board'. In Bux's telling, 'it was due to the kind courtesy of the merchants' that he reached Bombay.[93] With extraordinary tales of days and nights spent navigating the deserts and seas, Bux 'went straight to the barbershop of Karam Din in Bhindi Bazaar.'[94]

The epic tale that Bux told about hajj illustrates that there were many intersecting and diverging routes that *hajjis* travelled to Mecca. When Bux reached a three-way juncture in the wilderness, at a moment when British colonists were producing narratives seeking to reform hajj and Muslim modernists hoped to define Islam with precision, he took an arduous route that saw him draw on various storytelling practices to script a path out of the desert, illuminating for those to come another way to Mecca.

IV. Bombay to Somalia

Voyaging to the East African coast, Muhammad Bux returned with a story about an island of gold. Accounts of gold-rich lands have shaped how travellers have navigated the Indian Ocean at least since the writings of Greek geographer Claudius Ptolemy (d. 168), if not earlier.[95] In the Sanskrit tales of Sanudasa, a group of seven merchants reach a steep valley that can only be reached with the aid of goats. They kill their goats and sew themselves into the skins, large grey birds carrying the travellers disguised as lumps of meat 'in their beaks through the sky all the way to the gold country'.[96] In Arabic mariners' tales, abundance in gold is central to accounts of the fabular island of Waqwaq – a land at the farthest reaches of the Indian Ocean region that has featured in Arab mapping since the tenth century CE, always marking the edge of navigated waters.[97] In both European and non-European accounts of the Indian Ocean, the island of gold often operates as an imperial metaphor for frontiers.

After hajj, perhaps through the networks of former government employee Fojdar Khan, Bux met 'a person by the name of 'Bahadara' – one of the titles presented to South Asians from trading and landed classes who had demonstrated loyalty to the British Empire during the rebellion of 1857.[98] 'Bahadara' secured Bux a 'job on a government ship', whereupon Bux, contracting with the colonial government of Bombay, departed for Aden as a lascar.[99]

The government vessel remained stationed at Aden for a period of fourteen months, the South Asian crew running errands for the British garrison at Aden. With the British government annexing large portions of the Somali coast through the 1880s, the foodstuffs for the British military garrison and coaling station at Aden were sourced from the East African coast when Bux was labouring across these waters.[100] It was a fortuitous voyage for Bux. The *serang* of the ship fell ill and Bux was appointed to take his place, supervising more than 150 deck hands. Ever attentive to monetary details, Bux reported that his salary jumped from 18 rupees to 50 rupees per month.[101]

Bux began to enjoy closer intimacy with the white men inhabiting the upper echelons of the ship. He was informed that 'an officer from England had arrived who was to be taken around the smaller atolls for sightseeing.' After a voyage of two days from Aden, the ship reached 'British Somaliland'. Bux received 'orders to take ten ship hands along for this sightseeing by the VIP', along the eastern shores of the African continent. At an island off the Somali coast, they 'disembarked along with the visiting dignitary' with Bux as the headman of ten lascars.[102]

The official whom Bux accompanied was a surveyor in search of gold and other precious minerals. Over two days, the surveyor climbed the hills and mountains on the small island. Bux recalled that 'the VIP got up to the top of the mountain and surveyed for some time through binoculars. He used to pick up some rocks and pass them to us. We kept storing these rocks in a sack for him.' Over the course of the expedition, at the peaks of an island he doesn't name, Bux recalled that the officer 'told me he had been to Australia'. The surveyor informed Bux that 'she is a very fine country and exports gold to other countries'.[103]

By then, British colonies in Africa and Australia alike had become key suppliers of gold bullion, emerging as crucial to British imperial infrastructure in the Indian Ocean, particularly following the establishment of the International Gold Standard in 1871.[104] It was in this context that British officials surveying the Indian Ocean rim became one key group within a larger coterie of European knowledge producers mapping both Australian and African geographies as 'blank spaces' to be filled in – 'a white patch for a boy to dream gloriously over', in the words of nineteenth-century novelist Joseph Conrad.[105]

As British surveyors' narratives confirm, colonised people were often part of the teams producing survey maps across the Indian Ocean rim. For example, when a party of colonists were seeking gold in 1875 in Yolngu country on the northern Australian coast, near what is today Darwin, eight Aboriginal workers accompanied them. One of the surveyors wrote in his diary that coastal Aboriginal sailors had 'been from time immemorial connected with the Malay fishermen ... all speak Malay and look forward to their arrival with joy.'[106] Encountering an Aboriginal seafarer who 'knew the points of the compass in Malay and even spoke a few words of English', he wrote that the sailor 'gave us a great deal of information he had been to Macassar & Singapore with the Malays and had a great admiration for those places.'[107] While this account hints that alternative stories to gold-rich Australia were circulating the Indian Ocean with Aboriginal travellers, if not Malay fishermen, the idea of 'Australia' appeared on Bux's horizon as he began ascending labour hierarchies and increasingly seeing the Indian Ocean through 'imperial eyes'.[108]

Returning to Bombay after a lengthy period of service to the British government, Bux decided that 'I did not need any further travelling.'[109] He was discharged with excellent certificates of service. As Bux recounted, 'I had firmly made up my mind to go back home and join my ancestral trade.'[110] Even promotion to the rank of *serang* did not alter the fact that the 'quality of rations provided for consumption was inferior. The quality of rice was so poor that even the animals would not eat it. Pulse tasted bitter.'[111] Disembarking at Bombay with his purse full of riches, Bux did not return to Bhindi Bazaar. He made his way back to Lahore, determined to try his hand at silk weaving.

Decades later, likely sitting at one of his premises in Australia Chowk in Lahore, when Bux recounted this voyage to the Gulf of Aden, he omitted details about the local non-European populations he encountered for the first time in his memoirs. While he mentioned landing at Berbera on the Somali coast as part of a rescue operation, he recorded nothing about its inhabitants. This stands in stark contrast to his close descriptions of local goods, markets, traders, mosques, foods and sometimes brothels at other ports. Despite his claim that it was his 'usual habit to meet the locals at every port' the only reference Bux made to people from African countries was during another voyage, when he commented with derision that Somali seafarers 'called themselves Muslims'.[112]

V. Lahore to London

Voyaging to the English Channel, Muhammad Bux returned with a story about the border regimes guarding the West. In the weaving trade in Lahore, he lasted only three months. He reasoned with his father that 'if I stuck to this profession for the rest of my life, I might gain nothing but my daily bread.' With dreams of economic ascension and captivating his family with tales of a fabled gold-rich land, Bux cobbled together the train fare from Lahore to Bombay and 'set off for Australia'.[113]

On reaching Bombay, he was quoted 150 rupees as 'the charges per head … for the third class fare to Australia' – a sum equivalent to at least three months of wages as a *serang*.[114] These 'émigré fares' advertised by the Peninsular and Oriental Steam Navigation Company (P&O) targeted working-class Britons whose passage was subsidised by assisted migration schemes operated by British colonial governments in Australia. On realising these tickets were beyond his means, it was at shipping offices in Bombay that Bux first became aware of South Asians' exclusion from the story of the settler, or emigrant – the central character in schemas of Australian settler colonialism. First theorised by reformer Edward Gibbon Wakefield, the tale of the white emigrant combined two key planks of liberal thought: the story of 'free labour' and the claim that Aboriginal lands were 'unoccupied lands'.[115] The plan was first implemented in the colony of South Australia, and by the 1880s all Australian colonial governments were attracting émigrés from Britain through assisted migration schemes.

In South Asia, the 'emigrant' was at the centre of quite a different colonial project that was also structured around the story of 'free labour'. In the wake of the piecemeal abolition of slavery in the 1830s, an indentured labour scheme was negotiated between colonial companies and British governments to transport so-called 'free' workers from South Asia to former slave plantations and other imperial sites. The South Asian indentured labourers contracted to companies in Guyana, Mauritius, Fiji, Jamaica, Trinidad, Tanzania, Kenya, Uganda, South Africa and sometimes Australia were also defined as 'emigrants' in a series of Indian Emigrant Acts from 1871.[116]

With the lascar regime operating as the maritime counterpart of indentured labour schemes supplying South Asian workers to land-based industries, Bux decided that contracting as a lascar with a shipping company was his only means of reaching the Australian colonies. Given that companies only employed lascars on return voyages that began and ended in British India, Bux intended to dodge the racist rules barring South Asians from remaining at Australian ports. As he told his scribe decades later, 'I planned to leave [the ship] on reaching any port there. ... I tried my best but failed to get a job on any such ship.'[117] Despite excellent certificates of service and prior service to the British government, joining a ship headed for the Australian colonies as a lascar proved more difficult than Bux had anticipated. Despite his extensive networks of Punjabi men converging at Karam Din's shop in Bombay, Bux did not encounter a seafarer travelling to Australian ports.

Alongside the rapid expansion of camel transportation networks in the Australian interior, with some Australian firms and governments sourcing South Asian labour for camel, sugar, railway and pastoral industries, from the 1880s South Asians in Australia started to come under settler scrutiny. In response to pressure from Australian colonial governments to reduce the numbers of lascars jumping ship at

Australian ports, after 1887 the P&O 'decided not to engage Punjabi seamen on ships sailing to Australia'.[118] These shipping policies might have already been unofficially in place in 1883 when Bux began to seek contracts to the Australian colonies.

Unable to contract with a ship headed to Australia, Bux departed for London on a P&O vessel. However, when the ship docked at the port of Marseille, he missed the onward journey along with two other South Asian workers from the vessel: a washer-man and a sweeper. While Bux was 'terribly upset' when the sweeper 'started crying loudly', a French crowd gathered to observe the spectacle, mistaking his melodious wails for 'singing'.[119] They spent the night in prison and French police accompanied Bux and his co-workers to the P&O offices in the morning. According to the lascar regime, shipping firms were liable to pay fines of £100 for each lascar who jumped ship at European ports. After a week, when another P&O ship arrived, the three seafarers continued toward England, working their passage and eventually re-joining their original vessel in London. When Bux completed this contract, he was marked as a deserter on his return to Bombay. He was awarded no wages, and recalled that 'the service certificate given to me was so rotten that no one would allow me to stand near him. It broke my heart completely.'[120]

Unable to step into the roles of white emigrant or lascar, Bux narrated that he would 'go to the port daily, to work there, and would return in the evening.' Earning a pitiful 7 annas a day at the docks, Bux recalled that he 'kept on thinking I have wasted all my time and there is still no prospect of going to Australia.' With no other way forward, Bux 'prayed to the Almighty to show me some light'.[121] Not all of Bux's voyages saw him return with tales of riches and abundance.

VI. Lahore to Melbourne

Voyaging to Australia, Muhammad Bux returned with no stories about Aboriginal people. After many intervening voyages and fruitless attempts to travel to Australia, Bux finally jumped ship at the 'bustling and magnificent metropolis' of Singapore, which he had heard was 'nearest to Australia'.[122] He passed his nights in a mosque there and checked shipping offices during the day. When a vessel bound for Australia arrived,

Bux lamented that 'my efforts to enrol on it failed because it was totally manned by people from Malaya and I did not know a single word of Malayan language.'[123] With neither money nor proficiency in the working language of the crew, Bux stowed away, hiding 'between the emergency boats that were meant for the passengers.'[124]

Eventually, Bux 'was forced to come out due to thirst and hunger'. On finding him penniless, the captain informed Bux that he would have to work. Joining the Malay and Chinese crew, Bux drew closer to the place where he had once heard that 'they extracted gold'.[125] His first glimpse of the fabled land was of the northwestern Australian coast.

Seven nights after departing from the port of Singapore, the ship reached a port that Bux called 'Ralq'. When remembering this voyage from Lahore many years later, Bux recounted to his scribe, 'this place has pearls in abundance.' Perhaps he was referring to Port Walcott – one of the many pearling centres along the northwestern coast of the Australian mainland frequently visited by steam ships from Singapore since the 1860s. As Bux told his descendants, 'there we saw thousands of big launches, with Japanese and Malay crews. Their job is to take out the pearls.'

Remembering this port, Bux gave a detailed account of pearl diving operations, describing it as an 'extremely hazardous profession'.[126] Aboriginal and Indonesian divers harvesting oysters from the ocean floor were central to this industry. Bux explained that a 'wire-basket' was tied to the waists of the divers, who were lowered into the ocean with 'a rubber-hose' providing 'necessary breathing air'. When the basket was full, 'the diver jerk[ed] the string' and was raised with the 'mother-of-pearl'. On deck, 'a boat-official prie[d] them open with a knife' to reveal pearls 'of all sizes, big, small or even as tiny as a pin-head.'[127] If any of the divers whom Bux watched closely had been Aboriginal labourers, he neglected to mention it, at least in the English version of his story.

'At last,' Bux told his scribe, 'after leaving Port Ralq the ship reached Melbourne.' At 'Port Williamstown' where the Yarra River empties into Port Phillip Bay, Bux first stepped onto the Australian mainland in around 1885, docking at its southernmost port.[128] The locals informed him that 'there were many Indians in Melbourne,' with numbers of South Asians in the city exceeding 1,100 by 1891, according to settler records.[129] Bux boarded a train for one of the two neighbourhoods of South Asian traders. When he was stopped for not having a rail ticket, he appealed to the inspector 'that presently I had no money, but if he could take me to some Indians, I would be able to obtain money from them and pay the fare.'[130] At 11.00 p.m. that night, accompanied by a police officer, Bux knocked on the door of a boarding house on 79 Young Street in Fitzroy. The premises were leased by a man called Dervaish Alli: 'a Bangla-speaking fellow by the name of Dervaish came out. I narrated the whole of my story to him and told him that I have reached Australia at last!'[131]

A number of Punjabi and Bengali men lived at the boarding house on Young Street that Dervaish rented.[132] Two men from the village of Potohar in Punjab explained to Bux the next morning that 'Bengali Dervaish makes pickle' – a chutney that he cooked at the premises and supplied to his lodgers in 'filled bottles to sell in the market.' Bux was informed that 'Bengali Dervaish lets them have 5 shillings per pound as commission', and was offered the same job.[133]

Leaving the house with bottles of chutney, Bux sold 10 shillings' worth of pickles on his first day in the Melbourne markets. Paying only a shilling for meals that day, Bux saved a shilling and a half from the cut of the sales that Dervaish Alli gave him. Bux urged his readers to 'remember that a shilling is worth fourteen annas. Therefore, I had saved one-and-a-quarter rupee the very first day.' The conversion from pounds to rupees of Bux's profits on his first day in Melbourne suggested that he might earn up to 38 rupees in a month, well in excess of lascars' monthly wages of 18 rupees. In Bux's words, 'it showed me how good Australia was and that one could make a lot of money in that country.'[134]

As this highlights, Bux was accounting in two currencies, his many subsequent voyages to the Australian colonies consistently moving between rupees and pounds. Explaining how he made the conversions work for him, Bux conveyed the logic underpinning 'remittance economies', today a significant source of capital inflow into South Asian economies. Locating the future of his family's livelihood in translations between pounds and rupees, he recalled, 'I thought of calling over my close relatives to Australia, because there were ample opportunities to make a lot of money here.'[135]

Beginning with the profits he made on those jars of chutney, Bux commenced a long and prosperous trading career, threading together Australian markets to Indian Ocean ports and establishing an import/export business in Perth by 1895 (Fig. 8). In addition to acquiring a number of buildings and businesses in Perth, the Bux family also operated a camel business in Coolgardie in the Western Australian goldfields. While the British émigré's arrival on a landmass abundant in gold was a story about land, Bux's was a South Asian tale of economic ascension focused instead on the Indian Ocean.

What this story had in common with British colonial tales of the land of gold was the imaginative erasure of Aboriginal people. Today, a family with the name of Bux (or Bukhsh) is among the many Aboriginal families who left traces in the history of Fitzroy in Melbourne, confirming that in Victoria, as elsewhere throughout Australia, many South Asian and Aboriginal families came to be interconnected.[136] However, while Muhammad Bux lived, worked and traded in many areas with large Aboriginal populations, his lengthy recollections contain no traces of an Aboriginal presence, thereby systematically reproducing settler myths of emptiness.

Three months after having first arrived in the colony of Victoria, Bux prepared for his departure. Having disembarked with no money, he boarded another ship with a purse full of riches – £50, to be precise.[137] Through South Asian networks converging upon 79 Young Street in Fitzroy, Bux heard of a consignment of horses leaving Melbourne for the city of Madras. For wages of £10, he worked his passage back to British India, catching a train to Lahore. Casting himself as the dutiful son, Bux detailed that upon his return home, 'I gave all the money I have brought with me to my father and my stepmother. I did not consider at all that she was my stepmother.'[138]

VII. Lahore to Fremantle

Voyaging to Western Australia, Muhammad Bux and his wife Fatima Ghulam returned with different stories. They had married in around 1873 when Bux was sixteen years old, two years before his first sea voyage. It was a contract arranged by Bux's grandmother to heal a breach in the extended family. Bux sought solace in his grandmother's embrace in the aftermath of the violence repeatedly erupting in the family home, and she played a pivotal role in his travelogue in smoothing household disputes. As Bux recalled decades after her death, 'I always thought she was my real mother. She loved me more than my real mother.'[139] As Bux undertook voyage after voyage, his wife Fatima lived at her mother's home on Sultan Mahmood Street in the walled city of Lahore. In the long absences between Bux's return from ports, she gave birth to two daughters.

Domestic affairs bookend Bux's travelogue. With tales about his female relatives appearing at the beginning and end of some voyages, the very organisation of his memories maps masculinity to movement and femininity to stasis, drawing sharp class distinctions between the women in bazaars and women in the domestic sphere. While a schema of gendered partition that predates European colonial rule underpinned Bux's storytelling, across the British Empire during his lifetime, doctors, social reformers and temperance movements were colluding to increasingly demarcate discrete public and private spheres. In the South Asian context, locked in dialogue with British colonial reform discourse, many modernist South Asian men's movements targeted South Asian women as objects of reform.[140] Bux's lengthy voyages meant that Fatima and her daughters inhabited a somewhat autonomous women's sphere in Lahore. Whether or not this was his focus during his working life, after retirement Bux began increasingly drawing on South Asian men's reformist discourse to influence women's spaces, establishing a girls' school in Australia Chowk in Lahore in the 1920s.

As the construction of a number of monuments to ensure his legacy was underway, Bux recounted to his *munshi* that he had started to long for his family when he was in his early thirties in Australia. By the close of the 1880s, Perth was a city where 'no other Indian, Pathan or Sikh was seen.'[141] He reported 'going to a close-by river in Perth,' where he 'would always pray to Allah that he may let a time come that my close relatives arrive here to earn'.[142] When his father arrived in Perth in around 1890, Bux briefly found the companionship that he sought, as well as a reliable business partner. While he sold wares on the streets of Perth, his father kept the shop open and 'increase[d] the sales day by day'. Bux recalled:

> It became known to all people in Perth that an Indian shopkeeper had set up shop in William Street who hands out two wooden-pointers of 6-ft and 8-ft length to every customer entering his shop. He also provides a price tag of each item ... the shopkeeper is a gentleman and a nice person. Hearing such unusual thing[s] from each other, every woman paid a visit to the shop and bought something without any need.[143]

But Bux still missed the intimacy of family life, Fatima Ghulam and their children. Commenting on the relations he observed between South Asian men and 'those women who are white' in the Australian colonies, he warned his sons that 'when those Indians lose their wealth, the women left them too.'[144] Fearing that white women's affections were tied to capital, in around 1891 Bux convinced his wife to accompany him to the colony of Western Australia. Catching a train from Lahore with Bux, Fatima departed for Calcutta accompanied by her youngest daughter, who was seven years old. Bux's days of labouring across the Indian Ocean were behind him and in Calcutta he purchased freight for his merchandise and tickets for himself and his family.

On reaching Singapore the family rented a house from a trader and Bux 'procured goods consisting of silk and other items for sale in Australia.'[145] By that time, Bux was a powerful figure in his extended family, increasingly crafting futures for his younger relatives by dispensing advice, negotiating marriages and employment contracts and mediating disputes. Accompanying him on this voyage were three of his cousins – sons of his father's sister. He had offered to 'pay their entire traveling expenses for the journey for both ends.'[146] The terms of the engagement were that they would 'keep whatever they earned, but in case they earned less than 50 rupees in a month,' Bux would make up the balance.[147] Over the course of his many voyages, Bux facilitated the passage of over twenty-eight family members to Australian ports.

Fatima observed *purdah*, a regime separating women's spaces from those of men, which structured the architecture of gender relations in wealthy families across nineteenth-century South Asia. After a three-week voyage from Singapore, she and her daughter arrived in Fremantle before the sun had set. While Bux and his three cousins spent the afternoon in search of a shop for rent, Fatima and her daughter disembarked from the ship only when the city had been cloaked by dusk. Demonstrating how to maintain *purdah* in the Australian colonies, Bux tells his readers that 'it was done as planned, and no one came to know that an Indian had brought his family here.'[148]

Setting up shop in Fremantle, Bux's newly arrived cousins soon began hawking goods. As wares were transformed into shillings and pounds, delivering profits into the hands of Bux and his cousins, Fatima and her daughter remained in the upper quarters of the house, secluded from unrelated South Asian men as well as white men and women frequenting the shop. The circulation of capital that strung together Indian Ocean markets, in Bux's view, needed to remain beyond the walls of women's seclusion. Once it was established that a husband 'does not waste money', Bux opined, 'the wife should consider herself the owner of that income and should never think of accumulating money separately' – an interpretation of the marriage contract totally at odds with the property rights long guaranteed to married women in Muslim legal systems.[149]

While Bux repeatedly forewarns his sons and grandsons about the 'deluge of bad women in the cities' who might rob them of their capital, it is at the end of his travelogue that he delves into lengthy and cantankerous observations about women's economies within the domestic sphere, replicating key narratives in Urdu reform literature targeting women.[150] From the early 1900s, the *Bihisti Zewar* (Heavenly Ornaments) was one of the most influential Urdu texts directly addressing women in elite Muslim families.[151] Written by reformer 'Ashraf 'Alī Thānvī (d. 1943) as a syllabus for the modern Muslim woman, *Bihisti Zewar* consisted of ten volumes of detailed advice that sought to transform women's social relations with each other. The work comprises a major intervention into women's knowledge production.[152] Inventing new scripts according to which births, weddings, funerals and the raising of children should unfold, it was a text that drew systematic distinctions between 'Hindu' and 'Muslim' practices in the home.

Taking up many of the same topics that Thanwi addresses in the *Bihisti Zewar*, Bux told his scribe that he detested the 'ritual of *bhaji*', the exchange of fried vegetables between women of a household and within family networks.[153] He disapproved of the 'gathering of women for wailing' after deaths, arguing that 'an assembly of women often results in feuds'.[154] According to Bux, when women assembled they could have the most unfavourable influence on each other; he dictated to his scribe the evils of 'smoking hubble-bubble' among 'respectable women', which had 'become a sort of fashionable behaviour' in Lahore by the 1920s.[155]

On the issue of money in the domestic sphere, Bux complained that 'women have a system of collective savings called "committee" in most of the houses. That is harmful!'[156] He observed that 'women start contributing to these "committees" without taking permission from their husbands' and urged that wives should manage household money so that 'it will be available for the husband as and when required.'[157] He proclaimed that 'the vile rituals of marriage should be eliminated.' Bux particularly objected to the sums of money 'spent on preparing golden dresses' for the bride, brocaded gowns that he believed only rotted in boxes after the marriage ceremony, disused. It dismayed Bux that 'as a last resort nothing can be done except that the golden thread is separated and sold off. It fetches a price not in rupees but paisas.' Bux suggested an alternative he thought 'a thousand times better': 'that the couple is presented [the] equal amount of cash.'[158] On the topic of women's gold ornaments, he observed, 'If the same amount were invested in trade you would get it back with profit.'[159]

Reading these orations against the grain, we can glimpse the vibrant domestic sphere that Fatima inhabited in Lahore. Her experience in Australia, observing seclusion in the upstairs quarters of a shop, must have been very different from practising *purdah* in Lahore. With only her daughter for company, her brother in Perth some 12 miles away, and both her mother and eldest daughter across an ocean, Fatima gave birth to a baby boy in Fremantle in 1892.[160] As Bux narrated to his scribe, those were the days when an 'Englishman by the name of Vosper arrived to Western Australia from India', becoming one of the most active proponents of the idea of 'White Australia'. Friedrick Vosper 'gave lectures at each nook and corner, [in the] streets and markets', his ideas slowly gaining currency among settlers.[161] When hawkers' licenses stopped being issued to Asians in the colony of Western Australia in 1893, a measure sparked by growing white nationalist movements, Bux recalled that 'all the Chinese and Indians got extremely worried.'[162] At this point, Bux's three cousins who had accompanied him to Perth became jobless.

One morning, a policeman arrived at the shop with a court order, telling Bux that:

> people living around have reported that an Indian has opened a shop in their locality. He has brought his family with him and keeps them confined in the upper storey of that shop. They also had reported that this Indian man tortured his family and they keep hearing sounds of wailing from his house all the time.[163]

Whether it was the sound of Fatima crying that had escaped through the walls of the shop, or the wailing of her newborn son, white settlers had decided to use the Bux family's plight to make arguments against Asian immigration. As I will show in Chapter 7, whatever sympathies settlers had for South Asian women were inextricable from their racism toward South Asian men.

Bux ultimately translated the concept of seclusion in a Perth court in the early 1890s by appealing to 'tradition': 'I did not know the exact equivalent of "purdah" in English and also I failed to explain it properly. It was quite a fun [*sic*] in the court ... Sometimes the magistrate looked at me angrily and sometimes [he] would laugh on his own.'[164] The decision was deferred. Next time Bux appeared in court, an employee at the Telegram Office, F. A. Bailey, was asked to act as an interpreter. Having spent many years in British India, this man 'knew the Indian language well, as well as the traditions.' Thanks to Bailey, 'the magistrate got convinced that he had no jurisdiction in religious matters.' Bux was relieved when, in the end, 'the magistrate instructed me to take my wife out for a little walk [in] the dark.'[165]

On 13 January 1895, Fatima Ghulam departed from the port of Albany for British India, taking her daughter as well as her two young sons, who had been born in the colony of Western Australia.[166] As Bux continued to undertake voyages and as his Australian interests prospered, he soon began to long for married life in Perth once again. As he recounted to his scribe, 'I told my wife, the mother of Mohammad Rashid, my intention of taking her to Australia this year.'[167] Fatima, however, had other ideas. Bux recalled with irritation, 'She flatly refused to go with me, without thinking over the matter properly. She told me that she had no need to go to Australia and if I was adamant to take ... [a wife], I should marry someone else and take her along.'

Enlisting the sympathies of his relatives, Bux tried his best to sway her decision. He reported that 'a lot of counselling was done but it failed to move her.'[168]

Fatima might have had business interests of her own in Lahore that she wished to pursue without Bux's interference.[169] Or perhaps she enjoyed giving and receiving *bhaji* and other gifts that were exchanged by the women in Lahore. Maybe she liked participating in large gatherings of loud, gold-clad women at weddings. When she buried her son Mohammed Sharif, who died at the tender age of three years and four months in Lahore, she must certainly have appreciated grieving with her sisters and grandmothers, no matter how odious her husband might find the wails of South Asian women.[170]

A few years later, Bux entered into a second marriage with Janatt Begum with the express purpose of taking her to Australia. When Janatt Begum embarked on her first voyage to Perth at the dawn of the era of 'White Australia', reading between the lines of Bux's account suggests that Fatima Ghulam was relieved.

* * *

The most infamous merchant storytellers, as the tales of Sindbad show us, have long been able to captivate the poorest as well as most the powerful men across the Indian Ocean region. When Sindbad voyages to a distant and unknown island via a treacherous route of 'darkness and distress', the king of the foreign land marvels at both the pearls and the stories he brings, for, as he narrates later, 'I told him my story from beginning to end.'[171] When the king asks Sindbad about 'the way the Caliph rules in Bagdad', the answer so captivates him that he dispatches with Sindbad 'a magnificent gift for the Abbasid caliph Harun al-Rashid.'[172] When Sindbad returns to Baghdad with his purse full of riches and gifts for the ruler, the caliph summons the seafarer to his court. As Sindbad tells the porter, marvelling at his many voyages, Harun al-Rashid 'ordered the historians to record my story and deposit it in his library, so that whoever reads it may be edified by it.'[173]

Perhaps offering a clue to how Sindbad's voyages came to be written down, the episode hints that merchants' intimacy with power could ensure the continuing circulation of their tales. For centuries after he met 'death, the destroyer of delights, sunderer of companies, wrecker of palaces, and builder of tombs', the story of Sindbad continued to be shared across the Indian Ocean, leaving traces in the pages of many seafarers' travelogues, including a family history of the *Australiawallahs* spanning South Asia and Australia.[174] In 2004, Babar Malik, the most senior Pakistani diplomat in Australia, was captivated by the 'pioneering zeal' of and 'riches generated' by the family of Khawajah Muhammad Bux.[175] Malik wrote that the English translation of their history 'has at last set down for posterity the pioneering role of a family that excelled in establishing for itself a name.'

As I have shown through a close reading of seven of Bux's voyages, as a steam shipping revolution transformed the Indian Ocean, this lascar turned businessman rewired and appropriated many stories from this trading arena, while sidestepping others. Bux narrated his voyages with the hope of shaping the future trajectories of those about to inherit his wealth, and lay the blueprint for a form of South Asian masculinity that thrived within the particular structures of power relations established by British colonial regimes. The knowledge production of South Asian diaspora, as historians have recently cautioned, 'can serve the interests of imperial power, and is not, in itself, a mode of resistance.'[176]

In the decades since Bux was buried in the garden of the Australia Mosque in Lahore, his history has continued to circulate the Indian Ocean across generations. Bux's tale has been retold in texts titled 'Sawanih-E-Umri' (c. 1944), *Amazing Migrant* (2004), *Lahore Ka Sindbad* (2006), 'Muslim Australian Contributions' (2009), 'Under the Radar of Empire' (2011), 'The Memoirs of Khawajah Muhammad Bux, (Australian Businessman)' (2016), among others – some written by Bux's descendants, some by professional scholars.[177] In offering an addition to this growing list, I have argued for closer analyses of the complicity of elite South Asians in buttressing the most brutal regimes of contemporary violence across the Indian Ocean arena. As Jordana Silverstein shows in her account of Jewish diaspora in New York and Melbourne, 'the adoption of settler colonial ways of remembering and forgetting' too often underpins diasporic historical consciousness.[178] Accordingly, in the next chapter, I address the systematic erasure of Aboriginal people from South Asians' accounts of Australia.

4

THE TRAIN AT BELTANA

With the arrival of thirty-one South Asian men and 124 camels from Karachi, the first Australian camel depot was established in 1866 in the dramatic, colour-streaked peaks now known as the Flinders Ranges. Today these hills are the country of Adnyamathanha people – descendants of Kuyani, Bilaluppa, Jadliaura, and Wailpi families, among others, who survived the violence of colonialism (Fig. 9).

From 1866, more and more South Asians and their camels began arriving at Beltana – a pastoral property that colonised a patch of Kuyani people's land. Employed not only in camel transportation, but also in pastoral and mining industries, the South Asian workers and merchants pitched their tents at a bend on Warrioota Creek, the major waterway coursing through Kuyani geography (Fig. 10). The arrival of the Great Northern Railway in Beltana in 1881 in no way diminished the camel transportation industry. On the contrary, South Asians eagerly awaited the railway running from north to south, its extension creating new nodes from which camel lines could be launched 'for 1,000 miles east and 1,000 miles west', as one driver put it.[1]

As line after line of goods-laden camels departed from Beltana, and then from newer railheads, traversing deserts even further inland, Aboriginal knowledge producers keenly observed the South Asian drivers who arrived in their lands, as confirmed by the volumes of Aboriginal recollections about South Asians, in Aboriginal languages and English alike. In stark contrast, Aboriginal people very rarely feature in these South Asians' stories about Australia. As the absence of Aboriginal people from Muhammad Bux's detailed travelogue demonstrates, histories of South Asian migration sometimes replicate colonial discourse in their structured omission of Aboriginal people.

In this chapter I follow some of the first South Asians to travel into the Australian interior to investigate the asymmetrical schemas of seeing in Australian colonial settlements. Telling a history of Beltana, I highlight the contours of the contested epistemic terrain that belied every site of settler colonial incursion into Aboriginal land. What follows over the next pages is not a history of South Asians per se, but rather an account of the dense conjuncture of knowledge traditions that South Asians arrived in when they stepped onto Aboriginal land in the era of colonial rule. A transport and communications hub some 240 kilometres inland from the nearest seaport, Beltana was a site where the trajectories of different people from across the British Empire intersected. This crossover was apparent on the evening of 2 July 1881, when many people were awaiting the very first steam train to Beltana.

Schoolteacher Mrs Lewis was among the settlers who gathered at Beltana railway siding, welcoming the train with 'three cheers to the Queen'.[2] Many years later in 1925, she remembered the arrival of the train as a milestone in 'the march to progress'.[3] As she told an Adelaide journalist at the age of seventy-three, 'in those days blackfellows came from Central Australia, almost at Parachilna, for red ochre. It was not uncommon to see 200 natives on the trade route.'[4] It was one such group of distant traders, and not local Kuyani families, who had 'climbed to a hill top' the evening that the first train approached. In Mrs Lewis' account, 'the blacks ... crouched down with fear at the sight of the great black engine (or "black moora").'[5]

From flatter deserts in the north, the people gathered on the hill had walked for days and days to Beltana country, following the tracks of supernatural beings that the Kuyani people called *mura*, known as 'Dreaming creatures' in the field of Aboriginal history. The epic tales of *mura* travels, as Worimi scholar Dale Kerwin writes, described some of the 'arteries of an Aboriginal economic landscape'.[6] On the evening that the first steam train arrived, the locomotive, spurting spectacular volumes of steam, made such an impression on one of the travellers that he composed a song about it in Wangkangurru – one of the Aboriginal languages spoken in distant deserts in the north. On returning home from Kuyani peaks, he performed the song to his son, Mick McLean. A talented, multilingual storyteller by the time he was an octogenarian many decades later, Mick McLean in turn sang the railway song for linguist Luise Hercus in the winter of 1970.[7]

Putting these two memories of the first steam train side by side reveals that settlers and Aboriginal travellers arriving in Beltana along different pathways brought with them complex philosophies of movement that shaped their encounters with others. Focusing on these knowledges I piece together four distinct schemas of movement, which I refer to as 'tracks'. Put simply, a track is a story. I propose that tracks from different epistemological traditions circumscribed physical movement through Beltana, structuring settler and Aboriginal trajectories through Kuyani lands. Tracks not only underpinned the terrain of colonial encounter but also informed how people saw place and recounted the past.

By rendering visible some of the many tracks that converged in Beltana and at every colonial settlement, I challenge the logic of 'blank spaces' that continues to underpin the most powerful settler institutions today. The myth of uninhabited land was evoked by Australian Prime Minister Tony Abbott in November 2014, on the eve of the G20 Summit. Addressing British Prime Minister David Cameron in Sydney, Abbott celebrated 'the extraordinary partnership that our two countries have had since the First Fleet sailed into this magnificent harbor.' He remarked that 'back in 1788 it was nothing but bush ... they must have thought they'd almost come to the moon.'[8] Abbott's comments sparked angry protests outside the summit the following day. As the heads of the most powerful nation-states met, protesters outside burned Australian flags in rejection of a regime that continues to erase Aboriginal history and geography. While one television reporter lamented the burning of 'the symbol of our nation', activists marched through the streets chanting 'always was, always will be Aboriginal land'.[9]

As many writers have shown since the ground-breaking work of Patrick Wolfe, 'settler colonialism was distinctive for its structured imagining away, or cartographic genocide, of Indigenous peoples.'[10] However, while writers in settler colonial studies have produced the most sophisticated analyses of the colonial myth of unpopulated land, one curious feature of this field is that it sometimes replicates precisely the phenomenon it seeks to critique: the erasure of Aboriginal geographies. Using a Kuyani place-name and a Wangkangurru song as entry points into colonised epistemic terrains, I show that Aboriginal-language texts can offer glimpses into the imaginative geographies that Aboriginal peoples produced, offering a powerful corrective to this tendency.

I begin by piecing together the commodity track underpinning the movement of sheep from Beltana to Britian, examining an 1863 massacre of Aboriginal people at a waterhole on Warioota Creek. I go on to use linguistic methodologies to interpret the meaning of the word 'Beltana' – an English appropriation of the Kuyani place-name 'Palthanha'. Locating this as a site along a Kuyani track, I bring to light an artery of Kuyani imaginative geography. Next, turning to Mrs Lewis' memories in 1925 of the train in 1881, I consider her act of remembering as an instance of imaginative travel along the axis of time. Approaching the 'march of progress' as a track that structured her journey to the colonial past, I highlight the central role that progress narratives played in settler myths of blank space. Finally, examining a Wangkangurru track structuring the movement of goods through Beltana, I consider how this axis shaped Mick McLean's and his father's imaginative travel to the past.

I. Commodity Tracks

In 1856, the first flock of sheep arrived at Warioota Creek. Not long before, pastoralist John Haimes had signed Waste Lands of the Crown Lease no. 379 in the city of Adelaide. Including a survey of a blank patch of land, this leasehold title represented Kuyani geography for the first time as private property (Fig. 11). Legal theorists have described property as a 'construction of the human mind', defining it as a particular relationship of human dominion over objects.[11] Lease no. 379 classified both land and the sheep on it as property that Haimes had dominion over for 'pastoral purposes'. While it categorised sheep as 'stock' that the lessee had exclusive 'rights' to, lease no. 379 marked wild beasts as 'ferae naturae' to which Aboriginal people retained 'full and free rights'.[12] The title outlined 'that the Lessee shall not … change, alter, divert or obstruct the use of … roads, paths or ways', but did not acknowledge Aboriginal trade routes as 'roads, paths or ways', thus effacing their existence from colonial courts. With sheep, a powerful new schema of mobility arrived in Kuyani country: commodity tracks connecting Aboriginal geographies to London markets and funnelling lucrative profits to colonial firms.

From the 1860s, Adelaide-based pastoralist and parliamentarian Thomas Elder invested in the region, appending the Beltana sheep run to the assets of Elder, Smith & Company (ESCo), one of the most powerful companies in colonial South Australia.[13] The movement of sheep through Kuyani land remained inseparable from the movement of 'stock' along commodity tracks – a schema of motion that becomes visible if we follow the first bales of wool exported to Britain after ESCo acquired the Beltana sheep run.

First, Thomas Elder transformed his capital from money in Adelaide into commodities pastured on Kuyani hills, buying 17,705 sheep from Haimes for 13 shillings and 11 pence per head.[14] ESCo invested more capital in sinking wells and fencing paddocks, while the sheep grew fat on saltbush and drank from Kuyani waterholes. As more ESCo capital went into wages and freight, the fat sheep were shorn and the fleeces packed into 106 bales of wool commodity, which were conveyed to Port Augusta and loaded onto the ship *Ormelie*, consigned to a selling agent.[15] On arrival at the London wool exchange, each bale of Beltana grease wool sold for 9d per pound on 27 July 1863, transforming ESCo capital back into money from commodities.[16] Sheep featured in ESCo account books as one form that capital took on a track from money to commodities to money again, then back to commodities, and so on. Viewed over a longer duration of time, the total value of Elder's capital increased while moving along this commodity track, returning substantial profits to ESCo.

Between 1860 and 1865, as more pastoral and mining land leases imposed the imaginative geography of private property on Aboriginal land, facilitating the increasing motion of 'stock' along commodity tracks, Australian wool exports increased from 59 million lbs to 108 million lbs.[17] Concurrently, ochre continued to move through Aboriginal trading circuits, and in 1863 there was a confrontation between two economic systems at one of the few permanent water sources in Beltana. On 16 November 1863, after a visit to the ochre deposit at Parachilna, Aboriginal travellers had gathered at a waterhole on Warioota Creek when a white shepherd arrived with 1,300 sheep. The Aboriginal men stopped the sheep from getting to the water, killing three with boomerangs and driving the rest away, 'saying that [the] water was theirs' and eventually following the shepherds to the station kitchen.[18] There the manager of Beltana, Captain McKay, horsewhipped one Aboriginal man.[19] Tensions escalated over nine days with rumours spreading among settlers that 'between 200 and 300 natives [are] coming down.'[20] On 27 November, settlers with firearms confronted the traders at Warioota Creek. A witness later testified that Captain McKay had 'got off his horse to fire at the natives, as they were all about the creek.'[21]

Settler presses reported the deaths of only the three people whose corpses remained at Warioota Creek when police arrived, omitting the 'forty or fifty others [who] died of their wounds before they reached their own territory', according to Kuyani records.[22] In defense of the regime of private property, on 23 December 1863 the jury of eight settlers returned the verdict of 'justifiable homicide', unanimously ruling that the killers were 'quite justified in firing and shooting at the natives'.[23] McKay urged Elder to 'warn the Government to order up a sufficient force to protect the settlers … if not, they will be shot down like dogs, as the settlers must do so in defence of their lives and property.'[24] Between 1863 and 1880, police power increased across the colony as the returns on wool exports almost tripled from £715,935 to £2,009,171.[25] The result was that settlers continued to kill traders who were operating within the logic of Aboriginal economic systems. The shooting at Warioota Creek is one of a number of massacres along ochre routes characterised by unresolved discrepancies between settler and Aboriginal records.[26]

While waging war on Aboriginal economies in conflict with commodity tracks, colonists implemented a rations system to incorporate Aboriginal labour into the capitalist economy. By 1867 Beltana had become a ration depot, issuing tobacco, blankets and flour as 'compensation' for the dispossession of land. In practice, far from providing 'compensation', pastoralists used government-supplied commodities as substitutes for wages for Aboriginal labour.[27] While commodity tracks underpinned the way pastoralists saw both animals and land, and shaped how settlers arbitrated between legal and illegal acts in colonial courts, Kuyani people continued to see creatures embedded in distinctly different tracks, even as Aboriginal labour became incorporated into the pastoral economy.

II. A Kuyani Track

In deserts defined by the scarcity of water, both Aboriginal and settler tracks converged on Warioota Creek. 'Beltana' was an appropriation of the Kuyani place-name 'Palthanha' – a site along the creek. As linguists working with Aboriginal-language speakers have shown, place-names such as Palthanha often figure in tight sequences in Aboriginal narratives; situating place-names within tracks can reveal 'a way of looking at the land'.[28] Seeking spatial perspectives effaced by colonists' maps, I use linguistic methodologies to piece together a Kuyani track to Palthanha.

As British émigrés began to colonise Kuyani lands from the 1850s, through Kuyani people's stories they encountered *mura* – a concept Britons translated as 'good spirit, god or divine being'.[29] Travelling *mura*, or 'Dreaming creatures', not only leave tracks but also create the landmarks of Aboriginal geographies. Aboriginal place-names can sometimes refer to events signposting the travels of a Dreaming creature. This is demonstrated by linguists Jane Simpson and Luise Hercus, who use an example from Warumungu, a language spoken today around Tennant Creek in the Northern Territory: 'Warumungu ancestral women go to the place *Wittin* and leave a coolamon. That is visible now as a waterhole. *Wittin* means "coolamon" in Warumungu. They go east to another place, *Manaji*, where they dig bush potatoes. *Manaji* means "bush potato" in Warumungu.'[30] In these cases, which feature 'Warumungu ancestral women' as Dreaming creatures, the place-names Wittin and Manaji reference the creation stories of the sites and belong in a Dreaming track that unfolds in the strict order that the women travel in the story, hinting at the sequence of the places in Warumungu routes of motion.

Linguists suggest that Kuyani *Paltha-nha* can be translated literally as 'cloak place'. Their place-name research, however, has yet to shed light on the physical location of Palthanha or the Dreaming track associated with it.[31] From the 1880s settlers began to propose etymologies for

'Beltana', citing Kuyani speakers. As linguists insist, many differing etymologies written by settlers can, in fact, aid attempts to reconstruct the range of usages that Aboriginal-language words had. Nathanial Phillipson, the manager of Beltana, was the first colonist to record an etymology for Palthanha, writing that Kuyani workers informed him that 'BELT meant running and ANA water.'[32] This etymology has proved enduring, and draws attention to Warioota Creek as a key to the place-name's Kuyani meaning.

With the rise of the Beltana Pastoral Company, Aboriginal families continued to live near, hunt along, and tell stories about Warioota Creek. Docie Pondi, her son Billy, and his wife Rosie were one Kuyani family who spent their lives in the Beltana area. As one former Beltana resident wrote to an Adelaide newspaper in 1930, 'I played with the blacks' as 'a tiny girl' and 'Billy Pondi ... was a constant visitor to our home. ... Old Rosie did the washing for my mother.'[33] As interdependence increased between Aboriginal labour and pastoralists, Kuyani people often schooled settlers in Dreaming lore. One letter published in the *Register* in 1924 outlined a 'legend' of the 'Coollannie tribe' associated with the name 'Beltana'.[34] Written under the pseudonym 'Coollannie', he – or perhaps she – wrote, 'I was born at Beltana Station ... in the year 1884', and reminisced that 'I knew all the old-time blacks, and from them I gathered the following story'.

She or he wrote that 'Beltana Station stands on the south side of the Warioota Creek, on a high hill that slopes down to the creek.' Recounting that Warioota and Sliding Rock creeks 'junction ... in front of the station', the letter continued, 'just below the junction there arises a steep bluff, which seems to spring straight out of the creek's bed.' On most days both creeks were dry, stony paths. After the sudden thunderstorms that assault Kuyani hills, both would rise to rush westward toward Lake Torrens – the western boundary of Beltana station. Where the creeks meet, Coollannie wrote that 'in high floodtime the water divides, and a large portion of it swirls around this bluff.' Remembering the 'commotion' at the junction, Coollannie described that 'the swift straight current of the Warioota forces most of the waters of the Sliding Rock Creek to the north of the bluff, and they rejoin at the old Afghan camp' – the camel yard on the bed of Warioota Creek.

After detailing ecological motion along these creeks, Coollannie proposed that '"Ana" means water in the blacks' language and "Belta" means crossing.' Although not literally correct, Coollannie was not alone in claiming that 'Beltana' was a place associated with 'crossing-water'. In the 1920s, an elderly Kuyani man informed W. Reid, the manager of Beltana, that the name meant 'crossing of the waters'.[35] When Phillipson, Reid, and Coollannie's conversations with Kuyani people are all read together, as suggested by linguists, Palthanha emerges as the name for the junction of the two creeks.

The letter continued that 'the Coollannie tribe had a legend that the Warioota and Sliding Rock Creeks quarrelled when they met.' When Kuyani people told this story, it is likely it was Dreaming creatures travelling along the creeks who 'quarrelled'. As Adnyamathanha stories today confirm, the range of encounters between Dreaming creatures is extremely vast. Dingoes ripped an emu open to create an ochre pit. One lizard with two husbands had a jealous fight with another lizard with ten husbands. A kangaroo coming across a slumbering woman tucked her into its pouch and bounded away.[36] These encounters nevertheless all left their mark on places. Coollannie's account of the 'legend' of Palthanha continued that, on encounter, 'the Warioota lay down while the Sliding Rock waters passed over them, and then, after going around the bluff, the waters became friends again, and the[y] followed the creeks' natural course.' Almost from the moment that Europeans encountered Aboriginal people, they began to pen accounts of Dreaming creatures. Within the context of this literature, Coollannie's letter is recognisable as one settler's memory of a Kuyani track, albeit with some gaps.[37]

Significantly, Coollannie noted 'the strange part ... is that in high floods most of the Warioota's waters pass to the north of this bluff, while the Sliding Rock's waters pass to the south.'[38] While 'Palthanha' did not literally translate to 'crossing water', on rare occasions there was literally a crossing of waters there, as the two creeks reached equilibrium. Even if the letter contains gaps where Dreaming creatures usually feature in Aboriginal stories, that Coollannie replaced them with 'waters' hints that Kuyani storytellers told the tale as if mapping the motion of 'floodtime' waters. Coollannie's letter suggests that the Kuyani story of Palthanha contained details mapping ecological motion, suggesting that Warrioota Creek was one axis along which Kuyani people viewed place.

Kuyani tracks continued to structure Aboriginal spatial perspectives alongside the rise of pastoralism as their ability to see creatures' tracks – Dreaming and otherwise – became a valuable resource for pastoralists. Tracking dingoes and other animals threatening sheep became a crucial part of Kuyani labour, leading the Pondi family to become famous in Beltana for their tracking skills. Billy Pondi even extended an invitation to Warioota Creek in 1929, challenging white hunters who claimed superiority over Aboriginal trackers to 'come along and track a wild dog with us over the stones.'[39] Whereas the story of Palthanha fell out of circulation in settler records, it continues to be told by Adnyamathanha families today.[40] Though commodity tracks did not necessarily erase Aboriginal tracks, settlers deployed yet another track to imagine away Aboriginal presence, as they marched toward a destination point of 'White Australia'.

III. The March of Progress

From the moment it arrived at Beltana station in 1881, the steam train was understood by settlers as marking a break from the past. At inauguration celebrations colonists reminisced about 'former days' when deliveries to Port Augusta took 'three weeks', anticipating that 'the twelve hours … necessary in future … would give great impetus to the prosperity of Beltana.'[41] In 1925, the Adelaide *Mail* published one ageing settler's memories of that day. Consistent with European representations of steam trains as a symbol of 'progress', the report catalogued Mrs Lewis' account of the first train as one of a number of 'milestones in the march of progress'.[42] This process of remembering can be understood as an act of imaginative travel along the axis of time, from 1925 to 1881 – a journey that I show was influenced by a progress track. As Lorenzo Veracini has written, 'anticipatory geographies' of emptiness buttressed settler colonialism, and progress tracks played a central role in settlers' articulation of futures emptied of Aboriginal people.[43]

A tale first articulated by Immanuel Kant (d. 1804), 'progress' is a story of motion through time. European philosophers writing during the industrial and political revolutions of the late eighteenth century theorised progress as a timeline of collective human motion toward a better future, diverging from Christian timelines of approaching apocalypse.[44] While progress tracks arrived on Kuyani peaks with explorer John Edward Eyre in 1840, it was from the 1850s that British colonists increasingly began looking at well-watered sites like Palthanha and imagining their potential for progress toward prosperous settler futures.[45] Describing progress as 'the experience of a new time condensed into a word', German historian Reinhardt Koselleck has argued that 'progress became a modern concept when it shed or forgot its natural background meaning of stepping through space.'[46] It is precisely this faded figurative meaning that I evoke here to show that 'progress' comprised a schema of motion that settlers deployed to erase non-white tracks at Beltana.

In addition to the arrival of the steam train, the reporter from the *Mail* cited a number of 'milestones' in the 'march of progress', including 'the first arrival of camels from Afghanistan; the opening up of much unoccupied land, and many gold rushes and copper booms.'[47] Marking events that accelerated the motion of commodities, these milestones suggest that 'the march of progress' was a track closely entangled with commodity tracks. Intensifying capitalism across the Australian colonies was accompanied by growing populations of merchants and workers arriving from across the Indian Ocean and the China Sea. By the late nineteenth century, Beltana was a node of chain migration for South Asians working in the camel industry. With the onset of economic depression in the 1890s, racially exclusive movements gained momentum as settlers sought to exclude non-white people from the Australian colonies. Progress narratives articulated by nationalists envisioned a future 'White Australia', culminating in the federation of six British colonies in 1901 into the Australian nation. The new Commonwealth Parliament enacted legislation known today as the 'White Australia policy', controlling the entry, employment, and movement of non-white people. Published twenty-four years after colonials such as Mrs Lewis became nationals of 'White Australia', the newspaper article in the *Mail* reproduced the omissions and contradictions that buttressed the national spatial regime.

Whereas the 'arrival of camels' featured as a milestone of progress, the article in the *Mail* erased South Asians from the past by omitting camel drivers from the history of nineteenth-century Beltana, where they had a particularly large presence. The erasure of Aboriginal tracks was still more complex. First, imaginatively transporting herself back in time to the 1881 arrival of the train, Mrs Lewis remembered the 'hundreds of blacks, who lived about Beltana' and the regular arrival of '200 natives ... at a time' for ochre.[48] Yet, immediately afterwards, she recounted the 'opening up of much unoccupied land'.[49] How is it possible that so many Aboriginal people were present around Beltana if the land was 'unoccupied'? Precisely what constituted the occupation of land by a people according to settlers?

Intra-European debates about what constituted human 'occupation' of a place have long been central to changing notions of property, empire, and nation – licit forms of dominion in colonisers' legal traditions.[50] As historians of liberalism have shown, it was John Locke, the founding father of liberal thought, who defined 'occupation' as a relationship to land that increased its capital value.[51] With the aim of dispossessing Indigenous peoples from their land, seventeenth-century English colonists in Virginia first used this definition of occupation 'to invent the perception that the lands they were appropriating were void of exploitation and ownership.'[52] Settler colonists theorised 'occupation' as the movement of goods exclusively along commodity tracks – a redefinition that was crucial to the invention of myths of emptiness.

The Act of British Parliament in 1834 declaring British dominion over the colony of South Australia described Aboriginal geographies as 'waste and unoccupied lands', and accordingly Eyre described the country he saw inhabited by Aboriginal people as 'unoccupied' until it was 'occupied by stations'.[53] The article in the *Mail* in 1925 echoed these earlier declarations without actually denying Aboriginal presence in colonial Beltana. Rather, categorising Aboriginal relationships to place as falling outside the definition of 'occupation', the *Mail* draws attention to a key strategy settlers used to legitimise the theft of Aboriginal land.

Second, moving forward through time from the moment of the railway's arrival, the article portrayed a future emptied of Aboriginal people. The journalist wrote that the hundreds of Aboriginal people around Beltana 'died out quickly after the train came', suggesting that the train was an instrument that would realise settler fantasies about the erasure of Aboriginal people.[54] Just as colonists in Beltana in 1881 had imagined that the steam train would accelerate the arrival of goods at their destination, Mrs Lewis perceived that the train had hastened the arrival of settlers at the destination of 'White Australia'.

Whether it was the reporter or Mrs Lewis who announced the end of the 'Cooannie tribe' in 1925, the claim was not true. Undoubtedly, the 1920s marked a period of immense upheaval for Aboriginal people in the Flinders Ranges, with many communities being forced to move from their lands.[55] While it is important not to downplay the disease, upheaval, and violence caused by the ongoing processes of settler dominion, Kuyani people by no means 'died out'.[56] Not even all press accounts effaced Aboriginal presence from the Beltana region. One paper in 1929 published a photograph of four generations of a Kuyani family, from Docie Pondi, who had witnessed the arrival of the 'first whites', to her great-grandchildren – a striking statement of Kuyani resilience.[57] In addition, a corporate history of Beltana written in 1965 notes that Aboriginal people's presence 'has continued over the years until the present when they occupy the abandoned homes in the township.'[58] With Aboriginal families today continuing to live in Beltana, Aboriginal relationships to the area both predated and outlasted white settlement.

Imaginatively transporting herself to colonial Beltana from 1925, Mrs Lewis could see Aboriginal traders along ochre routes, and was also aware of Dreaming creatures (*mura*). That she equated the 'black engine' of the steam train with 'black moora' suggests that she used what she grasped about Dreaming creatures to imagine how people on the hill might have viewed the scene. However, narrating forward motion through time from the starting point of 1881, she disciplined her memories into a progress track, destined for 'White Australia'. Relegating Aboriginal people and 'moora' to the past and effacing non-white tracks from an imagined future, the newspaper article highlights how settlers used progress tracks to reconcile contradictions at colonial settlements between the blank spaces depicted on imperial maps and their lived experience of peopled Aboriginal lands. While settlers imagined that the train accelerated their march of progress to 'White Australia', another track structured Wangkangurru memories of the train.

IV. A Wangkangurru Track

In a tale recounted by many Wangkangurru storytellers, two dingoes chased an emu through deserts crisscrossed by creatures' tracks. Each time the emu changed direction, at each place it stopped to drink, each close escape from the dingoes' jaws – all created landmarks that Wangkangurru travellers followed for generations to Kuyani peaks. When British settlers and South Asian camel drivers and merchants alike began colonising land along the emu's escape route, Aboriginal storytellers repeatedly told them the saga of its getaway.[59] The numerous accounts of the story published in English confirm that it was on Kuyani peaks that the two vicious dingoes eventually caught the emu and ripped it open. There its blood gushed forth, staining the surrounding country red and coagulating in a cave near Parachilna.

From the 1850s, colonists started to describe the congealed blood of Dreaming creatures as 'red-ochre'.[60] Following the track of the Dreaming emu to Kuyani hills, Mick McLean's father, whom he sometimes referred to as 'Mathapurda', was en route to Parachilna in search of ochre when he witnessed the arrival of the steam train at the railway siding in Beltana. As historian Dale Kerwin has argued, ochre routes comprised conduits of innovation in Aboriginal geographies, as new goods, technologies, and ideas returned from distant lands with ochre traders.[61] Upon his return home to Wangkangurru deserts, Mathapurda sang about the 'railway', the steam train taking form in the imagination of his son. In 1970, Mick McLean recounted to linguist Luise Hercus, 'oh how I wanted to see the fire of a train! I wanted to see the smoke of that fire!'[62] While armed settlers defending private property wreaked havoc along ochre routes, public colonial paths – camel routes interlocking with the railway line – had different implications for Aboriginal tracks.

Employed in both the camel and railway industries from the earliest days, Aboriginal workers played a key role in ensuring the continued movement of ochre to distant deserts. Ben Murray, son of a Balochi man and an Aboriginal mother, recounted that in the 1910s, he used to deliver ochre along with the post to Killalpaninna on camels. He avoided being detected by missionaries by 'cut[ting] the corner of the flour-bag' and disguising ochre as a commodity.[63] Ochre also moved along the railway, and Ben Murray recalled that the train guard allowed ochre traders 'to travel in an empty truck concealed under a tarpaulin.'[64] The relationships that Aboriginal workers formed with railway staff and South Asian camel owners facilitated Aboriginal trade along these common routes where ochre traders were less vulnerable to the terror of armed settlers. As Wangkatyaka man Jimmy Russell recalled, by 1904 ochre traders 'walked to that hill and they came back on the train.'[65]

At times travelling the same physical routes as commodities, the congealed emu blood nevertheless remained embedded in a track distinct from commodity tracks. When Takaweejee, the head stockman at Cowarie station, told the Wangkangurru story in the 1920s, it began with two creatures springing from the earth: 'Emu jump up. Dog him live in hole. Chase'em emu. Emu run. Dog run.'[66] The chase had begun, and Takaweejee listed the sites the animals passed through – 'Pass'im Killalpaninna. Pass'im Dulkaninna. Pass'im Apawandinna' – stringing together Aboriginal communities connected by camel routes at this time. 'All time Emu run. Dog run.' Takaweejee continued, 'Pass'im Farina. Pass'im Beltana,' mapping the emu's escape along the railway line. 'Emu him run up big hills. Dog him catch'em emu. Kill'em. Blood him jump out. Ochre grow. Lot good ochre.' Even as settlers fantasised that the train had erased Aboriginal people from the Beltana region, Aboriginal traders were moving goods on the same train, while incorporating the railway into a Wangkangurru track.

While Mrs Lewis' memories of the first train were disciplined by a progress track, a close look at Mick McLean's performance of Mathapurda's railway song suggests that Wangkangurru journeys into the past were shaped by the Dreaming track featuring the fleeing emu. Before singing his father's song, Mick McLean reminisced about Palkuru in Wangkangurru deserts where he camped as a boy 'time and time again'.[67] He narrated in English, 'I was a boy then [my father] leave me along *Palkuru* [italics in original]. He came up for that red ochre over there at Parachilna.'[68] Switching to Wangkangurru, he reiterated that Mathapurda 'went off to Parachilna leaving me behind as a small boy. We went on staying in our camp [at Palkuru].' Returning to English, he continued, 'The end of that railway was along Beltana in that time *waru yarndi* (long, long ago),' and began to sing his father's lines, 'Railway *yarilu' waya'* Beltana *yarilu' waya'*.'

The lead-up to the song creates some ambiguity about when Mathapurda encountered the steam train – what Hercus describes as a 'chronological problem'.[69] The railway reached Beltana, Farina, and Marree in 1881, 1882, and 1884 respectively – events on the colonial calendar long before Mick McLean was born in around 1888. However, what Mick McLean recounted in English and reiterated in Wangkangurru suggests that he was a young boy when his father saw the train. How could Mick McLean have been born in 1888 and yet have been at Palkuru when his father witnessed the arrival of the first train at the railway terminus in Beltana in 1881? This is impossible according to the rules of chronology underpinning academic historical practice today.

While she highlights a timeline that did not correspond with Mick McLean's imaginative journey to the past, Hercus also draws attention to a track that did. She suggests that Mathapurda travelled to Parachilna on more than one occasion, both before and after Mick McLean was born. Upon returning from these epic excursions tracking Dreaming creatures, people told and retold their travel stories. Hercus concludes, 'it seems likely that he telescoped into one the two or more visits to Parachilna that he heard about as a child.'[70] While Hercus suggests that it was Mick McLean who 'telescoped' the various journeys into one, it could also have been Mathapurda who ordered the events along one narrative track.

Hercus' solution to the 'chronological problem' implies that the Wangkangurru track mapping the emu's escape not only described the route that Mathapurda traveled to Parachilna; it also formed an axis shaping how father or son, or perhaps both, imaginatively travelled to the site of the first Wangkangurru encounter with the steam train. While settlers' memories of colonial Beltana were structured by progress tracks entwined with commodity tracks, Dreaming tracks entangled with Aboriginal economic routes laid the paths for Wangkangurru movement to places in the past.

V. A New Track to Beltana

Historical storytelling consists of the act of imaginative travel between the present and the past. This was demonstrated not just by Mick McLean's performance of his father's railway song and Mrs Lewis' memories of the arrival of the steam train in Beltana, but also by Tony Abbott's claims in 2014 that Aboriginal geographies comprised of 'nothing but bush' in 1788. In narrating four tracks shaping how people remembered, recorded, and revisited events at one particular settler colonial site, this chapter can be read as a fifth track facilitating readers' imaginative travel to the past. In contrast to storytellers leading audiences along imperial tracks, arriving at blank spaces awaiting imperial penetration, this account of Beltana invites travel to the past with a clear view of the numerous tracks that converged at every site of settler colonialism.

The central problem with Abbott's view of the past is that it upholds an imperial tradition that envisions a future emptied of Aboriginal people – an outlook that can have disastrous implications for Aboriginal communities. As activists take to the streets to protest each discursive erasure of Aboriginal history and each renewed attempt to force Aboriginal people off their land, historians must pay greater attention to the geographical imaginations of colonised peoples. Understanding the past as a place crisscrossed by the tracks of numerous people and creatures is crucial if we are ever to glimpse futures beyond blank spaces.

5

THE CAMEL AND THE PROPHECY

During World War I, soldiers in the Australian and New Zealand Army Corps (ANZAC) helped to fulfil an 'Indian Prophecy', in the words of Hasan Musakhan.[1] Musakhan was a bookkeeper and legal advisor for some of the most prosperous South Asian merchants in the Australian camel business. In the aftermath of a war that killed an estimated 15 million people, including 72,000 British Indian soldiers, 60,000 Australian troops, and over 325,000 Ottoman troops, he penned a letter to the Adelaide *Register*.[2] He claimed that over a decade earlier, an 'Indian messiah' had foreseen in his dreams both the 'world war' and the 'downfall of the Turkish Empire'.[3] Musakhan was a prolific letter writer, and this was just one in a series of missives to Australian newspapers in which he would comment on political events through prophecies (Fig. 12).

Musakhan was part of the Ahmadiyya movement, one of the varieties of South Asian Islam that flourished along Australian camel tracks.[4] Its founder in Punjab, Mirza Ghulam Ahmad (b. 1835), claimed to be a prophet: both the messiah and the *mahdi*, who appears in Christian and Muslim eschatological narratives to signal the approach of the end times. From the 1880s, Ghulam Ahmad began to receive 'divine revelations' in his dreams, mostly in Persian, Urdu and Arabic and only occasionally in English.[5] One night in 1891, he dreamt that he was in a pulpit in the city of London. After preaching in English, he 'caught several birds who were sitting upon small trees and were of white colour.'[6] As he wrote in Urdu, their bodies 'resembled partridges'. Interpreting the dream as a prophecy that he would never travel to England, but that his writings would, Ghulam Ahmad began disseminating his divinations in Britain and across the Anglophone world, through his extensive South Asian networks stretching outwards from Punjab.

As the Ahmadiyya movement was growing, Musakhan arrived in the Australian colonies in 1893 at the height of the camel trade. With camel transportation remaining crucial to pastoral and mining industries in the first two decades of 'White Australia', Musakhan became an increasingly energetic 'Muslim missionary' while negotiating the contradictions between white nationalism and promises of citizenship of the British Empire. As one Chicago-based publication noted, by 1922 Musakhan was 'sending communications in favour of Islam and the Ahmadia movement to the periodicals of Australia at the average rate of one every day.'[7] In this way, the dreams that Ghulam Ahmad had in Punjab left ample traces in Australian presses, as Musakhan embedded English-language translations of Persian, Urdu and Arabic prophecies in his letters.

Prophecy is a mode of storytelling that often responds to crisis.[8] Particularly at times of calamity, messianic figures have long provided popular narratives that order chaos into meaningful stories, organising events into grand arcs connecting past, present and future. The phenomenon is not peculiar to Muslims. In the aftermath of the attacks on 11 September 2001, US President George W. Bush frequently used prophetic narratives to secure popular support for the American invasions of Afghanistan and Iraq.[9] Within this context, over the last three decades Australian governments have deployed episodes from World War I to place warfare at the centre of Australian national identity. While constructing the twenty-first-century Australia–US alliance, for example, Australian Prime Minister John Howard repeatedly evoked the 1918 Battle of Hamel as the site where Australian and American soldiers first fought side by side.[10]

Since then, alongside a series of US-led military interventions into 'Muslim majority countries', a global Islamophobia industry has produced an 'Islam versus the West' binary across the English-language public sphere. In this chapter I counter the simplistic dichotomies used by Western states as instruments of war-mongering by telling a history of the rise and fall of the Australian camel industry, while plotting the circulation of Ahmadi prophecies across the Indian Ocean.

* * *

Hasan Musakhan was from a wealthy trading family in Karachi that claimed a genealogy to Afghanistan. His uncle Khan Bahadur Moradkhan was the first South Asian merchant to supply camels to the Australian colonies. From the 1830s, Moradkhan supplied camels to British colonists in the Province of Sind, the 'post and palankin routes' of the Mughal era comprising 'the arteries of British India'.[11] He climbed the ranks of colonial bureaucracy during the 1857 Rebellion. Led by South Asian soldiers in the British Imperial Army known as 'sepoys', many disparate groups unified in revolt against British East India Company rule over North India. What British observers at the time called the 'Sepoy Mutiny', South Asian historians have long described as an 'anti-colonial war'.[12]

During the uprising, South Asian trading classes mostly sided with British colonists.[13] Moradkhan was no exception. He deployed nearly 10,000 camels and organised part of the camel relay from Karachi to Delhi that supplied rifles, bullets and British troops, including soldiers dispatched from the Australian colonies, to the seat of the uprising in Delhi.[14] After British forces regained control, tens of thousands of South Asians were executed. As historian Shahid Amin writes, 'strung-up rebels, the dead stripped to skulls and bones ... held the *ghadar* (rebel) up as an object lesson for all colonial times to come.'[15] By Royal Order issued from London, the British East India Company was disbanded and the final vestiges of Muslim political authority were dismantled in Delhi with the sacking of the last Mughal sovereign.[16] The formation of the British Raj in 1858 marked the beginning of a new chapter in the history of British colonial rule in South Asia.

The new political order established a direct relationship between the queen and her South Asian subjects for the first time, and Moradkhan was amply rewarded. The British Raj granted him land as well as the honorific 'Khan Bahadur' – one of the titles presented to South Asians who had demonstrated loyalty to the British Empire during the uprising.[17] From 1859, when Australian colonists started to arrive in British India with interests in camels, they were directed to Bahadur

Moradkhan in Karachi, Australian presses describing him as 'a respectable native'.[18] Departing from Adelaide in 1862, South Australian pastoralist Samuel Stuckey travelled to Karachi to purchase camels for Elder, Smith & Company (ESCo) – one of the most influential stock and station agents in the history of Australian capitalism.[19] Stuckey was an agent of ESCo and 'claimed the distinction of having been the first child born to white parents' following the proclamation of the colony of South Australia in 1836.[20] As he wrote in his diary, he travelled to Moradkhan's estate 'on the River Hubb on the boundary of Persia.' Staying in a tent 'furnished with table, seats, bedsteads' Stuckey met with 'Morad Khan and his interpreter, who was a Scotchman, and two native secretaries.'[21]

Some time after Moradkhan had contracted to supply camels and workers to ESCo, his sister-in-law Gool Bashra Kamal became pregnant with her first child.[22] She gave birth to Hasan Musakhan in Karachi in May 1863.[23] By then, Stuckey had left British India, without any camels. Shipping costs were too high with the American Civil War underway. In a move to force British recognition of the new secessionist Confederate States, an embargo was placed on cotton exports from the Southern slave plantations of America to Britain. In response to the 'cotton famine', British firms began sourcing this raw material from South Asia. Stuckey wrote in his diary that 'freights were ruling high in consequence of such a large quantity of cotton awaiting shipment from Bombay.'[24]

On reaching Adelaide, Stuckey travelled north to the desert ranges where ESCo had interests in a number of pastoral leases on lands inhabited by the ancestors of Adnyamathanha people today. The first Australian camel depot was planned in this mountainous region, which featured on many long-distance Aboriginal trade routes and is known today as the Flinders Ranges. One of the Aboriginal men living there was well known among white settlers by the name Pompey. With many connections to Aboriginal families in the hills as well as the flatter deserts further north, Pompey was involved in many instances of Aboriginal resistance against British pastoralists' activities from their first arrival with their sheep.[25] Stuckey described him as a 'very powerfully built, fine grown man … notwithstanding [that] he had one leg withered below the knee from the effects of a wound he could run like a deer.'[26] On 18 January 1864, with 13,000 ewes dramatically reducing supplies of water in the middle of a drought, Stuckey met Pompey at Titree Creek. There was a confrontation, and a few hours before dawn, Stuckey shot Pompey in the chest.[27]

Stuckey's plans to return to Karachi were delayed by having to stand trial for the murder of Pompey. At a coroners' hearing a 'jury consisting chiefly, if not exclusively, of the personal friends or servants' of Stuckey unanimously acquitted him.[28] At a second tribunal, the jury passed a sentence of 'justifiable homicide' and Stuckey was discharged 'amidst the cheering of the spectators.'[29] Though he escaped having to serve a prison sentence, Stuckey complained in his diary that the 'case cost us £360' and settlers petitioned the South Australian parliament to reimburse his costs.[30] A letter of support from Stuckey's 'fellow colonists' argued that the only way to prevent 'lynch law' on 'the distant stations' was by increasing police numbers, drawing on the logic of racialised violence that had emerged in the American South.[31] With Australian colonial governments steadily increasing police resources in interior regions alongside the exponential growth of Australian wool exports, many of their decisions from the 1860s led to the presence of greater numbers of armed officers backing settler industries, changing the terrain of power on which white pastoralists and miners encountered Aboriginal people.

Before Samuel Stuckey departed for Karachi, settlers severed Pompey's head from his corpse and it was 'placed in the South Australian Institute for the inspection of students in ethnology.'[32] As historians have shown, the scientific assertion of difference between colonisers and colonised peoples, through various disciplines, such as ethnology and anthropology, was one British response to a decade of uprisings across the Empire, beginning with the 1857 Sepoy Rebellion. In response to the Fenian Uprising in Ireland (1867), the Morant Bay Rebellion in the Caribbean (1865), the Maori Wars in New Zealand, and countless Aboriginal retaliations against Australian colonists, colonial ideology across the British Empire shifted from a 'universalist to a culturalist stance'.[33] With the collapse of the belief that civilising missions could transform colonised peoples into liberal subjects, from the 1860s colonial regimes increasingly claimed that colonised peoples could not be civilised, not only because of their adherence to what the

British called 'tradition', 'custom' and 'religion', but also because they were biologically different.

When Stuckey reached Karachi, Moradkhan sold him 124 camels. Moradkhan also brokered employment contracts between ESCo and thirty-one South Asian camel drivers. They were contracted for a period of three years and departed for the colony of South Australia in 1865. On completion of their contracts, all thirty-one workers returned to British India on the *Kohinoor* in 1868, overseeing a cargo of twenty horses and one emu.[34] Within months, a second batch of forty-two contracted workers supplied by Moradkhan headed to the Australian colonies.[35] Each group of workers was accompanied by a *jemidar* – landed South Asian headmen in charge of the South Asian workers employed by Australian colonists. As newspaper records confirm, from the earliest days, camel drivers went on strike or challenged their white employers in Australian courts when the terms of their contracts were breached, sometimes with the support of the *jemidar*, at other times without.[36]

While Moradkhan belonged to the elite classes of South Asians who sought to secure their prosperity in service to British colonists, for many others the era of the British Raj precipitated a larger crisis in what historian C. M. Naim describes as the 'collective Muslim psyche'.[37] The overthrow of the Mughal crown by the British in 1857 had marked the highly theatrical, symbolic end to a dynasty of rule established in 1527. The upheaval left in its wake a vast archive of storytelling strategies for making sense of crisis. Over the decades that followed, prophetic dreams about future Muslim kingdoms emerged as a pervasive feature of South Asian political discourse.[38] An outpouring of revelations predicted the arrival of a messianic figure who would illuminate the way forward. Forecast events were often pegged to significant units of millenarian time on the Muslim Hijri calendar (H), like centuries, or blocks of forty days.[39]

Emerging in around 1300 H, or 1883 CE, the Ahmadiyya movement was one of the many Muslim 'reform' movements to spring up in British India at the turn of the Hijri century. Its founder Mirza Ghulam Ahmed belonged to the aristocratic Mirza family descended from Mughal households. Once the rulers of the walled city of Qadian in Punjab, during the Sepoy Rebellion Ghulam Ahmad's family had supported British colonists.[40] He first began to have particularly vivid dreams after his father's death in 1876, which made concrete the passing of an age.[41] Like many of the sovereigns whom the Mirzas claimed a lineage to, Ghulam Ahmad started compiling a dream book of 'divine revelations'.[42] Over several decades, he developed a framework to interpret his dreams, drawing on many textual traditions alive in Punjab. Issuing prophecy after prophecy, Ghulam Ahmad soon established a reputation as a charismatic Muslim reformer who could foresee the future.

On some key points, Ghulam Ahmad's views diverged from the many Muslim reformers who were publishing prophecies in the newspapers of late-nineteenth-century British India. Based on a particular reading of the Quran, he claimed that Jesus had not been killed at the time of crucifixion, but had subsequently travelled to India. Drawing on the narratives of Russian orientalist scholar Nicolas Notovitch, Ghulam Ahmad argued that Jesus was buried in a tomb in Kashmir.[43] With his dreams regularly featuring elements rich with Christian symbolism, such as white partridges, Ghulam Ahmad repeatedly dreamt that both his character and appearance had a strong resemblance to 'Jesus, son of Mary'.[44] These were interpretations that Ghulam Ahmad formulated and published in direct dialogue with Christian missionaries. When countering the arguments of Hindu reformers, Ghulam Ahmad cited dreams in which Hindus kneeling before him informed him he was 'an avatar of Krishna', his revelations often featuring Indic characters.[45] Casting himself as the messianic figure at the centre of many textual traditions, Ghulam Ahmad wrote that 'when the thirteenth century came to a close and the fourteenth century was about to dawn, Allah the Almighty informed me by revelation: you are the *mujaddid* (renewer) of this century.'[46] According to Muslim knowledge traditions, a *mujaddid* appeared every century to illuminate the path forward. By the 1890s Ghulam Ahmad was not only prophesying the future, but, controversially, he was also claiming to be a prophet.

While these declarations were formulated as defences of Islam in the era of the British Raj, some of Ghulam Ahmad's arguments had precedents in the 'millennial epistemology' of the Mughal dynasty.[47] Many Mirzas before Ghulam Ahmad had claimed to be the long-awaited messiah arriving at the turn of the century.[48] From the establishment of the

Mughal administration to the era of British colonial rule, Mughal iconography remained 'obsessed with Jesus', as Azfar Moin puts it, and Mirzas were repeatedly cast as Christ reborn.[49] In addition, as engagement with Sanskrit literature also formed a key element of Mughal self-fashioning, poets commissioned by Mughal courts frequently characterised Mirzas as avatars of Indic gods.[50] While Ghulam Ahmad's self-identification as both Jesus and Krishna was entirely consistent with the personas of past Mirzas, these sorts of claims were increasingly dismissed by the late nineteenth century. As this signals, belying the various modernist Muslim and Hindu reform movements that emerged during the rule of the British Raj was a deeper shift in the epistemic grounds on which South Asian selves were being constituted.

The close of the thirteeth Hijri century in 1883 gave rise to a range of millenarian movements in South Asia, a moment that coincided with the beginning of a new era in the Australian camel trade. One of the best-known *jemidars* at the time was Faiz Mahomet, who was joined by his younger brother Tagh Mahomet in the Australian colonies in the 1870s.[51] Following Moradkhan's death, in the 1880s the Mahomet brothers devised an alternative scheme to meet growing Australian demand for both camels and South Asian workers. Entering into a business partnership to form Faiz and Tagh Mahomet, Camel Proprietors and Carriers (F&T), the brothers began operating as subcontractors for ESCo. With a shipment of 225 camels to Adelaide in 1884, F&T resumed the camel trade, with their drivers camping at Crystal Brook on the way to the northern deserts of South Australia (Fig. 13). As one settler observed, from the 'rugs, carpets, and quilts which they spread round the camp fires ... they treated the spectators to music from a guitar, and a gaily ornamented species of violin, varied with songs and improvisations.'[52] Accompanying South Asian travellers heading inland, the Ahmadi variety of Islam was one of many that circulated along Australian camel tracks over the next decades.

In British India, in the first decade of the fourteenth Hijri century, Moradkhan's nephew Hasan Musakhan graduated from N. J. Highschool in Karachi, winning a scholarship to attend Bombay University.[53] While his uncle had conducted his business affairs in Persian, employing interpreters to communicate with English speakers, Musakhan, in contrast, reached adulthood after colonial reforms had instituted English as the medium of elite education. As Gauri Visawanathan has shown, British scholarships financed university education for students from 'learned Indigenous classes ... targeted for eventual induction into government service.'[54] Educated as an 'orientalist scholar of five languages' in this new era, Musakhan took up the post of headmaster of the 'Anglo-Vernacular and Technical School' in Sind – an institution for boys established by the British Raj.[55]

In around 1893, when he was thirty years old, Musakhan departed for the Australian colonies and secured a job as a clerk for F&T.[56] The firm was prospering, as it secured more Australian government contracts to deliver stores to outback stations. The drivers F&T contracted in British India were remunerated at £2 per month in addition to rations, their wages rising each year.[57] Many of these drivers owned some of the camels they brought on board the ships. When contracting with F&T, they paid a deposit that was returned to them on reaching Australian camel camps with their animals. As the expanding firm borrowed money from ESCo at an interest rate of 10 per cent per annum, it then lent capital to its South Asian employees at a rate of 12.5 per cent.[58] It was a business model that saw many F&T subcontractors form competing camel-carrying companies. Narrating his early impressions of the Australian colonies, Musakhan wrote to the *Punjab Observer* in 1895 that while there were scant opportunities for an 'Entrance passed Indian gentleman', there was always money in the camel business, or the drapery or grocery lines.[59]

As camel transportation became a crucial adjunct to Australian pastoral and mining industries, South Asian merchants began patronising different spiritual guides – figures key to the mediation of disputes not just between employers and employees or debtors and creditors, but also between competing carrying companies.[60] Writing to two Perth newspapers in 1896, one South Asian merchant insisted 'that the true and only priest here is Mirza Khan' – a mullah from Calcutta.[61] Listing Mirza Khan's superior credentials over a rival in Perth, the writer claimed that 'Mirza Khan is a missionary' and 'continually wears the dress of a missionary or priest.'[62] With the self-styling of Muslim spiritual guides mirroring the language and garb of Christian evangelism, the arguments that mullahs made were often direct refutations of British missionaries. As the letter writer in Perth continued, Mirza

Khan was 'prepared to argue' with his rival 'in the presence of Jews, Hindoos, Christians and Mohammedans, and will also explain the religion in five different languages.'[63]

In the late nineteenth century, debates between faiths were staged both in packed halls as well as in the pages of newspapers, across the British Empire as well as in the United States. The theatrical style of debate itself spread with Christian evangelists and Muslim travellers. John Alexander Dowie, for example, who was ordained as a Baptist minister in Adelaide, delivered sermons to large audiences in Melbourne and Sydney that some settlers described as 'bombastic'.[64] After moving to Chicago in 1888, where he was influenced by the thriving evangelism of post–Civil War America, Dowie founded the city of 'Zion' in Illinois, one of the many precursors to the emergence of the Pentecostal Church. From the 1890s, claiming that he was a Christian messiah, he began describing himself as 'Elijah the Faith Healer'. As Dowie wrote in his own periodical, 'my mission is to gather people from the East and the West, the North and the South, and fill this city and all other places with Christians until the time comes when Islam should be swept away from the face of the earth.'[65]

In Punjab, it was in direct dialogue with such declarations that Ghulam Ahmad formulated both his arguments and his persona as a prophet. In 1893, for example, he engaged in a public argument on the topic of Jesus' ascension with a Christian missionary that went on for fifteen days, hundreds of people purchasing tickets each day to witness the debate.[66] It was from these sites of contest that Ghulam Ahmad issued his dream-based prophecies, at times tailored specifically to Christian, Muslim and Hindu audiences. First publishing them in local newspapers, he disseminated these prophecies through a growing global Ahmadiyya community. Harnessing print publication networks to shape how his followers interpreted astral signs, Ghulam Ahmad prophesied in 1894 that a lunar and solar eclipse during the month of Ramadan would confirm two things: the approaching end of time and that he was the final messiah.[67]

When the full moon was partially eclipsed at midnight on 21 March 1894, Hasan Musakhan was at the F&T camel camp in Marree in the colony of South Australia. It was the month of Ramadan in 1311 H and people fasting at camel camps across the Australian colonies were particularly attuned to the Hijri calendar.[68] Three days later, F&T launched a new camel line from Marree to the town of Coolgardie in the colony of Western Australia. One settler recalled there was a 'good deal of embracing' among the 'crowd of Afghans' as the camels commenced a journey of over 2,000 kilometres.[69] Musakhan did not join the camel drivers heading west, and travelled instead to Adelaide. A fortnight after the lunar eclipse, a solar eclipse was sighted in British India on 6 April 1894, during the last days of Ramadan. At the Eid celebrations Musakhan attended at the Adelaide Mosque on Little Gilbert Street, it is likely that the two eclipses were accepted by some as fulfilling Ghulam Ahmad's prophecy, rejected by others, and debated by many (Fig. 14).

From Adelaide, Musakhan travelled to Perth by sea, proceeding to Coolgardie by camel with F&T camel owners.[70] Establishing a Coolgardie branch on 24 July 1894, F&T secured its stronghold on camel lines throughout Western Australian goldfields. It was in response to settlers' increasing agitation against 'Asiatics' in the Western Australian goldfields that Musakhan appealed to his larger networks of Muslim reformers. In 1894, when one white settler in Coolgardie shot dead two South Asian camel drivers, he was acquitted of both murder and manslaughter. Protesting 'persecution by certain white people', Hasan Musakhan wrote to Punjab and forwarded to Australian newspapers his ensuing correspondence with Hamid Snow, a British man who had embraced Islam.[71] Snow was a leader of one of the many Muslim reform movements in British India and was well connected to a community he described as 'the English Muslims of the Church of Islam'.[72]

Musakhan's protest to Snow about the 'safety and security' of South Asians' 'life and property' invoked citizenship of both the British Empire and the state of Afghanistan.[73] According to some interpretations of the 1893 Durand Line Agreement demarcating the border between British India and Afghanistan, Afghan diaspora were guaranteed free passage throughout British imperial territories.[74] Aware of the multiple regimes he could petition, Musakhan requested help from his 'brethren in India and Afghanistan ... by bringing this matter to the notice of the English parliament and also to that of the Ameer of Afghanistan.'[75] Snow replied from Punjab with plans for 'a monster protestation meeting next week' regarding 'the treatment of our brethren in Australia'.[76]

The promises of British imperial citizenship were collapsing for many South Asians across the world as white settlers were drawing a global colour line. It was in the American state of Mississippi that a literacy test was first introduced in 1890 as a measure to deny suffrage to African Americans after the abolishment of slavery plantations.[77] With strategies of white dominion travelling across the Anglo-sphere, a dictation test was introduced in the British colony of Western Australia soon afterwards in 1897 as a tool of racial arbitration wielded by customs officials. Musakhan secured an exemption from the dictation test armed with both his 'passport' and 'matriculation certificate', pointing to the emergence of university degrees as one of the instruments South Asians used to negotiate white border regimes.[78] In one of his increasingly frequent letters to Australian newspapers, Musakhan reproached the settler regimes for denying his rights as a British subject despite the fact he was 'well educated in English'.[79]

Over the next few years, Musakhan regularly appeared as an interpreter or advisor in 'test cases' in Australian courts as South Asians challenged piece after piece of racist legislation. In 1898 he married Sophia Blitz, a woman from a German Jewish family in Adelaide. She gave birth to their daughter in Coolgardie, a son and daughter in Perth, and a son in Broken Hill, and the family frequently travelled between camel camps. When six Australian colonies formed the new nation of Australia on 1 January 1901, Musakhan was still employed by Faiz Mahomet, who was in Karachi procuring camels for the Western Australian government. In March 1901, Australian officials cabled Faiz Mahomet declaring that the 'importation of camels into Australia' was 'strictly prohibited', bringing to a close the era of the South Asian camel trade across the Indian Ocean (Fig. 15).[80]

The news led many of those who had been engaged in supplying camels to invest their capital in the less lucrative camel-carrying business within Australia. As some Australian state governments – formerly colonial governments – acquired camel yards once owned by South Asians, a new class of power brokers emerged in the camel industry in the era of 'White Australia'. In Marree, Moosa Balooch was appointed to oversee the South Australian government camel depot, at times drawing the ire of earlier 'camel kings'. It was during this aggressive period of white nationalism that Musakhan began describing himself as a

'Muslim missionary'. A registered newsagent, distributing many local dailies and overseas periodicals from a shop at 95 Brisbane Street in Perth, he began disseminating tracts on Ahmadi thought in English-language presses. With Faiz Mahomet, he also threw his energies into the construction of a mosque in Perth from 1904.[81] As political movements for sovereignty across the British Empire were being shaped by the newly invented formation of the independent crown dominion, Musakhan began to articulate a vision of a future Muslim dominion.

Ghulam Ahmad received ample coverage in English-language newspapers of the time, as Ahmadi missionaries in Australia, South Africa, Britain and the United States translated and disseminated materials they received from Punjab. With sensational duels sometimes unfolding in the English-language public sphere, the Adelaide *Register* in 1903 reported on a debate between 'Rival Messiahs'. Reproducing Ghulam Ahmad's declaration that 'I am the true Messiah who was to come in the last ages', Australian presses paid particular attention to his debates with evangelist John Dowie, given the latter's Australian past.[82]

Dowie never travelled to British India, but his calls to 'Exterminate Islam!' still caught Ghulam Ahmad's attention in Punjab.[83] As Dowie wrote in 1900, 'There is in India a stupid Muslim Messiah who writes to me oft and oft again that the tomb of Jesus the Christ is in Kashmir.'[84] In his correspondence, Ghulam Ahmad repeatedly challenged Dowie to a 'prayer contest'.[85] Dowie refused to respond, declaring that it was beneath him to 'answer gnats and flies on whom if I were to stamp my foot I would crush them to death and destruction!'[86] As one Perth newspaper noted with displeasure, Ghulam Ahmad's retaliations included the claim that Dowie 'was for a short time a convict in Tasmania.'[87]

With Ghulam Ahmad's style of messianic Islam mirroring Dowie's variety of charismatic Christianity, one Australian press dubbed him 'Dowie's Double'.[88] After a particularly vituperative exchange of insults, Ghulam Ahmad foresaw in his dreams that Dowie would 'leave the world before my eyes with great sorrow and torment.'[89] His prophecy was published in newspapers across the Anglophone world in 1903.[90] Four years later, on 9 March 1907, while delivering a sermon in Zion city John Dowie was 'struck with paralysis', according to Ahmadi literature.[91] After several hours of violent spasms, he eventually died. Musakhan was among the many letter writers worldwide who informed presses in Chicago, Boston, London, Adelaide, Melbourne, Cape Town and Perth that Dowie's painful death fulfilled Ghulam Ahmad's prophecy.

Discussions of Turkey also loomed large in Muslim reform movements emerging from South Asia. After the Sepoy Rebellion of 1857, many Sunni Muslims understood the Ottoman caliphate as the only remaining sovereign power that could trace its lineage to the political system established in the lifetime of Muhammad. The invocation of the names of Ottoman caliphs at Friday prayers in many South Asian and Australian mosques alike bestowed on 'them a sanctity they did not have earlier', as Naim writes.[92] Turkish political developments were keenly followed in British India, giving rise to a number of social movements.[93] Participating in these debates by day, Ghulam Ahmad had a dream on the night of 2 January 1904 prophesying the future of the Ottoman Empire: 'Turkey will be defeated in a land hard by [*sic*], and after defeat she will be victorious in a few years.'[94] Four years later, as South Asians were closely following the Young Turks movement, Ghulam Ahmad had another dream. Musakhan summarised this third prophecy in a Melbourne newspaper: 'After the victory, she will again be defeated.'[95]

After eighteen years in the Australian camel industry, when Musakhan briefly returned to British India in 1911 he continued communicating with Australian presses. From the city of Khairpur, Sind, he wrote to Perth that perusing the Western Australian *Sunday Times* 'brought back to my recollection all the pleasant as well as unpleasant experiences of my life in Australia.'[96] Commenting on the paper's review of 'Turkey's hopeless position in the affairs of European politics', Musakhan outlined for Australian readers the three prophecies that shaped Ahmadi interpretations of Turkish political events. He picked up the correspondence when he returned to Australia and announced that the first two of Ghulam Ahmad's three prophecies about Turkey had been fulfilled during the Balkan Wars.[97]

Following the outbreak of World War I in 1914, Musakhan again cited the Ahmadi prophecies about Turkey and articulated his visions of the ideal Muslim polity. He wrote that Turkey 'must become a protectorate under the British government, like Afghanistan and other Muslim dominions, in order to reap the full benefit of peaceful civilization.'[98] As this confirms, Musakhan's schema of reform envisioned a Muslim dominion under the protection of the British imperial flag. With the Ottoman Empire entering the war as a German ally, Musakhan opined that 'Turkey has of her own foolishness ... lost all chances now of remaining an independent Moslem power ... she cannot remain safe from evil influences of the neighbouring military European powers, who are always preparing for bloodshed and plunder.'[99] For Musakhan, the fall of the Ottoman Empire was a necessary step toward building what he called an 'independent Moslem power'.[100]

Musakhan's vision of the future was produced at a moment when many South Asians were anticipating that British India would be granted independent dominion status with the end of the war. In 1916, when ANZAC troops were among the Allied forces who defeated Ottoman soldiers in both Baghdad and Jerusalem, Musakhan rejoiced. When the war ended, he wrote to the *Register* celebrating 'Peace day' and drew attention to 'the capture of Jerusalem on December 8, 1916, in which the Australian soldiers took a particularly large and foremost share.'[101] It was at this juncture that the third Ahmadi prophecy about Turkey's fate was fulfilled, wrote Musakhan. The actions of the ANZACs, he continued, even though they were unaware that 'they were helping in carrying out the fulfilment of the Divine Prophesy [*sic*]', meant that Australian soldiers were 'entitled to God's blessings for so sacrificing their life and all.'[102] As Musakhan wrote from the small town of Warialda in northern New South Wales, 'the Anzac Day and its anniversary will always excite a deep and joyful interest in the hearts of the followers of the Indian Messiah because it perpetuates the memory of the revelation ... about the final fate of the Turks.'[103]

In the aftermath of World War I, British India was not granted dominion status or any other form of independence from British colonial regimes. It was in this context that Mohandas Karamchand Gandhi united the Khilafat and Non-cooperation movements, bringing together different South Asian reformists to articulate an anti-imperial nationalism. Watching these developments from Australia, Musakhan continued his energetic outpourings over the next decade. His articles to English presses in Australia circulated across the globe through a network of Ahmadi 'missionaries', which by the 1920s had roots 'all over India, Burma, Ceylon, China, Mauritius, Mesopotamia, Persia, Arabia, Egypt,

England, United States of America, East & West Africa, Australia.'[104] Sometimes weighing in on race relations debates unfolding at global sites, he wrote articles for English-language presses in Perth, regularly sending them a one-page pamphlet called *The Moslem Sunshine*.[105]

With the self-fashioning of Ahmadi missionaries undoubtedly mirroring the Christian evangelists they were refuting, plotting the circulation of Ahmadi stories from South Asia to Australian interiors highlights a variety of Islam that continued to draw from multiple textual traditions even as different 'religions' were increasingly defined in opposition to each other. As the trail that his writings left in Australian presses confirms, Musakhan published Punjabi Ahmadi prophecies while engaging with Australian settler narratives about World War I, racial exclusion, Christian thought, national boundaries and the camel industry. It is even possible to glean a little about his relationship to Aboriginal people and knowledges from an article he sent to Australian periodicals that appears to have found no space in settler newspapers. Citing the latest edition of the Perth-based *Moslem Sunshine* in July 1922, the editor of the Chicago-based Ahmadi magazine *Moslem Sunrise* summarised that Musakhan 'had a strange experience of giving the Message to the original inhabitants of Australia where lying sick in a forest camp, he was miraculously helped by Allah.'[106]

Over the course of Musakhan's life, however, the bitterly oppositional ground of inter-religious debate in British India hardened, as the perception of the Ahmadiyya as 'heretics' became more entrenched. By the twentieth century, the most vicious attacks on Ahmadiyya were not being launched by Hindus, Christians or the racially exclusive Western borders enacted by the 'global colour line', but rather by other reformist varieties of Islam.[107]

In Perth, Musakhan's wife Sophia died in 1923. She was buried 'at the Jewish portion of the Karrakatta cemetery'.[108] From this point, Musakhan's letters to Australian newspapers grew increasingly melancholy, coinciding not only with the rise of motorised transportation and the decimation of the camel-carrying industry from the mid-1920s, but also the increasingly aggressive persecution of Ahmadiyya in South Asia. Throwing his energies into the compilation of a history of the camel industry, Musakhan recounted the era that had passed (Fig. 16). He catalogued the names, and sometimes the brief biographies, of the South

Asians who had arrived in the Ausralian colonies contracted first by Khan Bahadur Moradkhan and then by Faiz and Tagh Mahomet, producing a comprehensive administrative history of the mosque they constructed at the crossroads of William Street and Robinson Street in Perth.[109]

As state governments across Australia passed camel destruction acts, Musakhan published a sweeping historical narrative titled 'Like Ships in the Night Afghan Life Passes to the Mists' in a Perth newspaper.[110] Noting that 'the motor cars and motor wagons have started to capture all the carrying trade', he cited 'the Divine Prophesy [*sic*] that camels will be abandoned in later days.'[111] After travelling to the Western Australian goldfields, he wrote to the *Mirror* that the people he knew and loved were 'one after another saying goodbye to "White Australia" for ever.' He reflected that 'The surviving members of that hardy Afghan community ... are nearing the completion of the term and span of their natural lives', describing the passing of a generation whose lives and selves had been profoundly shaped by their negotiations of sharpening borders.

For the ageing South Asians in Coolgardie, the homelands they had left far behind across the Indian Ocean no longer existed. As they faced the uncertain journey ahead, Musakhan wrote to the Perth *Mirror* that they could be heard singing a song:

> Yea;
> The Persian maids with black hair locks,
> The Indian darlings with narrow waists,
> Have stolen my heart, have captured my heart.
> And.
> Here at Coolgardie I am a prisoner.
> Is there any hope for me to ever,
> Return to my own sweet home?
> My old, sweet home, old sweet home.[112]

6

THE BOOK OF SAND

In 1895, the southbound train on the Great Northern Railway would stop once a week at Alberrie Creek siding – a station in the northern deserts of the colony of South Australia.[1] Late one Tuesday afternoon, two young Aboriginal women were waiting by 'the long black water tank' at Alberrie Creek for the 5.46 p.m. train.[2] They were sisters. As they waited to catch the train back to the town of Marree, two South Asian men appeared on the horizon with a string of camels. To the sisters' dismay, 'the train was running late'.[3] Their subsequent encounter with the two camel drivers at Alberrie Creek railway siding was a story that was told and retold by Aboriginal women and men for decades.[4]

In the 1960s, Mona Merrick recounted the well-known story in Arabunna – one of the many languages spoken by Aboriginal people around Marree. Linguist Luise Hercus recorded Mona's retelling on tape and published it in the journal *Aboriginal History* in 1981, accompanied by an English translation. As Mona narrated, with a long night's trek to Oodnadatta ahead of them, 'two Afghans (*Abigana*) came past with their camels (*gamulu*)'. The two men were on their way to the dam near Alberrie Creek railway siding to water their camels. When they saw the young women by the railway tank, they brought their animals to a halt. In Mona's account 'they asked – they asked straight away! – "Undo your clothes and show us your breasts – we want to see your breasts!"'[5] With no sign of their belated train, in desperation, 'the two of them showed their breasts'.[6] The girls wondered, 'When is this train coming – these whitefellows (*wadjbala*) are making us show our breasts!'[7]

The frightened girls had 'brownish-red bodies, not absolutely black'. As Mona specified 'they were both very plump'.[8] The men demanded, 'Lift up your clothes so we can see your thighs – show'm leg!'[9] In response, the sisters 'showed and showed their thighs, oh how they went on showing and showing!'[10] The sisters were frightened not just of impending violence but also of something still more alien, for the men did not grope them. 'They are not even putting their hands anywhere near – they are just looking!'[11] Unnerved by their gaze, the two women wondered why the men made them bare their light, plump flesh but did not try to touch them. It became evident to the girls that it was '*palku*', their flesh, their meat, that the men hungered after. They concluded 'those two want to eat both of us, you and me!'[12]

This Arabunna story is part of a much larger archive of Aboriginal-language histories of South Asians produced over the seven decades that camels were the main form of long-distance transportation in interior Australia. Sometimes containing fragments of South Asian-language songs, sayings, words and *surahs* from the Quran, today Aboriginal oral archives continue to offer startlingly detailed observations of these travellers from across the Indian Ocean. Born in around 1912, Mona Merrick heard the Arabunna story about the two sisters at Alberrie Creek from her Aboriginal mother Barralda. Alberrie Creek railway siding marked one of the bounds of the Finniss Springs pastoral property that Mona's white father held a title over. The story about the two camel drivers at Alberrie Creek was not the only one that Barralda told featuring the possibility that South Asian men might eat Aboriginal women.[13] From the 1960s, Hercus recorded these and other Arabunna-language accounts and published some of them with English translations over the decades that followed.

When the railway was extended to Marree in 1884, the town became one of the major camel communication centres in Australian interiors. Some of the most powerful camel-carrying firms set up yards in Marree from the late 1880s and many Aboriginal people came to be employed by South Asian camel owners. As Mona Merrick recollected, lots of Aboriginal people 'used to work (with camels) and then go back to Oodnadatta: the Afghans just paid them money (but stayed in

Marree)!'[14] To describe South Asian merchants and workers, who often arrived in Aboriginal lands as employees of white settlers and colonial governments, Mona Merrick used the term *Abigana* – an appropriation of the settler term 'Afghan'. Other phrases Aboriginal people used around Marree were *wadjbala madimadi* (white fellows with hair-string) and *gadabu ŋara-ŋara* (head tied up), drawing attention to the turbans worn by some South Asians.[15]

By the 1910s and 1920s, when Mona and her brothers and sisters were growing up near Alberrie Creek some 30 kilometres to the west of Marree, many Aboriginal and South Asian families were intricately interconnected through intimate and family relationships as well as employment contracts. As Mona recalled, the train to Marree eventually arrived and the two sisters boarded to go home. She concludes that 'The two Afghans didn't want that train (to come) – they only wanted a girlfriend.'[16] It is a closing line that captures Mona's ultimate ambivalence toward South Asian men, having spent a lifetime in close proximity to many camel camp families.

This Arabunna story of encounter cannot properly be understood today if it is simply inserted into existing English-language historical narratives – the accounts of the past found in Australian history books that we already take for granted as true. Instead, Aboriginal-language stories can reveal glimpses of the epistemological ground on which Aboriginal people narrated the past. While histories of non-white migrants in the settler offshoots of the British Empire are too often written as dramas about 'pioneers' or 'aliens' that unfold on the 'blank spaces' underpinning settler colonial regimes, Aboriginal-language archives point to alternative imaginative geographies that have long structured historical storytelling about South Asians.

When I came across an English translation of the story about the two women and two men at Alberrie Creek in the journal *Aboriginal History*, my first reading situated the text in the context of the twentieth-century settler policies of child removal well documented by Australian historians.[17] During Mona's childhood, settler regimes seeking to control Aboriginal people's most intimate relations always threatened to interrupt the lives of those at Finniss Springs. In the early twentieth century, at the height of the settler project of 'White Australia', many children's homes were established across Australia with the aim of absorbing lighter-skinned Aboriginal people into white working-class Australia. Like the two young women in the story, both Mona and Barralda were light-skinned. Their lives unfolded against the ever-present possibility that government administrators, police officers or Christian missionaries might remove Aboriginal children from Finniss Springs to so-called 'half-caste' homes. When Mona was about twelve years old, the Colebrook Children's Home was established at Oodnadatta, a few railway stops north of Alberrie Creek.[18] Barralda's telling of the two sisters' story might have been part of a larger archive of Arabunna anecdotes that warned light-skinned Aboriginal children about the various dangers at Alberrie Creek railway siding.

As Mona's retelling of the Alberrie Creek encounter hints, South Asians brought with them their own ideas about skin colour that were distinct from, but always entangled with, British colonial regimes of racial hierarchy. Mona's narrative repeatedly returned to the detail of the two sisters' skin colour, and her mother Barralda might have used the story to warn her light-skinned daughters about South Asians' schemas of difference. One interpretive strategy is to historicise the story. By placing the tale in its temporal context, we can investigate whether encounters between different colonised peoples at Alberrie Creek were shaped more broadly by the 'global colour line' being drawn in the early twentieth century.

Another possible interpretive strategy is to examine the conditions, purpose and institutional context in which the Arabunna story was recorded, translated and ultimately published by Hercus in the journal *Aboriginal History*. This is a line of enquiry that draws attention to the movement of orientalist reading strategies between South Asia and Australia. Born into a Jewish family that fled from Nazi-era Germany to Britain in 1938, Luise Hercus was trained in 'Oriental Studies' at the University of Oxford, focusing on Sanskrit and Prakrit.[19] Eventually relocating to Melbourne, she began working with Australian Aboriginal-language speakers in the 1960s.[20] As one of the founding figures of the field of Australian linguistics, over the course of her career Hercus produced an astounding number of linguistic studies of many Aboriginal languages, using and extending an interpretive framework that had grown out of orientalist scholarship in British India. By following the movement of linguistic research methodologies across the Indian

Ocean, we can read this Arabunna tale to investigate connections between the operation of knowledge-power in South Asia and Australia.

Yet, when I tried to read Mona Merrick's Arabunna story through these historical and linguistic interpretive lenses, something disappeared: the imaginative worlds of the Aboriginal women who told this story. More specifically, historicising the story could not answer the question that most puzzled me: Why did the Arabunna girls waiting for their train at Alberrie Creek railway siding deduce that the two South Asian men were going to eat them? It is possible to imagine the way those men stared at the young women. In response to their gaze of possession and desire, the sisters' terror and confusion is comprehensible. But why in this moment of sexualised encounter did the women intuit that they might be eaten? This twist in the story continued to trouble me. It is unlikely that South Asian men actually ate Aboriginal women. There are no references in English or South Asian-language records about cannibalism among camel merchants or drivers in the Australian colonies. Why then did two young women draw this conclusion when the men commanded them to bare themselves? It was a detail that only started making sense to me when I travelled through Arabunna country with Barralda's grandson, Reg Dodd.

I first met Reg Dodd when I was chasing the Bengali book found at the Broken Hill mosque. In July 2009, I began contacting the descendants of the South Asian families who used to live in Broken Hill. The old camel camps throughout Australia continue to be tightly interconnected through family networks. Lal Zada, who lives in Port Augusta today, is the great-grandson of Khan Zada, a lascar from Karachi who found work as a camel driver in Broken Hill. Many of Lal's family live in Port Augusta, and they invited me to join them on a road trip to Marree for the Camel Cup, an annual occasion for the descendants of South Asians to reunite. The transcontinental train, or 'Afghan express', no longer runs through tiny Marree. The newer railway connecting Adelaide to Darwin is still known as the 'Ghan', while the disused original route is locally called the 'old Ghan'. Across abandoned railway tracks and camel routes, I travelled the first leg of the journey to Alberrie Creek with the Zada family.

The frenzied activities of the Camel Cup include three days of camel racing, a dance on the second night, and the reunion of the 'Afghans', culminating in a third night of feasting. At some point during the festivities, Lal introduced me to Reg Dodd. The two men are roughly the same age. From the 1950s, they were both employed at the railways, where they went on to work together for many years. Now in his late seventies, Reg Dodd is one of the older living members of Mona Merrick's family, and can recall hearing Arabunna stories about the fear that South Asian men would eat Aboriginal women. Reg is the chairman of the Arabunna People's Committee in Marree. As a charismatic and prominent Aboriginal spokesperson in the area, he plays a crucial role in the Arabunna-language revitalisation programs underway at Marree Aboriginal School today.[21]

I had my first opportunity to talk to Reg on the morning that I was leaving Marree. Setting up a couple of foldout chairs outside the Arabunna People's Community Centre, Reg doused a few wooden blocks in petrol and set them alight for some warmth that bitter morning. By then, I had come across many Aboriginal-language stories about South Asians. Recorded, translated and published by linguists between the 1960s and 1990s, they were tales that offered startling, detailed accounts of encounters between South Asians and Aboriginal people. In my attempts to read the Aboriginal-language texts using historical and linguistic methodologies, I had started to realise that reading these stories in English translation was insufficient. I tried to articulate to Reg my reasons for wanting to talk to him. I aspired to learn about language, history and place. Could I talk to him about Arabunna?

He answered with a query. 'You have to ask yourself,' he said, 'why have you come here?' I was the latest in a long line of researchers with an interest in Arabunna and Reg challenged me with a series of difficult questions. 'Why do you want to know about my language? Why should I tell you about my language? Unless you want to be an expert in my language, why would you want to write about it in a book?'

For this last question, I did not have a satisfactory answer. The question exposes the inescapable power dynamic at the heart of all 'research' encounters with Aboriginal people. I was writing in order to get accreditation as a historian from a university. In the era of native title, when writers are endorsed as 'experts' on Aboriginal people and, in particular, on their languages or country, scholarly testimony and written material presented in courts of law can have disastrous and unexpected results for Aboriginal people. The subject of who has expertise on Aboriginal languages and places is therefore a particularly sensitive one. Lurking beneath it are highly charged questions of ownership and boundaries generated by native title legislation in the 1990s, which began treating the relationship of Aborginal people to land through the framework of property relations.

I still wanted to talk to Reg about Arabunna. To write a book about non-English-language sources in Australia while ignoring Aboriginal languages would only replicate the systematic erasure of Aboriginal people and knowledges from English-language scholarship in Australia. On the other hand, to write about Aboriginal-language texts risked partaking in the production of 'expert' scholarship deemed to have a higher truth-value in Australian institutions than Aboriginal people's ongoing and dynamic knowledge creation about their own land and selves. None of my answers satisfied Reg. Going around in circles, we returned again and again to his question, 'But why have you come here?'

Eventually, I answered Reg in the most direct way that I could. I told him about finding the Bengali book in Broken Hill. *Kasasol Ambia* was a songbook, I told him. It was not read silently. Rather, the poetry was written to be sung and performed to an audience. I wanted to know whether any of the older descendants of South Asians at the Camel Cup reunion might remember what their grandfathers and great-grandfathers used to sing in towns like Broken Hill, Bourke, Marree, Beltana and Coolgardie. Reg listened intently as I told him about my ongoing search for the reader who had brought the compendium of Bengali stories of the prophets to the Australian deserts. It was this search that brought me to Arabunna country. It was why I had come to Marree.

'Well?' he eventually demanded. 'Did you learn anything? What did they say? Do they remember?' I told him that many people at the reunion had described, or even performed, what they could remember of the sliding scales so characteristic of South Asian music. I was in the middle of happily telling him about a number of leads on how the Bengali book might have travelled to Broken Hill, when suddenly he steered the conversation in an alarming direction off the safe path of historical research. 'Can you sing?' he asked me. 'Sing something from the book.' Horrified, I desperately asked myself where Lal Zada had gone. Surely it was time to hit the road. Eventually Reg softened his approach. He cajoled me, asking only for 'a couple of lines.' I protested, 'it's in a much older form of Bengali to what I know! It's a difficult text. I have no idea how I would sing it.' He offered to bring his guitar. It turned out that he was a country music singer.[22]

In the end, seeing no escape, I did sing, but not from *Kasasol Ambia*. I really did not know how to sing the verses in that book. Instead I sang the song I was most familiar with from the handful of Hindustani classical *ragas* I knew: *Vrindavani Sarang*. Popularly believed today to have been composed by the poet Haridas (d. 1575), the lyrics narrate Radha wandering through the forest of Vrindavan, singing of her search for Krishna as she strains to hear his silent flute. Reg listened intently. Through the melody of her song, Radha evokes the tune of precisely what she seeks: Krishna's flute. Singing it that wintry morning in Marree changed something. Sitting back on his chair, Reg began to reminisce about the camel drivers and merchants who had grown old during his childhood. 'There are so many stories about them,' he told me. 'We grew up with them and they were always around and working with us.' He recalled a string of names, 'Moosha, Dadleh, Bejah …' They were South Asians whose grandchildren and great-grandchildren I had met during the Camel Cup festivities.

During that first conversation with Reg, I began to understand that while the history of encounters between South Asians and Aboriginal people was riven by various asymmetries, it was nevertheless a long relationship of coexistence at the margins of 'White Australia'. Beginning with the camel industry, many successive industries as well as increasingly interconnected family relationships shaped lifetimes of negotiations between these colonised peoples from different parts of the British Empire.

'We received your letter,' Reg eventually revealed. The letter that I had dispatched from Sydney through activist networks had reached Arabunna poet Kevin Buzzacott – Reg's cousin – who had delivered it to the Dodd family, telling them to expect me soon at Marree.

By the time Lal Zada arrived to pick me up for the six-hour drive south to Port Augusta, Reg and I had covered a lot of ground: language movements and mother-tongues, mining politics, uranium, BHP-Billiton, country music, contested national borders, East and West Pakistan, war in South Asia in 1971, and Arabunna. It seemed like we had only just got started, but it was already time to leave. 'You should come back!' Reg said. He invited me to return the following spring on a camping trip through Arabunna country.

* * *

A few months later, at the end of September 2010, I travelled back to Marree and then on to Alberrie Creek. It was spring. The desert was in full bloom. Marree locals were saying that the surrounding country was greener than it had been since 1975. Heavy monsoon rains beginning in December 2009 had watered the Indian Ocean coastline of North Queensland and the Northern Territory. The rains had brought to life the circuit of sandy beds that lead inland to Lake Eyre. Along the way, record levels of water had gathered, fed by unusually high levels of local rainfall. Lake Eyre was full (Fig. 17).

Today, mining and tourism are the two main industries near Marree and Alberrie Creek. Reg Dodd operates an Aboriginal-owned business that takes outsiders through Arabunna country. Through this business Reg constantly travels to significant places as part of a larger strategy of Aboriginal land management.[23] His trips provide the infrastructure for an important meeting ground for the Arabunna community to build alliances and support networks with outsiders and wider social movements. My seven co-travellers were a group of legal practitioners working in Aboriginal land rights.

Our camping trip with Reg began and ended at the extant Alberrie Creek railway tank, over a century after the two Arabunna sisters had waited there for their train. Since the 'old Ghan' stopped running in 1981, the tank has acquired some curious appendages (Fig. 18).[24] The rusted body of a Ford Chrysler and a thin metal rod have transformed it into a giant dog that wags its 'head' when desert winds pick up. Standing by this water feature, it is possible to see the faint outline of the route via which 'the Ghan' would have arrived from Oodnadatta. The rails are long gone. On the first night of our camping trip, we used railway sleepers for the campfire at Alberrie Creek.

In 1989, Reg Dodd and historian Jen Gibson wrote that Scottish-born Francis Dunbar Warren had acquired the pastoral title to Finniss Springs in 1918.[25] The Warren-Hogarths were an influential family of pastoralists who held leases over the heartland of Arabunna country to the west of Lake Eyre. Reg's grandmother, Barralda, had a number of children with Francis Dunbar Warren, and Mona Merrick was their eldest. Over the course of Mona's life, Finniss Springs became a convergence point for many Aboriginal people whose land had been usurped and who negotiated livelihoods in pastoral and camel industries. Reg was born in 1940 and during his childhood Finniss operated as a 'labour bureau for surrounding pastoralists'.[26] When F. D. Warren, whom Reg calls 'old grandfather', passed away in 1954, his Aboriginal children and grandchildren inherited the pastoral title to Finniss. Many of Barralda's descendants continue to live on this property. It is the unusual story of a white pastoralist who was incorporated into a large Aboriginal family.

Leaving Alberrie Creek early the next morning, we headed northwards along the road to Oodnadatta. This unsealed road was once the camel track. Today it meanders alongside the abandoned railway line, entangled with many Aboriginal storylines. As we travelled, we got to know Reg's family through his stories about the places where they had once lived. At Anna Creek pastoral station I caught glimpses of the various Arabunna women whom I had only ever read about. It was at Anna Creek that Barralda had first built an extremely important political and intimate relationship with F. D. Warren. When Reg pointed out where Barralda had given birth to his mother, Amy, I began to grasp something of the intimate lived significance of the places we were travelling through.[27]

After arriving at the now defunct railhead at Oodnadatta we doubled back, heading southwest toward the town of Coober Pedy. By day we travelled Arabunna country to the places that Reg wanted to show us. Each night the discussion veered toward the politics of land and country, settler law versus Aboriginal lore, colonisation and history. Having followed in the footsteps of the South Asians I was chasing, I was simultaneously something of an interloper, a participant and a contributor to a longer conversation about what was central to ongoing Aboriginal experiences of colonisation: alienation from the land. On the last leg of the journey, we cut eastwards across the vast territory encompassed by Anna Creek. It had once been a pastoral property; today BHP-Billiton holds a mining lease over the land, while members of the Arabunna community hold the native title.[28]

1. The Kasasol Ambia at Broken Hill. (Photo © Samia Khatun, 2009.)

2. Unloading Camels at Port Augusta, c. 1893. (Photo Courtesy of the Port Augusta Public Library.)

The language of the translator, Reza-ullah, will be illustrated by the following extract, in which we have 17 foreign for every 24 Bengáli words.

B 1 F 1 B 2 B 3 F 2 F 3 F 4 B 4 B 5
শুন হো মোমিন ভাই করিয়া খেয়াল। আখেরে সাফৎ তাঁর হইবে
F 5 F 6 F 7 F 8 F 9 F 10 F 11 B 6 B 7
নেহাল॥ মহাম্মদ মোস্তা নবি আলায় হেস্তালাম। পয়গম্বরী হৈল তাঁর
B 8 F 12 F 13 F 14 B 9 B 10 B 11 B 12 F 15 B 13
উপরে তামাম॥ নবুওত দরিয়াতে সেই মোতি ভারী। দেখিতে ছেফত তাঁর
B 14 B 15 B 16 B 17 F 16 B 18 B 19 B 20 B 21 B 22
আমি কিবা পারি। আপনা নুরেতে তারে আপে নিরঞ্জনে। প্রথমে করিয়া
F 17 B 23 B 24
পয়দা রাখিল গোপনে॥

3. Rajendralal Mitra's Analysis of Munshi Rezaulla's Poetry. (*Journal of the Asiatic Society of Bengal*, 1864.)

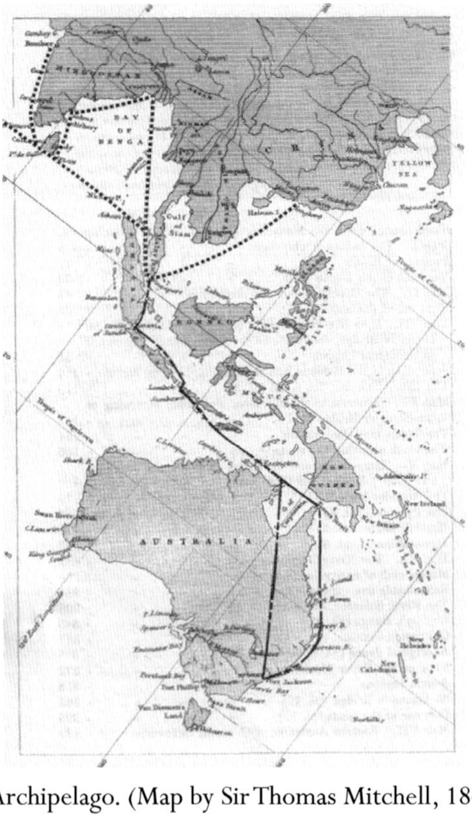

4. The Indian Archipelago. (Map by Sir Thomas Mitchell, 1848.)

5. The Mosque at Marree in South Australia, c. 1884. (Photo Courtesy of the State Library of South Australia.)

6. Abdul Sattar as an Aged Cloth Merchant in Fremantle, 1931. (Photo Courtesy of the National Archives of Australia.)

7. Reconstructed Building of the Australia Mosque, Founded by Muhammad Bux in 1925, McLeod Rd, Lahore. (Photo © Manan Ahmed Asif, 2016.)

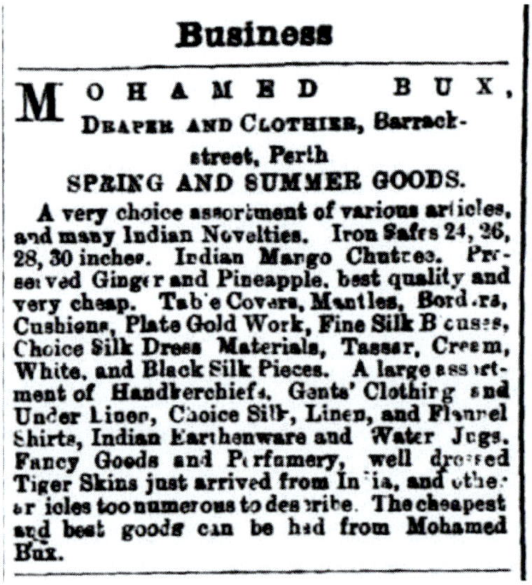

Business

MOHAMED BUX, DRAPER AND CLOTHIER, Barrack-street, Perth

SPRING AND SUMMER GOODS.

A very choice assortment of various articles, and many Indian Novelties. Iron Safes 24, 26, 28, 30 inches. Indian Mango Chutnee. Preserved Ginger and Pineapple, best quality and very cheap. Table Covers, Mantles, Borders, Cushions, Plate Gold Work, Fine Silk Blouses, Choice Silk Dress Materials, Tassar, Cream, White, and Black Silk Pieces. A large assortment of Handkerchiefs, Gents' Clothing and Under Linen, Choice Silk, Linen, and Flannel Shirts, Indian Earthenware and Water Jugs, Fancy Goods and Perfumery, well dressed Tiger Skins just arrived from India, and other articles too numerous to describe. The cheapest and best goods can be had from Mohamed Bux.

8. Advertisement of Wares Sold by Muhammad Bux. (West Australian, 3 October 1895.)

9. The Flinders Ranges in the Distance. (Photo © Samia Khatun, 2014.)

10. Camel Yard on Warioota Creek, Beltana, 1870. (Photo Courtesy of the State Library of South Australia.)

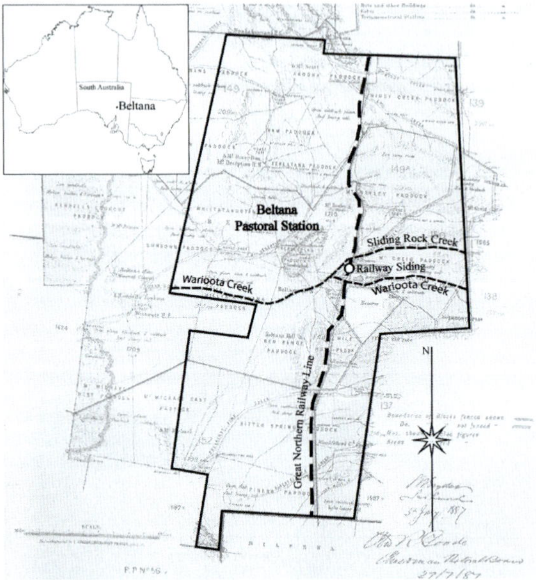

11. Map of Beltana Pastoral Station, c. 1887. ('Second Annual Report of Pastoral Board,' *South Australian Parliamentary Papers* 56, 1887.)

12. Mohamed Hasan Musakhan. (Published in M. H. Musakhan, Islam in Australia, 1932.)

13. Shipment of Camels From Karachi to Port Adelaide for Faiz Mahomet, 1884. (Photo by James Taylor, Courtesy of the State Library of South Australia.)

14. The Mosque on Little Gilbert Street, Adelaide. (*South Australian Chronicle*, 1 September 1894.)

Form No. 21. **COMMONWEALTH OF AUSTRALIA.** No. 94/06

DUPLICATE. *Immigration Restriction Acts 1901-1905 and Regulations.*

CERTIFICATE EXEMPTING FROM DICTATION TEST.

I, John James Broomhall the acting Collector of Customs for the State of West Australia in the said Commonwealth, hereby certify that Faiz Mahomet hereinafter described, who is leaving the Commonwealth temporarily, will be excepted from the provisions of paragraph (*a*) of Section 3 of the Act if he returns to the Commonwealth within a period of Three Years from this date.

Date 14 May 1906 J J Broomhall Actg. *Collector of Customs.*

DESCRIPTION.

Nationality Indian Birthplace Quetta

57 Complexion Dark

Height 5' 6½" Hair Black

Build Medium Eyes Black

Particular marks Left leg broken

(For impression of hand see back of this document.)

PHOTOGRAPHS.

Full Face :— JJHS Profile :— JJHS

Date of departure 16.5.06 Destination Singapore

Ship S S Charon

Date of return .... Ship ....

Port ....

....

Customs Officer

By Authority: Robt. S. Brain, Government Printer, Melbourne.

15. The certificate that allowed Faiz Mahomet to land at Australian ports in the era of 'White Australia' was an early form of a passport, 1906. (Photo Courtesy of the National Archives of Australia.)

16. Camel Sign on Approach to the Flinders Ranges. Today over one million feral camels roam Australian deserts. (Photo © Samia Khatun, 2014.)

17. Lake Eyre in Spring. (Photo © Samia Khatun, 2010.)

18. Railway Tank at Alberrie Creek. (Photo © Samia Khatun, 2011.)

19. Sandhill at Anna Creek Station. (Photo © Richard Wilson, 2010.)

20. Reg Dodd and Samia Khatun at Anna Creek. (Photo © Richard Wilson, 2010.)

21. Tracks of a Creature at Anna Creek. (Photo © Richard Wilson, 2010.)

22. Tracks of Two Creatures Crossing. (Photo © Richard Wilson, 2010.)

23. Reg Dodd Telling the Stories of the Tracks. (Photo © Richard Wilson, 2010.)

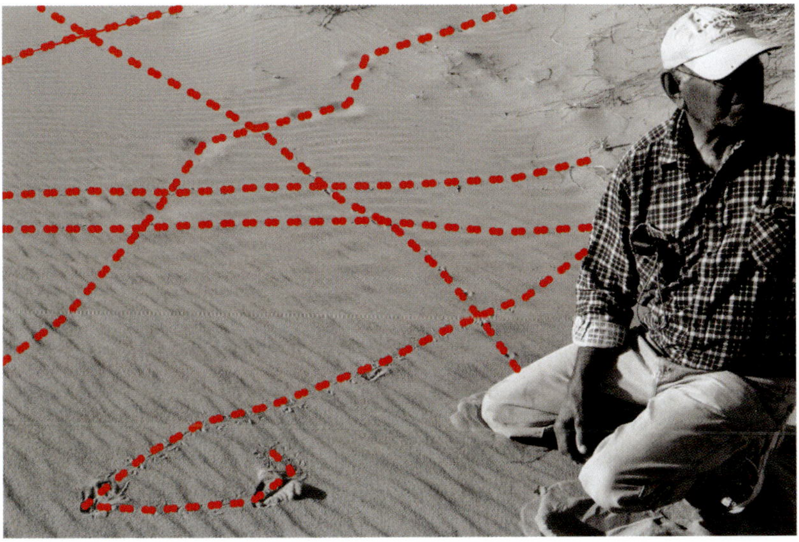

24. After following a single creature's tracks for some time, suddenly it becomes visible that the entire sandhill is crisscrossed with tracks. (Photo © Samia Khatun, 2018.)

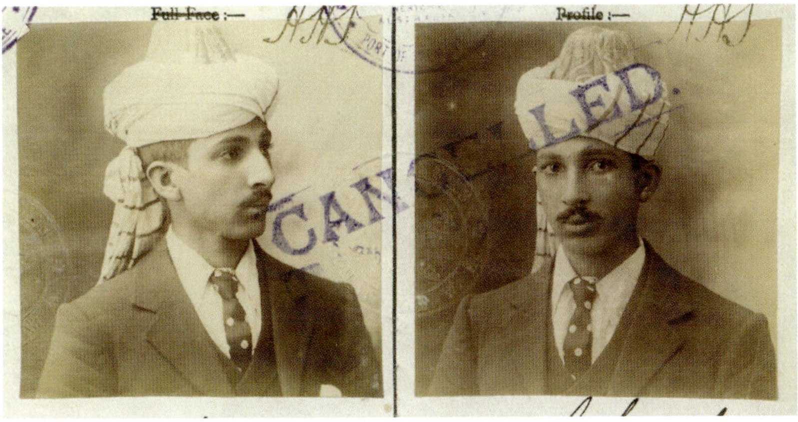

25. Ghulam Faiz Mahomet, 1907. (Photo Courtesy of the National Archives of Australia.)

26. Adelaide Moosha with her Children in Marree, c. 1913. (Photo by A. M. Hopewell. Courtesy of the State Library of South Australia.)

27. Akbar Khan and Lallie Matbar Arrive in Adelaide. (*Mirror*, 10 November 1928.)

28. The House With the Steep Stairs, Road 8/A, Dhanmondi, Dhaka. (Photo © Samia Khatun, 2018.)

29. Children of Sajeda Khatun and Kazi Motahar Hossain, 1942. From right to left: Kazi Mahbub Hossain, Zobaida Mirza, Zaheda Khatun, Kazi Iqbal Hossain, Kazi Mokbul Hossain, Khorsheda Khatun, Kazi Anwar Hossain, Sanjida Khatun, Fahmida Khatun (on lap) and Obaida Saad. (Photo © Family of author, courtesy of Elli Mama and Milli Khala.)

One morning, Reg found a windbreak between some shrubs and called me over. We were at a creek near Oogelima springs. He nursed a fire back to life while I made porridge. I brought up the story I had read about the two sisters waiting at Alberrie Creek, and Reg's eyes lit up in recognition. 'See, the woman who told that story about the camel men, that woman and my mother, they were sisters,' Reg said. Clearing a patch of ground in front of him, he began telling me the story of the encounter at Alberrie Creek. Planting two sticks in the ground next to each other to represent the sisters, he recalled, 'See, when the old women told these stories they would be talking so fast. And at the same time! Just talking and talking. Oh! they would just sit there and tell the story so fast.' He remembered that in his early years, he and the other children would always be listening. Without even being aware of it, they picked up innumerable stories. That was how the Arabunna tale of what happened at Alberrie Creek travelled between mothers, sons, daughters, sisters and aunts at Finniss Springs.

As he retold the story about Alberrie Creek, Reg mapped the events in the sand, marking the camel transportation centres in relation to the stick-sisters stationed at the railway siding. Nearby Marree operated as a hub from which many new camel lines to distant deserts were launched from the 1890s. Reg explained that camel lines connected South Asians' camps in New South Wales, Queensland, and Western Australia. I realised that at every encounter with a South Asian camel driver along the Oodnadatta track or the Birdsville track, there was a chance that Aboriginal children could end up very far from home – whether or not they wanted to. No doubt this was a possibility that watchful mothers and other elders worried about, even if young people did not. As Reg explained, elders would relay these stories because they contained lessons for younger listeners. They were memorable cautionary tales, and worked by warning Arabunna children to keep their distance from the camel men who navigated the vast deserts.

During the era of camel transportation, many different types of intimate relationships between Aboriginal women and South Asian men flourished along the camel tracks. Like Mary Eileen Josephine, the Aboriginal woman from Wilcannia who married Khan Zada in Broken Hill, many Aboriginal women became part of South Asian camel camps.[29] In other cases, children born to Aboriginal women sometimes spent their whole lives without being publicly acknowledged by their South Asian fathers. As Ben Murray, son of Balochi camel driver Bejah Dervish, remembered as an aged man, 'We didn't go by his name because he wasn't interested in looking after us. Mother had to carry on herself.'[30] At the same time, as Reg recalled, there were South Asian men like Munjaloon, a camel driver with a store at Oodnadatta, whose name was taken on by Tommy Munjaloon – one of the Aboriginal children he adopted and looked after. Today, when Aboriginal people and the descendants of South Asians in Australian desert towns speak of each other, they often do so through concrete experiences of extended family relationships – some happy, others less so. After telling the story of the encounter between two women and two men at Alberrie Creek, Reg concluded by recalling a string of South Asian names familiar in those parts: 'Moosha, Dadleh, Zada …' and so on.

Listening to Reg's account of the meeting at Alberrie Creek clarified why older Aboriginal people transmitted the story over many generations. As he explained, Arabunna stories were told for a purpose, with the reasoning sometimes hidden in the stories themselves. While the motivation for repeating the account of the sisters at Alberrie Creek was ultimately to care for young people, other stories had different morals and messages, perhaps teaching children how to look after certain trees or the land. Yet, my original question remained unanswered. Might it be because they had already heard such cautionary tales about *Abigana* men that the two sisters had deduced that they were going to be eaten? Or maybe Barralda or other storytellers had embellished the events with this detail in their own retellings, so that their children would keep their distance. Still, why was being eaten the apt metaphor for everything that could happen in an encounter between South Asian camel drivers and young Aboriginal women?

I began to literally see a possible answer at the end of that long day that started at Oogelima Creek. After a late breakfast, we made our way back toward the 'old Ghan' railway line, veering off the path to chase every animal track and every storyline that caught Reg's attention. Driving across the vast breadth of Anna Creek pastoral station – larger than the size of Belgium, locals will tell you – we stopped at the base of a series of crimson sandhills that almost looked ablaze in the late afternoon sun. After we had set up camp, Reg led us up to the crest of the sandhill on foot, as the sun sank lower and the country developed ever deeper hues of red (Fig. 19).

'See, this is your classroom!' Reg Dodd announced. Here, wandering the dunes, watching, listening and following creatures in a particular way, he imparted the first lesson in how to read places as he did (Fig. 20). 'See here,' he announced, pointing out a track in the sand. 'See where he is going?' In a split second, Reg had taken off on the creature's trail. By looking at its tracks, Reg could recreate every minute detail and dramatic twist along its path. Picking up the track of a three-toed, two-footed creature, I tried to follow Reg's example. It was an animal I was unfamiliar with, but whose prints my untrained eyes could easily follow (Fig. 21). As I became immersed in following one particular thread and moved along the trail, the intense drama that storied every inch of the sandhill unravelled before my eyes.

Creatures on the move across the dunes have thrilling lives. They meander through the landscape of plant life and water sources, sometimes encountering other creatures. They lay eggs, shed their entire skins, and bury themselves in the earth to slumber at sundown. Sometimes they drop dead, only to become a convergence point for other creatures to feed on, who in turn defecate, reproduce, and so on. My three-toed creature was having an uneventful day and only left its droppings in its wake. Nevertheless, as its tracks continuously crossed others with no consequence, it became clear that I had little idea who came first in these intersecting stories. To wonder when the track had been laid was a somewhat meaningless question (Fig. 22).

It is where creatures suddenly and unexpectedly meet that drama erupts, initiating a tale of pursuit and escape. Soaring above the dunes for some time, predatory birds leave precise, brutal prints. When they escape from the clutches of these hungry hunters, pursued creatures leave behind shallow elongated tracks as they speed across the sand. There came a moment when, suddenly, I could see that the sandhills were entirely crisscrossed with tracks of innumerable beings on the move (Fig. 23 and 24). The layer of sand that was visible to me was a tactile medium that recorded with exceptional detail the multi-dimensional history of living beings that moved through it.

Reading the sandhill as an archive of stories, Reg would often break out into Arabunna, naming creatures and describing their actions. My untrained ear could not commit their names to memory. I tried, but my clumsy tongue could not wrap itself around the Arabunna words that rolled so easily off his. The creatures' paths soon disappeared into the earth, slipping from my gaze far more quickly then I would have liked. Just as it takes years to learn to read and even longer to write stories in Bengali, it must have taken Reg years to learn how to decipher sand tracks and tell Arabunna stories. In addition, it was a lifetime of living in and close to Arabunna country that had maintained his literacy. As I crawled through the dunes, mesmerised by animal tracks, I realised that for Reg and his family, living on Arabunna territory went hand in hand with nurturing this particular knowledge relation – a way of knowing the land.

At sunset, Reg stopped suddenly at the crest of a dune. Something had happened. He pointed out the track of a lizard travelling down the hill, and so began the last chapter of the lesson. The even weight and spacing of the footprints revealed that the creature had been moving at a leisurely pace, unaware that it was being observed and sized up by a soaring predator. Fixing the lizard in its gaze, an enormous bird suddenly swooped in on its prey, leaving behind prints in the earth that reveal that it was an eagle. The lizard managed to escape and sped away. 'See how he got away here?' Reg decoded the hounded reptile's tracks. The hungry bird bore down a second time with more force, creating a deep furrow in the sand. The disturbed sand revealed the site of struggle where the lizard had torn itself away from the eagle's beak and scampered away, injured. The third attack the bird made upon the lizard was its last. Here the captive lizard struggled in the clutches of the eagle's claws, creating a shallow and wide circle around the site which Reg translated as the 'poor fella thrashing about'.

This episode of high drama that Reg decrypted in the sand lies outside the bounds of what are recognised as significant events in most English-language history books today. In conventional histories of this Arabunna sandhill, the lizard and the eagle would not feature as central actors. And yet, it was this asymmetrical encounter between two creatures that gave me an invaluable insight into some of the principles of Arabunna storytelling. Beginning with the predatory gaze of the eagle, the central motif of these sand dune dramas was one of pursuit and escape, actions that left a trail in the sand. Like so many other narratives imprinted on the sandhill, the tracks of the lizard ended with dismemberment, consumption and disappearance from the face of Arabunna geography. Eating! Here, being eaten, the apprehension of being eaten, and the pursuit of other creatures in order to eat were ever-present prospects shaping how creatures moved across the land.

Being pursued by a hungry predator was practically integral to any good Arabunna story. Could this sandhill represent Arabunna geography in microcosm? What if Arabunna country in its entirety was one such sandhill writ large? Could boulders, hills and valleys be marks left by creatures of giant proportions? Did water from sudden thunderstorms travel along the tracks left by enormous travelling creatures? Might smaller creatures travel to the places where larger creatures lay dead, their blood staining the earth till it coagulates?

Having only spent a brief amount of time with Reg, I cannot, of course, hope to grasp the intricacies of Arabunna philosophies. What is clear is that learning to decipher tracks in minutiae and tell stories of this form was crucial to the day-to-day livelihoods, sustenance and survival of Arabunna people throughout the era of the camel industry and beyond. Although Aboriginal people came to be the principal workforce in the pastoral industry in these parts from the 1860s, the meagre rations that colonial and later state governments offered as compensation for alienation from land was never enough to sustain families.[31] In the 1940s and 1950s, Reg recalled, 'we got a bit of flour and jam and sugar and tea, that's all. Apart from that you lived off the land.'[32] Were these sandhills the classrooms where Aboriginal children were taught how to subsist off the land? It must have been here, chasing creatures across the sand dunes, that the two Arabunna sisters at Alberrie Creek, Barralda and her children Mona and Amy, and the children of Reg's generation had all learnt to read and tell Arabunna stories.

After my first lesson on the sandhill, I began to see why the Arabunna sisters had thought the two cameleers were going to eat them. Their story follows the logic of many of the narratives that Reg described on the hill. It begins with an encounter at the water tank. In response to the unnerving, greedy gaze of the South Asian men and their sizing up of the girls' bared flesh, the sisters deduced, 'we know they want to eat us!' – this being the next logical step in the grammar underpinning many of the Arabunna stories of encounter that I heard on the sandhill. To the relief of the two girls, the train finally arrived, and they escaped, leaving the railway track behind them.

My first lesson in how to 'read' Arabunna stories and places had come to an end. Reg's classroom was a very different learning environment to the university libraries, syntax tutorials and state archives from where I had been attempting to read Arabunna-language sources. As the sun was setting that evening, I realised with sudden clarity that Arabunna country was a history book that Reg could read. For him, part of living there was to be able to nurture an intimacy with land that in fact constituted a relationship to knowledge quite distinct from Enlightenment epistemes. Over the seven days I spent travelling with him, I caught a glimpse of how those two sisters waiting for their train at Alberrie Creek might have learnt to read deserts. These were deserts underwritten by a vast library of narratives that Aboriginal people could draw on to story their encounters with others.

After nightfall, when it had become too dark to read the tracks in the sand, Reg said to us, 'See, if there is a dust storm tonight, it will be like turning a whole new page. And all the stories? Oh! They will start all over again.'

7

THE BOOK OF MARRIAGE

Tuesday, 24 May 1904 was a bright moonlit night at Marree railhead in the northern deserts of South Australia.[1] When Sher Khan, a 35-year-old camel driver from Kabul, alighted from the 8.40 p.m. train, he hid in the shadows waiting for Moosha Balooch.[2] Three months earlier, camel owner Moosha Balooch had become engaged to Adelaide Neackmore Khan amid much celebration.[3] Since then, the news of Adelaide's pending marriage had haunted Sher Khan at every turn. On that night in May, Moosha was on his way home from the Marree post office when he saw Sher Khan at the railway turnstile. Moosha held out his hand. Instead of shaking it, Sher Khan yelled, 'I'll kill you, I can't leave you alive!' and shot Adelaide's fiancé five times.[4] One of the bullets pierced Moosha's chest.

In 1904, Moosha Balooch and Sher Khan were both working in the camel industry. At the time of the shooting in Marree, both claimed that they were engaged to 14-year-old Adelaide, the daughter of camel driver Surwah Khan and his white wife. Adelaide's story has been recounted in many histories of Muslims in Australia; Christine Stevens' history of the camel industry contains the lengthiest account. Writing in 1989, Stevens claimed that 'Surwah Khan agreed to his fourteen-year-old daughter marrying Sher Khan and the brideprice was set at £150.'[5] According to Stevens, Sher Khan had already 'paid a deposit of £100' when 'Moosha offered Surwah Khan £200 for his daughter.'

When he received the higher offer, 'The greedy father accepted the money' and 'word of deceit spread fast ... until it reached Sher Khan.' Today 'brideprice' narratives like these feature at the centre of many histories of Muslim women in Australia.[6]

In this chapter, I challenge the use of brideprice narratives to describe gender relations between Muslim men and women. 'Brideprice' is an anthropological category invented in British colonial texts about colonised people, and I propose that people of Muslim heritage and feminist scholars alike need alternative stories about gender relations to those produced for the purpose of buttressing Anglo imperial regimes. The transactions Australian historians have called 'brideprice' were actually described as '*mahar*' payments on marriage contracts signed at camel camps. I trace the Arabic legal concept of *mahar* to the literary/juridical texts titled *Kitab al-Nikah* (The Book of Marriage, pl. *Kutub al-Nikah*) – the Arabic and Persian volumes of historical precedents about marriage that were once found in legal libraries across South Asia. The Muslim intellectual tradition of *Kitab al-Nikah* offers us a model for feminist history writing. By using its architecture, I construct a history of marriage explicitly for use by people of Muslim heritage to make sense of our lives today, spanning across the national, imperial and racial borders of the colonial present.

Rethinking 'Motion' in Indian Ocean Historiography

While scholarship about the Indian Ocean world has burgeoned around the analytic of motion, historians in this field have been slow to respond to feminist calls for 'gender-inflected analyses of mobilities'.[7] As Engseng Ho writes in his study of Hadrami merchants, 'most were men ... a diaspora in the etymological sense of a scattering of seed'.[8] Erasing the women central to the family genealogies and economies spanning the Indian Ocean, Ho's analysis is consistent with key texts in this field, offering little insight into the lives and worlds of women in these households or the gendered regimes of power that shaped their histories. The result is that leading scholars have implicitly equated masculinity with motion and femininity with stasis. In this chapter, I rethink the definitions of 'motion' that underpin Indian Ocean histories by reading marriage records as an archive of women's motion.

For Adelaide, like many other daughters in Australian camel camps, marriage was accompanied by a physical move of only a few streets to a new family home. For other women, engagement to South Asian men propelled epic journeys across the Indian Ocean and Australian deserts, negotiating what scholars of legal pluralism have described as a 'marital patchwork' of legal systems.[9] As extant marriage contracts confirm, these agreements citing 'Mohamedan law' did not require women to convert to Islam. Resisting any easy categorisation as 'Muslim women', they all crossed various borders at marriage: some women negotiating tightening national borders at Australian ports, others crossing the racial boundaries between 'Asiatics', 'Whites' and 'Aborigines' that buttressed 'White Australia'.[10] Stories about gender relations profoundly shaped the trajectories of these border-crossing women, 'brideprice' comprising one of the tales that work to buttress Western imperialism in contemporary South Asia.

The Story of 'Brideprice' and the Colonial Present

In concluding that 'Afghans brought and sold their wives', Australian historians replicate an orientalist story about gender relations that has circulated across two centuries of Anglo imperial discourse about Afghanistan.[11] As Edward Said wrote, 'Orientalism is after all a system for citing works and authors', and Stevens' account of 'the Muslims of Afghanistan and the north and west of India' cites ethnographies spanning from Mountstuart Elphinstone's writings during the first British mission to Kabul in 1808 to Fredrik Barth's essays produced from US bases at the Afghanistan–Pakistan frontier during the Cold War era.[12] In his *Account of the Kingdom of Caubul*, which laid the foundations of contemporary Western knowledge about Afghanistan, Elphinstone opens his chapter on women with the claim that 'the Afghauns purchased their wives'.[13]

Beginning in the late nineteenth century, the analytic of 'brideprice' was yoked to the tale that Afghan men buy and sell women. With the emergence of evolutionary anthropology, brideprice was theorised as a payment common to both 'ancient' European societies in the past and 'traditional' societies at contemporary colonial frontiers.[14] As anthropological discourse is organised around stadial narratives of human progress from savagery to civilisation, the category of brideprice is inextricable from notions of progress – a powerful story of collective human motion along the axis of time. With Enlightenment thinkers theorising the status of women as a key marker of civilisational progress from the eighteenth century, 'brideprice' from the late nineteenth century became one of a constellation of indicators that colonised societies languished at the stages of 'tradition' or 'savagery' far behind British arrival at 'modern' and 'civilised' marriage.[15]

In more recent imperial history, the story of brideprice continues to be produced at the contemporary Afghan battlefront, the very fact of its repetition across two centuries lending it the appearance of unquestionable truth. For example, in a newspaper series coinciding with the period that Australian troops were deployed to Afghanistan in 2001, Australian foreign correspondent Paul McGeogh reported that, 'bought and sold, denied basic rights, women in Afghanistan are treated only slightly better then farm animals'.[16] As Lila Abu-Lughod has shown, the cry to 'save Muslim women' comprised a key strategy to mobilise Western popular support for the US-led invasion of Afghanistan in 2001.[17] As part of a discourse that claims that Western military intervention is a means of improving women's rights, accounts of 'brideprice' in Afghanistan have circulated alongside narratives of 'honour crimes', 'polygamy' and 'forced marriages'.[18]

Feminist thinkers have long played a crucial role in the production of these imperialist narratives about non-white women.[19] Since Gayle Rubin's 1975 essay on 'The Traffic of Women' heralded a new era of feminist intervention into anthropological discourse, many writers have made use of the term 'brideprice' in feminist analyses of marriage.[20] There has, however, been no shortage of critiques of 'imperial feminism' and of the use of anthropological universals to produce 'monolithic' accounts of 'third world women' in need of Western intervention.[21] Writing from South Asian contexts, some scholars have used descriptors from colonised knowledge traditions, including activist Flavia Agnes, who has deployed the terms *mahar* and *stridhana* from South Asian legal discourses in order to devise pro-women outcomes in Indian courtrooms.[22] However, as Abu-Lughod argues, even activists engaged in creative dialogue with non-European epistemes have tended to locate the cause of gendered violence in 'tradition', thereby situating people at an earlier stage of civilisational progress.[23] The result is that across a wide range of feminist scholarship today, pro-women arguments remain beholden to imagined trajectories from 'tradition' to 'modernity' – or progress narratives.

Alternatives to Orientalist Narratives

Non-European storytelling templates about gender relations loosen the grip of progress narratives on feminist thought. While stories about Muslim women have long been fashioned to buttress Anglo imperial regimes, for even longer Muslim women told stories to resist and escape power regimes. As Moroccan writer Fatima Mernissi reminds us, the ingenious use of stories by Muslim women to negotiate husbands' power over them is perhaps as old as Scheherazade, the legendary storyteller who escaped death for 1,001 successive nights with 1,001 tales that captivated her own captor, her cruel husband King Shahriar.[24] By treating Scheherazade as an archetype of the many Muslim women resisting and negotiating marriage through storytelling, Mernissi situates her own feminist writing within a genealogy of stories told by divorced aunts, wives and widows in the maze of upstairs rooms in her childhood home. Drawing inspiration from raconteuses from Scheherazade to Mernissi, and following in the footsteps of a long line of storytellers critiquing marriage in my own family, from my great great-grandmother Moslema Khatun to my mother Eshrat, in this chapter I piece together the stories that shaped five women's marriages into Muslim families.

Reading the marriage contract signed in 1917 by Myrtle Mary at Bourke camel camp, I trace the '*mahar*' payment it outlines to the Muslim literary/juridical discourse of *Kitab al-Nikah* (The Book of Marriage). I redeploy this Muslim intellectual tradition to propose a model of feminist historical storytelling – a 'Book of Marriage' – that documents the stories shaping women's trajectories to their marriage homes. I then shift my focus onto the Indian Ocean world, and trace Shamsulnissa's voyage from Karachi to Western Australia in 1906. Collating legal narratives that shaped Shamsulnissa's journey, I highlight some power regimes that South Asian women negotiated during the era of 'White Australia'. I then follow Adelaide's trajectory to her marriage home in Marree, revealing the ways South Asian men scripted her into employment contracts as well as nationalist plots. Tracing Lallie's 500-mile walk across Western Australian deserts to marry Akbar Khan in 1928, I also illustrate that Aboriginal women sometimes contracted marriages to South Asian men as part of their escape from settler regimes. Finally, by exploring Eshrat's dreams of escape from her marriage in Australia to Bangladesh, I show that contemporary Muslim women's archives contain narrative pathways out of the 'prisonhouse of orientalism'.[25]

As Chicana writer and queer theorist Gloria Anzaldúa argued, the dreams of *la mestiza*, or the border-crossing woman, offer a powerful point of departure from the narratives of 'the gringo, locked in fictions of white superiority'.[26] Eshrat's dreams of crossing the Indian Ocean to reach a maze of upstairs rooms in her home in Dhaka highlights the chasm between Muslim women's stories about marriage and the racist stories about marriage contained in Australian histories of Muslims. Drawing on Anzaldúa's insights, I seek to answer a number of questions raised by Eshrat's dreams: How do we write histories that we can use today to make sense of the marriage archives of Muslim mothers, grandmothers and grandfathers without having to label loved ones as 'traditional' and 'uncivilised'? If we are to do away with racist progress narratives of savagery to civilisation, how are daughters, sons and granddaughters of South Asians in Australia to make sense of where we have come from and where we are going?

I. Myrtle Mary

Born in 1899, Myrtle Mary Dee was the daughter of country storekeepers in the colony of New South Wales. When Myrtle married Morbine Perooz, she moved to 'Perooz camel camp' in the town of Bourke. Morbine had arrived from Peshawar in the Australian colonies in around 1893, establishing a camel business with his brother Paleel.[27] It was in the difficult months after Paleel's death that Morbine became involved with Myrtle, a student at Bourke Convent School.[28] A month after Myrtle's fourteenth birthday, she gave birth to Morbine's son.[29] A Catholic priest at Bourke refused to marry the new parents despite the pleas of Myrtle's mother. Three weeks later, a Presbyterian minister united Myrtle and Morbine in holy matrimony.[30]

Just before her eighteenth birthday, Myrtle participated in a second marriage ceremony. In January 1917, at Perooz camp, she and Morbine signed a marriage contract citing 'Mohamedan law', which specified the payment of a '*mahar*'. Like the many white women who married Muslim men in Australia, Myrtle negotiated not only settler marriage laws but also Mohamedan law – an orientalist discourse produced at the intersection of British common law and *shari'a* systems. Of the many stories that shaped women's trajectories through their marriage homes, definitions of licit sex – or marriage – were some of the most powerful.

From *Shari'a* to Mohamedan Law

Both the *mahar* payment and the definition of marriage articulated in Myrtle's contract with Morbine were first theorised in the legal discourse of *shari'a* – an Arabic word literally meaning 'the way to water'. Prior to European imperial expansion across the Indian Ocean, at the centre of *shari'a* legal systems was a growing library that jurists consulted and added to as they arbitrated between legal and illegal courses of action. As historian Wael Hallaq has written:

> *Shari'a* was not only a judicial system and a legal doctrine whose function was to regulate social relations and resolve disputes, but a discursive practice that structurally and organically tied itself to the world around it in ways that were vertical and horizontal, structural and linear, economic and social, moral and ethical, intellectual and spiritual, epistemic and cultural, and textual and poetic, among much else.[31]

The earliest *shari'a* libraries comprised the Quran and volumes of prophetic precedent detailing the acts and words of Muhammad. With the growth of Islam, scholars developed methodologies for determining the legal course of action – or *shari'a* – in novel situations. These new works of jurisprudence (*fiqh*) became the third corpus of texts in *shari'a* libraries.[32] Ordered into 'books' on various topics, each volume of *fiqh* included a book of marriage, or *Kitab al-Nikah*, which contained a chapter on *mahar*.

As Islam spread to new lands, new volumes of *Kitab al-Nikah* were penned with every new work of *fiqh*. The growth of the *Kitab al-Nikah* genre was propelled by laypeople's questions and jurists' answers. For example, in a *shari'a* court in Delhi, during the reign of Sultan Firuz Shah (d. 1388), disputing parties questioned whether marriage payments in addition to *mahar* were legal.[33] Consulting existing *Kutub al-Nikah*, the judge answered that money or sweets paid according to community expectations were legal, although appropriations of these payments by others were illegal.[34] As Hallaq has shown, legal narratives produced in *shari'a* courts were collated into volumes of precedent and added to *shari'a* libraries for future consultation.[35] Accordingly, this narrative about one fourteenth-century marriage in Delhi remains in *Kutub al-Nikah* held in libraries in Aligarh, Patna and London.[36] Expanding in the process of a question-and-answer dialogue with the libraries it was housed in, the *Kitab al-Nikah* literary genre was a growing archive of historical precedents produced by real marriage disputes – a compendium of juridical stories that profoundly shaped Muslim women's trajectories.

Following the establishment of East India Company rule over Bengal from the late eighteenth century, orientalist scholars invented a new relationship to *shari'a* libraries. The introduction of a new legal hierarchy, with British administrators and judges at the top, marked an epistemic break in the *shari'a* system.[37] Funded by the Company, the first *Kitab al-Nikah* that orientalist scholars translated into English was contained in *Al-Hidaya* (The Guide) – a *fiqh* text penned in 1159. Starting with the English publication of this text (*Hedaya*) in 1791, the English codes produced for use in the colonial courts of British India came to be known as 'Mohamedan law' and circulated across a wider imperial terrain beyond British India.[38]

In 1917, in the Australian inland town of Bourke, when Myrtle signed a marriage contract citing 'Mohamedan law', she was inserted into a story that can be traced to the *Kitab al-Nikah* that emerged with Islamic jurisprudence. Myrtle and Morbine's contract specified that 'I, Perooz, shall pay to the said Myrtle Mary Dee on demand at any time now and hereafter the sum of £10 as "*mahar*" or marriage consideration according to the Mohamedan law'.[39] *Mahar* is a compulsory transfer of property from husband to wife in Muslim legal traditions, forming part of the larger circuit of gendered motion defining the marriage contract.[40] However, Morbine's agreement to pay this amount 'on demand' did not necessarily mean that £10 was physically transferred to Myrtle's purse. As historian Kecia Ali shows, marriage contracts in Muslim legal traditions set in motion not physical entities but rather relationships of dominion (*milk*).[41]

While English 'dominion' is a central concept in liberal thought, Arabic '*milk*' is a key category in Muslim legal traditions – both terms describe the asymmetrical power relation between a person and their property, among other relations.[42] In her marriage contract, while a relationship of dominion (*milk*) over the *mahar* amount moved to Myrtle, in exchange, *milk* over her sexual organs moved to Morbine. In her critique of marriage, Ali argues that sex is only licit in Muslim legal traditions if men possess a type of gendered *milk* over a woman's sexual organs. However, as she points out, marriage does not transform women into property.[43] The range of relations denoted by '*milk*' in legal discourse spanned the word's wide range of semantic usages, encompassing the asymmetrical relationships between Allah and Muslim, person and commodity, master and slave, and, as Ali shows, husband and wife.

While Myrtle's contract confirmed that some women at Australian camel camps were scripted into this circuit of *milk* relations, the tale of dominion was only one of many stories that shaped Myrtle's life. After all, when Myrtle gave birth, the definitions of licit sex articulated by her mother, the Catholic priest and the Presbyterian minister powerfully shaped her onward trajectory from this vulnerable juncture. Myrtle's lived experience suggests that many stories shaped the path of each woman who married a Muslim man. For those of us looking to the past to understand power relations, the imperative question is how and why these stories were told and enforced. Four years after marrying according to settler law, why did Morbine and Myrtle sign a contract citing Mohamedan law? Did Myrtle ever demand her *mahar* entitlements, or Morbine his rights to sexual intimacy? Did settlers tell the story of this marriage differently from South Asians? In 2004, why did a politician claim in Australian Parliament that 'Myrtle was sold into wedlock to an Afghan'?[44] What stories did Myrtle tell about her days and nights with Morbine as she moved across the racial borders dividing Bourke?

I propose that the answers are contained in a history book titled *The Book of Marriage* – a multi-authored compendium of historical precedents that continues to expand to this day. Analogous to books of *fiqh* with the same name, *The Book of Marriage* is both like and unlike *Kitab al-Nikah*. Like *Kitab al-Nikah*, it resides within a library of knowledge that is not underpinned by the progress narratives central to orientalist thought. The historical discourse I describe, like *Kitab al-Nikah*, is a repository of stories that powerfully shaped women's trajectories through their marriage homes.

Unlike *Kitab al-Nikah* however, *The Book of Marriage* is a feminist text that was not produced to enforce the schema of gendered *milk* defining marriage. Rather, it contains stories told for the purposes of challenging the range of dominion relations women negotiated when marrying. While *Kitab al-Nikah* contains narratives exclusively penned by jurists, *The Book of Marriage* includes tales told by a much wider range of storytellers. Some say that for each woman who entered a marriage contract citing Muslim legal traditions, *The Book of Marriage* comprises all the narratives she was ever scripted into, critiquing stories that buttressed power regimes and highlighting stories that did not. Others say that in housing all the stories that Muslim widows, divorcees and wives articulated to negotiate difficult marriages, the compendium contains all 1,001 tales that Scheherazade told over 1,001 sleepless nights. It is beyond the scope of my book to conclusively prove the existence of this ever-growing volume. Instead, in the remainder of this chapter, I offer some additional entries to *The Book of Marriage* from the Australian context.

II. Shamsulnissa

On 28 February 1907, 17-year-old Shamsulnissa departed from Karachi for Western Australia.[45] With Shamsulnissa in the passenger saloon of the SS *Century*, 516 camels travelled in the 'tween decks' with fifty South Asian workers.[46] Based in Karachi, Shamsulnissa's family of Afghan traders had good working relationships with governments in British India, Australia and Afghanistan.[47] Like Shamulnissa, many South Asian women from well-connected merchant families continued travelling the Indian Ocean during the era of 'White

Australia'. The collation of legal narratives that Shamsulnissa was scripted into serves to highlight how some power regimes shaped South Asian women's Indian Ocean crossings.

Shamsulnissa was the daughter of Bibi Ismat and Tagh Mahomet, the younger brother and partner in the firm Faiz and Tagh Mahomet, Camel Proprietors and Carriers (F&T). As F&T established itself as one of the most prosperous South Asian companies in the Australian camel business, Faiz and Tagh arranged a future marriage between their eldest children in Karachi: Ghulam and Shamsulnissa. However, on 10 January 1896, while 11-year-old Ghulam and 5-year-old Shamsulnissa were likely still asleep in Karachi, their futures were thrown into uncertainty. As dawn was breaking across the Western Australian goldfields, Tagh Mahomet was murdered at Coolgardie Mosque by a camel driver from a competing camel company.[48]

As Faiz departed for British India with his brother's remains in a 'leaden coffin', the grieving family must have grappled with a number of questions: Who would inherit Tagh's assets? What did the future hold for Tagh's daughters, Shamsulnissa and Kamernissa?[49] When the family gathered at Karachi, Faiz proposed some answers. Declaring that he intended to honour Tagh's plans for his eldest daughter, Faiz announced Shamsulnissa and Ghulam's future marriage as part of a larger story plotting future prosperity. At a moment of terrible uncertainty, Faiz's announcement was met with 'great rejoicing'.[50]

The Karachi Family Court interpreted Tagh's will citing 'Mohamedan law'. The settlement 'approved in India' was executed in Australian courts, and Faiz was appointed as the legal guardian of Tagh's daughters.[51] The estates of Shamsulnissa, Kamernissa and their mother Bibi Ismat were to be invested in the Australian camel business and annual sums remitted to Karachi.[52] Not everyone was happy with the settlement. Bibi Ismat's brother and legal attorney, Abraham Mahomet, claimed that Australian courts should interpret Tagh's will according to 'English law', not 'Mohamedan law'.[53] The press speculated that settler law might have delivered more assets into the control of Abraham Mahomet, another trader in the Australian camel industry.[54] As historians have shown, litigants frequently engaged in 'forum shopping', exploiting fissures between legal discourses in search of advantageous outcomes.[55] Despite

Abraham Mahomet's challenge, Australian colonial courts upheld Mohamedan law.

In 1900, Faiz departed for Karachi, having secured permission from the Western Australian government to import camels. However, on 1 January 1901, six separate British colonies federated into 'White Australia', a settler dominion independent from British rule. As the new Commonwealth Parliament introduced pieces of legislation that sought to restrict the movement of Asian merchants, workers and their capital, the terrain of family politics was transformed for many South Asians. In Karachi, workers had loaded 500 camels onto a steamer when Australian officials cabled Faiz Mahomet 'that the importation of camels into Western Australia is strictly prohibited'.[56] Leaving the camels in Karachi, Faiz returned to Perth in 1902, suing the Western Australian government for 'breach of contract'. He claimed damages of £13,463.[57]

Shamsulnissa's inheritance of £3,600 was part of a much larger sum of non-white capital circulating the Indian Ocean that the regime of 'White Australia' brought to a halt. Faiz permanently left Australia in May 1905, handing over the camel business to his son Ghulam.[58] In October 1906, news reached Ghulam in the Western Australian goldfields that Abraham Mahomet was importing 500 camels from Karachi, having secured government permission.[59] Abraham's plans to 'swell his bank balance' also included a bid for guardianship over Tagh's daughters. On 7 March 1907, Ghulam departed for Karachi, most likely intending to marry Shamsulnissa (Fig. 25).[60]

Boarding different vessels, the betrothed children of Faiz and Tagh crossed the Indian Ocean without meeting. Shamsulnissa, who was then seventeen years old, landed in Western Australia on 22 March 1907 with Abraham Mahomet and his younger sister Bachi Bibi.[61] They stayed in Perth in the house of Nellie Mahomet – Abraham's white wife. Observing Shamsulnissa, Nellie began to suspect she was 'acting under the coercion and in fear of the said Abraham Mahomed'.[62] She approached the police and stated that 'I surprised my husband by discovering the said Shamsulnissa and himself together in a bed he had placed on the kitchen floor'.[63] Nellie claimed that Abraham had replied that he was acting 'out of revenge to Faiz Mahomed and Goolam … affianced husband of Shamsulnissa'.[64] Highlighting the vulnerability of women embroiled in property battles, Abraham's likely assault of Shamsulnissa comprised one of his many challenges to Faiz and Ghulam's legal claims of *milk*.

The way that settlers responded to Nellie's allegations reveal another set of legal narratives in which Shamsulnissa became entrapped in Australia. On 30 April 1907, police arrived at Nellie's house with a doctor who took Shamsulnissa into a private room for the two-finger test.[65] The test involved the insertion of fingers into a woman's vagina, a methodology for constructing women's sexual history that was routine in rape trials in colonial India and Australia alike.[66] As is well documented, the British common law system and its colonial variants systematically put raped women on trial rather than their male attackers, in what Pratiksha Baxi has described as 'state-sanctioned assault'.[67] With Dr Gertrude Mead's certificate declaring Shamsulnissa's sexual organs as '*virgo intacta*', police did not charge Abraham Mahomet.[68]

While police, doctors and the press did not hesitate to construct Shamsulnissa's sexual history, Australian judges disagreed on whether they could produce legal/illegal narratives about South Asian women. On 3 May 1907, when Abraham appeared in the Supreme Court of Western Australia seeking to be appointed the legal guardian of Tagh's daughters, Justice Burnside challenged the original appointment of Faiz as Shamsulnissa's guardian. He ruled 'that the decree of July 29, 1897, made by Justice Stone was bad', declaring that 'the wards were not then, and never had been, within the jurisdiction of the court and the judge had no power to appoint a guardian or remove Faiz Mahomed from an office he had been improperly appointed'.[69] Hearing that Shamsulnissa was waiting outside court chambers, Burnside refused to admit the testimony of a 'prohibited immigrant' and ordered her immediate return to British India.

Burnside's ruling had caught the attention of legal professionals, and Abraham was in court again within a month, his counsel including Justice Stone.[70] Representing Faiz, Richard Haynes proposed that Abraham had in fact assaulted Shamsulnissa and that the medical assessment was wrong. Haynes argued that Dr Mead had not examined Shamsulnissa but rather Bachi Bibi, and that Abraham had switched the young women.[71] After the hearing, police accompanied Dr Mead once more to Nellie's house, where Abraham was 'weeping and wailing at the prospect of such a scandal'.[72] Whether or not the cries of her likely tormentor reached Shamsulnissa in the room where 'the doctress was ready to make the necessary examination', presses reported that 'Shamsulnissa point blank REFUSED!' to be examined.[73]

On 18 July 1907, Shamsulnissa's fiancé Ghulam returned from Karachi to Western Australia.[74] The day before Shamsulnissa's final departure from Perth, a fight broke out between Ghulam and Abraham – the young woman had again been caught in a family inheritance dispute, exacerbated by the regime of 'White Australia'.[75] In Australia, Shamsulnissa was forced to navigate a maze of narratives that she was scripted into by others, South Asian uncles and Australian judges bitterly contesting who had the authority to dictate her future. In rebuffing Dr Mead's examination, she had refused 'point blank' to be inserted into any more settler narratives. The last detail that can be gleaned about her from archival records is that she left Australia at the age of seventeen with 22-year-old Ghulam, their fathers having prescribed their marriage years before, while they were both children in Karachi.[76] Perhaps she was later able to narrate the story of her journey on her own terms to her sister Kamernissa, or to her mother Bibi Ismat.

III. Adelaide

Adelaide Neackmore Khan was born on 8 March 1890 in the city of Adelaide.[77] Daughter of Ellen Khan, *née* O'Brien, and camel driver Surwah Khan, she spent her first days in one of the travellers' cottages on Little Gilbert Street adjoining the Adelaide Mosque.[78] Most of Adelaide's childhood was spent in Marree. During family visits to Adelaide, the mosque compound, which boasted a pond with '350 fish – gold, silver and red', was a focal point.[79] On 17 February 1904, a month before her fourteenth birthday, Adelaide was engaged to camel merchant Moosha Balooch at one of the cottages on Little Gilbert Street.[80] The celebrations ended abruptly when settlers began throwing stones at the house, shattering the windows.[81] Since that day, settlers, Aboriginal people and South Asians have told and retold stories about Adelaide's marriage.[82] Here, I outline some stories told by South Asian men that shaped Adelaide's trajectory to her marriage home.

Moosha Balooch was from Balochistan, a border region between British India and Afghanistan where his family had a history of service to the British imperial army.[83] He arrived in Australia as a camel driver, and by 1902 managed a South Australian government camel depot near Marree.[84] Moosha's family prospered in an era when state governments (formerly colonial governments) continued to contract South Asians to maintain the camel transportation network while nationalist legislation erected racially exclusive borders. In this precarious context, Adelaide's father arranged her marriage to Moosha, a government employee. As part of marriage negotiations, Surwah Khan secured a position for himself managing Moosha's camels for 'two pounds a week'.[85]

Many South Asians disapproved of the match. Shortly after his engagement, Moosha was told that Sher Khan, a younger Afghan camel driver, had previously been engaged to Adelaide.[86] Whether or not Surwah Khan actually negotiated an earlier contract between his daughter and Sher Khan in 1902, claims that this agreement had been breached began circulating after Adelaide's engagement to Moosha. Sher Khan confided in his Punjabi friend Rahim Bukhsh that 'my friends give me the shame calling me all sorts of names ... through this girl.'[87] Most of the men mocking Sher Khan were Afghans, leading Rahim Bukhsh to reply, 'I can't do anything about this as they are your country people.'[88] Agreeing that Rahim Bukhsh had better not intervene, Sher Khan lamented, 'they won't stop it for me ... Moosha will have to shoot me or I will shoot Moosha.'[89] Before Moosha departed for Marree, another merchant, Gunny Khan, warned him, 'look after yourself.'[90]

Based in Broken Hill in New South Wales, Gunny Khan was a merchant and Afghan nationalist operating extensive camel lines throughout Australia.[91] From the 1890s, 'camel kings' such as Moosha Balooch and Gunny Khan were increasingly divided according to their alliances to British India or Afghanistan, in step with wider imperial developments. After the Durand Line was drawn by treaty in 1893, this imperial–national border demarcating the boundaries of Afghanistan and British India increasingly featured in the politics of Australian camel camps.[92] Nation-building rhetoric appealed to the Afghan diaspora throughout the world to return, particularly after the appointment of Habibulla Khan as the king of Afghanistan in 1900.[93]

Attuned to nationalist calls across the Indian Ocean, Gunny Khan drew distinctions between 'Afghans' and 'British Indians', particularly when responding to white nationalists. For example, on returning to Broken Hill after Moosha and Adelaide's engagement, Gunny Khan interjected in press debates about 'Afghans' by protesting settlers' use of the category. He insisted that 'in Broken Hill it would be impossible to find a dozen men who are Afghans', writing, 'I call the people who belong to the State of Afghanistan Afghans'.[94] Insulting people from Balochistan and other border regions of British India, he wrote that 'on the borders of Afghanistan there are many savage tribes, whose only law is force'.[95] Situating Afghan nationals alongside British imperialists in a schema of civilisational progress, Gunny Khan's letter, published on 23 May 1904, claimed that those people from the border regions 'are gradually being conquered and civilised by England and Afghanistan, and it is not fair to call these savages Afghans'.[96]

The night after Gunny Khan's letter was published, drawing a border between 'savages' and 'civilised' across camel camps, Sher Khan arrived at Marree railway station on the 8.40 p.m. train. Cloaked by shadows that moonlit night, the younger man from Kabul awaited Adelaide's fiancé from Balochistan with a loaded gun and shot Moosha Balooch five times across an imagined border between Afghans and British Indians.[97] A few months later, when Sher Khan was tried for 'shooting with intent to kill' at Port Augusta, Gunny Khan was appointed as his interpreter. Moosha protested this appointment, testifying, 'Gunni Khan is not my friend.'[98] Not only did Gunny Khan operate camel lines in direct competition with Moosha, he also had a reputation as an 'unreliable interpreter', having taken on many other camel merchants through this role in settler courtrooms.[99]

At first Sher Khan pleaded 'not guilty'. However, as evidence mounted against him, he changed his plea to 'guilty', strategising with Gunny Khan to construct a story featuring Adelaide. The court typist recorded that Sher Khan 'had, he explained, received great provocation' for shooting Moosha, 'as he had been (by Afghan law) married to the girl, Adelaide Nakemor, daughter of Surwah Khan, and that Moosha Balooch had stepped in and supplanted him'.[100] Sher Khan's legal team 'appeal[ed] to the Judge to deal leniently with him', claiming Sher

Khan 'had provided [Adelaide's] parents with £200 to educate her. Moosha Balooch, however, took the girl away'.[101]

It is unclear what marriage payment Sher Khan's defence evoked by citing 'Afghan law'. With Islamic jurisprudence coexisting with multiple other legal epistemes across South Asia, in early-twentieth-century Afghanistan, *walwar*, *toyana*, *peshkash*, *shirbaha*, *qalin*, and *malpreg* were some of the marriage payments in circulation in addition to *mahar*.[102] While the claim may have been that Sher Khan had paid a *mahar* of £200 to school Adelaide, his lawyers did not have Adelaide's property rights in mind in constructing this narrative. Rather, aiming to lessen Sher Khan's sentence, their defence suggested that his rights over Adelaide had been violated, and claimed that Moosha had breached 'Afghan law'. With settler courts increasingly unsympathetic to claims of legal pluralism, Sher Khan was sentenced to '10 years with hard labor', understood as 'a heavy sentence' by one settler newspaper.[103]

The bullet that had pierced Moosha's chest had narrowly missed his heart. As the trial went on, it was removed from his back.[104] He survived. On 8 April 1906, a Methodist minister married Adelaide and Moosha at Marree camel camp (Fig. 26).[105]

Examining Adelaide's trajectory from daughter to fiancé to wife shows that some South Asian men used their daughters' marriages to secure their own livelihoods and establish relationships with power brokers in a precarious industry. Men also scripted women into Afghan nationalist narratives, as the distinctions between 'Afghans' and 'British Indians' were drawn in response to both white nationalism and imperial developments in South Asia.

Ever since settlers hurled stones at the cottage on Little Gilbert Street at Adelaide's engagement, stories about her have repeatedly appeared in English print. Over time, settlers fused Sher Khan's defence narrative with other South Asians' stories about Adelaide to construct a tale that historians labelled as one of 'brideprice' from the 1980s. If the narrative of *mahar* was ever articulated in order to demand Adelaide's dues, it did not make it into the public record. Rather, the stories that circulated were those told in the service of property battles and nationalist projects – of both settlers and South Asians.

IV. Lallie

In the winter of 1926, Lallie Matbar travelled to Mount Morgans in a truck driven by her fiancé Akbar Khan.[106] Lallie's mother Jirgullu insisted that her family accompany her. So the young Aboriginal woman rode with relatives – elders from her Wongatha family living in the eastern goldfields of Western Australia.[107] Born in Karachi, Akbar had arrived with his father in the Australian colonies in around 1894 as a 14-year-old camel driver.[108] Akbar later invested in a motor lorry when they 'cut into the trade of the camel teams'.[109] Known to some as Jack Akbar, by 1924 he was delivering supplies throughout the region from his shop at Mount Morgans.[110] While Lallie's family agreed to her marriage to Akbar, according to settler law in Western Australia, Aboriginal women needed government permission to marry non-Aboriginal men. To negotiate a marriage across three legal epistemes, in late July 1926, Lallie's family accompanied the couple to Mount Morgans' police station.[111]

During the era of 'White Australia', government regimes sought to control Aboriginal people's most intimate relations. In Western Australia, the 1905 Aborigines Act defined 'any person being the offspring of an aboriginal mother and other than aboriginal father' as 'half-caste'.[112] According to this legislation, the legal guardian of all 'half-caste' girls and boys under the age of sixteen was the chief protector of Aborigines – a post held by Auber Octavias Neville from 1915.[113] Consistent with the global rise of eugenics discourse in the 1920s and 1930s, Neville constructed plans for 'half-caste' women's systematic marriage to white men, seeking to 'merge them into our white community and eventually forget that there were any Aborigines in Australia'.[114] This regime outlawed intimacies between 'Asiatics' and 'half-castes'. Aiming to absorb so-called 'half-caste' children into 'White Australia', police systematically captured and removed children from their Aboriginal mothers, imprisoning them at 'half-caste' institutions. Collating stories that Lallie told shows how some Aboriginal women envisioned marriage to South Asian men as a way to escape settler regimes.

Lallie Matbar was born in a creek bed just like her mother Jirgullu before her.[115] Born to a white father, Lallie and her brother Snowy spent their childhood with Jirgullu in the 1910s. As Lallie's grandson

David wrote in a poem in 1992, Jirgullu 'raised them in desert, the place of the *Tjukurpa*' – a word he translates as 'the Dreaming'.[116] An episteme as complex as *shari'a*, *Tjukurpa* is an archive of stories about animals and people travelling great distances. Crisscrossing the Australian mainland, many Dreaming narratives are tales of pursuit and escape along routes known as 'Dreaming tracks' in the field of Aboriginal history.[117] Through Wongatha country, as elsewhere, the epic Dreaming tracks connecting waterholes map long-distance routes of Aboriginal travel.

By the time that Lallie and Snowy were learning their first *Tjukurpa* stories from Jirgullu, many settler institutions were surveilling 'half-caste' children. By piecing together information from these surveillance records, historian Pamela Rajkowski has deduced that Lallie was pregnant in 1926 when her family accepted Akbar's marriage proposal.[118] At Mount Morgans' police station with Lallie and her family, Akbar applied for permission to marry Lallie. But Lallie had long been on Constable Samuel Perk's list of children for removal to Moore River Native Settlement, a 'half-caste' institution near Perth.[119] Outnumbered, Perks did not attempt to capture Lallie that day. However, he declared Lallie's relationship with Akbar illegal, citing the Aborigines Act 1905 (WA).[120] The drive away from the police station must have been a sad one as it dawned on the family that Lallie, pregnant and unmarried, would now be under stricter police surveillance.

Following this meeting, Akbar hired a lawyer to petition Chief Protector Neville. In contrast, Jirgullu fled from settler law. Taking Lallie to Mount Margaret, Jirgullu embarked on an escape from police pursuit across deserts inscribed with older stories of escape and pursuit. As Christian missionaries at Mount Margaret recorded, 'Lallie and her brother Snowy Bradley ... arrived from Linden' in early September 1926. With 'their faces blackened with charcoal because they were part-white ... Jirgullu brought them to Mount Margaret in the hope that they would not be caught and sent to Moore River Settlement'.[121] At dawn on 7 October 1926, at Mount Margaret Mission, Lallie went into labour, giving 'birth to a premature three-and-a-half pound baby'.[122] He was stillborn. Six days later, Perks arrested Lallie, charging her for breaching several sections of the Aborigines Act 1905 (WA).[123]

Lallie was imprisoned at Moore River Native Settlement. She escaped three times. Sometimes alone, sometimes with others, she began embarking on epic flights across unknown deserts without Jirgullu.[124] Each time, she was recaptured. In November 1927, Lallie made her final escape from Moore River.[125] As she told the press later, 'I went on foot for hundreds of miles searching ... [for Akbar Khan], and found him by enquiring at the camps of blacks to see if he had passed.'[126] Lallie's own account of escape diverges significantly from the route Rajkowski has reconstructed from police records.[127] Raising her age to 'nearly 24' and omitting how Akbar, among others, aided her escape, Lallie told her story carefully, negotiating the labyrinth of legal/illegal narratives contained in the Aborigines Act 1905 (WA).[128] She told the press that, learning from Jirrgullu that Akbar was headed for the Western Australian border town of Eucla:

> I went from Laverton through Kalgoorlie to Balladonia, walking, and staying at the camps of blacks on the journey ... at last I got to Eucla, after having been two months on the track. The distance, as the crow flies, from Kalgoorlie to Balladonia is 200 miles, and from Balladonia to Eucla, 300.[129]

When Akbar reached the border in his truck heading for South Australia, Lallie recounted, 'I persuaded him to take me.'[130]

Arriving in Adelaide, the couple found refuge at one of the cottages adjoining the mosque on Little Gilbert Street.[131] Lallie married Akbar on 23 May 1928 at a civil registry in Adelaide, travelling soon afterwards to Farina camel camp to contract a marriage according to Mohamedan law at the house of camel owner Gool Mohamed.[132] However, with Akbar maintaining correspondence with friends in Western Australia, it was not long before government bureaucrats learnt Lallie's whereabouts.[133] Police arrested the couple in early October 1928, charging both Akbar and Lallie for breaching the Aborigines Act 1905 (WA).[134] Their journey back to Western Australia under arrest must have been a devastating one.

With newspapers condemning the waste of 'good money ... to separate two dusky lovers', on 8 November 1928 the city court of Perth upheld the validity of Lallie and Akbar's marriage.[135] Lallie was 'released on her husband's bond of £500', and Akbar signed a contract with Neville agreeing to 'prevent the said Lallie Akbar from returning to Western Australia'.[136] When the couple returned to Adelaide by steamer, the *News* reported that 'two smiling brown faces peered over the rail toward the shore' (Fig. 27).[137]

Lallie's marriage to Akbar offered some respite from settlers' regimes of racial persecution. Their eldest daughter Mona Wilson recalled in 2012, 'that was the time they ... took all the Aboriginal children away. So we were little Muslim kids weren't we? Can't touch us.'[138] Raising four children at the Murray River town of Renmark, Lallie continued to try to return to Wongatha deserts with Akbar's help. As her mother Jirgullu was ageing, on 15 June 1939 Lallie wrote to Mount Margaret Mission that she longed 'to go home sweet home'.[139] However, Neville refused to grant her re-entry to Western Australia.[140] Jirgullu died while her daughter was trying to return.[141]

Eventually, Akbar's adherence to legal/illegal narratives diverged significantly from Lallie's approach to power regimes. As Mona recalled in an interview with historian Peta Stephenson, 'I was supposed to marry one of Gool Mohamed's sons ... but then I went and got pregnant.'[142] Akbar insisted that 15-year-old Mona leave the home and give her baby up for adoption. As their children remembered for years, the course of action that Akbar laid out for Mona was very difficult for Lallie, who had spent a lifetime escaping regimes separating mothers from their children.[143] While Mona was away giving birth, Lallie left Akbar in 1946, returning to Jirgullu's country with her younger daughter Shirley.

Lallie continued and extended the escape that her mother Jirgullu had begun across Wongatha deserts for the rest of her life, far beyond her birth country, adding to a much older archive of epic tales of escape. When Lallie visited Mount Margaret, where her first child with Akbar Khan was buried, missionaries informed police that she had returned to Western Australia.[144] Neville had retired. However, the new commissioner of native affairs opened a file observing the movements of 14-year-old Shirley Akbar, thereby renewing the cycle of state surveillance that continues to persecute many Aboriginal women today.

V. Eshrat

With the 1791 English translation of *Al-Hidaya* (The Guide) in Calcutta, British orientalists commenced an epistemological invasion of *shari'a* libraries that ultimately sought to dismantle an entire discursive system used by many people across South Asia to make sense of their lives. A few years later, in 1808–09, Mountstuart Elphinstone partook in a military expedition to Kabul, where he encountered some women. Whoever they might have been, and regardless of how they storied their lives, the East India Company official inserted them into narratives that lay the foundations of orientalist knowledge about Afghan women. Since then, two centuries of Anglo military interventions have fuelled a growing corpus of English-language sources about Afghan women at battlefronts. While these orientalist narratives continue to structure most Australian histories of Muslim women, many alternative storytelling templates can be found in the knowledge traditions of colonised people.

In compiling Myrtle's, Shamsulnissa's, Adelaide's and Lallie's histories as additions to *The Book of Marriage* compendium, I have outlined a model of feminist history analogous to the Muslim intellectual tradition of *Kitab al-Nikah*. I have treated marriage records as an archive of gendered motion and pieced together stories about marriage for the purposes of challenging the many overlapping power regimes shaping women's trajectories. Offering my mother Eshrat's story as one more entry to *The Book of Marriage*, I conclude by demonstrating that for people of Muslim heritage, interpreting marriage archives using Muslim narrative traditions offers glimpses of an entire episteme that today structures some of our most significant dreams.

Eshrat was born in East Pakistan into a family where many people had intricate, detailed dreams and some even knew how to interpret them. Like many of his contemporaries across South Asia, her paternal grandfather, Mirza Mohiuddin, could foresee the future.[145] Interpreting his own dreams, he articulated highly structured three-part prophecies in the 1920s that continue to be told and retold today by his descendants. Eshrat's maternal grandfather likewise interwove elaborate dreams and their interpretations into his recollections of the past.[146] Dreams have long operated in South Asian knowledge traditions as powerful tools with which to make sense of the world. They are embedded throughout works of Muslim historiography, as historian Tayeb El-Hibri shows.[147]

Though my mother was only a child when a palm reader first saw travel by water etched on her hand, it was only after marriage that she began imagining futures across the Indian Ocean. Her father, Mirza Abdus Sattar, was a scholar of Persian and Arabic, trained in Calcutta during the 1930s. In the 1960s, he built a house in Dhanmondi in Dhaka city on land granted to his wife Zobaida, an English teacher employed by the Pakistani government. When she married, Eshrat left the house on road no. 15 in Dhanmondi behind. She returned there when my father travelled to the United States and Saudi Arabia to train and work respectively. In 1990, Eshrat departed from the Dhanmondi house a second time when she left Bangladesh for Australia as a married woman with children.

By then, entry into Australia was no longer managed according to the regime of 'White Australia'. New visa systems were reinventing the border regimes of the prosperous settler offshoots of the British Empire. In Australia, following the release of the FitzGerald Report in 1988, immigration officials began issuing permanent residency visas based on a class-based points system measuring 'human capital'.[148] In 1990, travelling by air, Eshrat was classed as a 'dependent' on her husband's 'professional category visa'. That year, many miles below Eshrat's Qantas jet, forty-seven women without visas, some with their children, crossed the Indian Ocean on boats, only to be imprisoned at Australian shores.[149] They were among the Cambodian refugees whose arrival saw the Australian government formulate a new policy of mandatory detention of asylum seekers arriving by sea. Navigating these new gendered, class-based definitions of legal and illegal motion across the Indian Ocean, Eshrat entered 'Multicultural Australia' at Sydney airport.

After a decade of married life in Sydney, as ongoing public hysteria about 'boat people' alongside Australian involvement in wars in Iraq and Afghanistan transformed narratives about 'Asians' and then 'Muslims', Eshrat began to dream of escape, one sweltering spring day in 2002. At the time I was a student, making a short film for a class. While I was testing out some new audio equipment, I happened to pick up the phone to call my mother. By chance, having just worked out how to connect a Digital Audio Tape recorder to the landline, I ended up with a recording of Eshrat's account of a dream she had had the previous night.

Crossing an ocean in her sleep, Eshrat dreamt that she was at the bottom of the stairs of the Dhanmondi house in Dhaka. Unable to find her footing up the narrow staircase, she could not reach the upstairs rooms she had once inhabited. Her deceased father stood nearby, watching. They were close. 'Why have you built these stairs like this?' (Fig. 28)[150] Eshrat asked her father. 'They are so steep.' 'Yes,' he admitted quietly, 'they really are designed very badly.' He offered no real answers. After narrating her dream, my Amma pleaded with me, 'Does this mean I will never find my way home?' I, too, had no answers. Often mesmerised by the vivid dreams Eshrat recounted to me, I used that recording as the soundtrack for a short film.

After another decade and many attempts to leave both her marriage and Australia, one autumn afternoon in Sydney in 2011, Eshrat dreamt that a guide would show her the way home. By then I was a history student, despairing at the failure of Australian history books to offer adequate precedents for the contemporary experiences of South Asian migrants. When she told me her dream, I asked Eshrat if I could record it on my mobile phone. She recounted it to me a second time, and later, I uploaded the MP3 file to the internet so that her family overseas could hear it too.[151]

She dreamt that she was walking with my father through the streets of Dhanmondi after rain. In all of her efforts to avoid muddying her sari while crossing the road, she lost him. Recognising that she is near Dhanmondi Lake, Amma assured herself, 'If I enter the lake grounds using another gate, I will soon reach that bridge I know and I can find my way to the Dhanmondi house.'[152] Alone, she began her search for the entrance. 'Sparkling with light,' my mother explained, 'the scenic lake area' drew in anyone walking past, particularly 'near the house of Sheik Mujibur Rahman' – the founding father of the Bangladeshi nation. 'I didn't enter through that gate, though,' Eshrat said.

Amma was lost when she met a young girl who was 'about twelve or thirteen years old.' The girl asked her, 'Where are you going?' When Amma said, 'I am headed to road no. 15 – the one renamed 8/A,' the girl replied, 'I am also going that way, to road no. 19. Let's walk together.' Amma and the girl try entrance after entrance. 'At the first entrance there is a big lock on the gate. The next gate is by a mosque and a *janaja* (funeral) is underway. That way is blocked. Past five or six different gates, some locked, some grilled shut, there is an open gate.' Entering the grounds, Eshrat finally manages 'to get onto the no. 8 bridge and over the water.'

She knew the way from there. Reaching a 'shining high wall' past the first two houses on road no. 15, Eshrat wondered, 'Can't I get in there?' Then she spied a 'hidden entrance' in the corner. She told me, 'I quietly slip in and on the other side in the courtyard I find my mother. Amma is playing badminton with her colleagues' – teachers from the Eden Girls' College in Dhaka. Eshrat was surprised to find that her deceased mother Zobaida was not entirely happy to see her after so many years. Gently, my mother explained to me that it was as if Zobaida were saying, 'You? You left your children there and came here?' Zobaida nevertheless invited Eshrat in. My mother climbed the stairs to Zobaida's high-ceilinged room in a building that seemed at once very old and very new. Beautifully arranged, the room had a sewing machine, a table for reading, and a bed covered in a biscuit-coloured velveteen spread, similar to a spread Zobaida had once brought back from England. My grandmother's room 'leads into another room ... Perhaps it is the room prepared for me,' my mother suggested. Eshrat awoke from her dream with her future in sight. Packing some belongings, she told my father, 'I am happy to be leaving this house for the last time.' She died a few days later.

Guiding her across difficult borders, Eshrat's final dream exposes the gap between contemporary Muslim women's stories and the narratives contained in orientalist histories of Muslim women. Her dreams of crossing the water render visible what both Indian Ocean scholarship and Australian histories often efface: that non-white women move. They not only cross multiple borders, but also tell stories in a particular way to make sense of their travels. Disciplining these stories into progress narratives of 'tradition' to 'modernity' does not do justice to the archives of border-crossing women.

Rather, Eshrat's dreams are better interpreted as pages belonging to a still-expanding volume titled *The Book of Marriage*. Without reproducing the racist logic of progress narratives, this alternative history of marriage is an archive of precedents that people of Muslim heritage today can use to see patterns and continuities between diverse women's experiences of crossing racial, national and imperial borders. For example, like Shamsulnissa's unhappy journey to 'White Australia', Eshrat's dreams of escape from 'Multicultural Australia' reveal that Australian national narratives do not contain the answers to many South Asian women's questions. Like the early-twentieth-century Afghan nationalist narratives that Adelaide was scripted into, Eshrat's dream gently warns border-crossing women that contemporary South Asian nationalist narratives do not signpost the way forward. Instead, like the story Lallie scripted back to Jirgullu's country, Eshrat's dream suggests that a more fruitful strategy is to return to and continue the stories told by loved ones who escaped power regimes. Most importantly, interpreting Myrtle's marriage archives alongside Eshrat's dream-archive illuminates a pathway to the libraries whose ruins belie colonised geographies.

In my reading of my mother's dream today, I can see that Eshrat was searching for the way to the water (*shari'a*) from where she knew her way home – a legal route out of her marriage and into a happier home. Like many, many women before her, she sought escape from the maze of narratives spanning from South Asia to Australia. Yet, if it was *shari'a* that Eshrat desired, out of her marriage and Australia, why could her father not answer her questions about the narrow stairs in 2002? Not only did he build the house Amma longed to return to; my grandfather spent the last decade of his life absorbed in his Persian and Arabic texts. However, as we have seen, many fathers – just like legal guardians, historians, state bureaucrats, police officers, journalists, legal professionals and doctors, not to mention military invaders – embedded in gendered power relations with women, have systematically long produced inadequate narratives featuring Muslim women.

I do not know much about the guide (*al-hidaya*) who finally did show Amma the way, only that she was twelve or thirteen years old. Who was she? After reaching Zobaida's upstairs room, when Amma asked the girl her address, her guide mumbled, 'In time, all in good time,' before slipping away. Since my mother's last dream, I have often wandered the labyrinth of Dhanmondi's named and renamed roads in search of road no. 19, wondering where that girl lives. Is she from one of the propertied families inhabiting the towering flats of Dhanmondi today, or does she sleep on the kitchen floors and storerooms where domestic maids dream of return to their village? What was her name? And how did she know the way?

By the logic of dreams, if the guide (*al-hidaya*) knew the way to the water (*shari'a*), then the search for her will lead to the library central to the *shari'a* episteme. For this reason, when I find her, I expect that she will be in a library somewhere on road no. 19 in Dhanmondi. It will be quite different to Mirza Abdus Sattar's library – for he didn't know the answers to Eshrat's questions. No, I believe that while browsing another such library, the girl found a hidden entrance into another chamber – past the illusion that no answers exist beyond orientalist narratives, past the volumes containing Muslim men's unsatisfactory answers to generations of women, and through a concealed entrance into another vast library.

For in this inner chamber resides a history titled *The Book of Marriage*. I believe that browsing this volume, before she met my lost mother circling Dhanmondi Lake, the girl read my mother's life story. It contained directions: 'At the first entrance there is a big lock on the gate. The next gate is by a mosque and a *janaja* (funeral) is underway. That way is blocked. Past five or six different gates, some locked, some grilled shut, there is an open gate.'[153] I can see now that soon, I will meet a woman who will remember that once, when she was younger, that is how she guided Eshrat over the no. 8 bridge and across the water, so that my Amma could slip past the wall to greet her own Amma once again.

8

TO HEAR

Beginning with 'Hear the Book of Prophet Yusuf', the *Kasasol Ambia* in Broken Hill tells us that Yacub had eleven sons and Yusuf was the youngest.[1] When Yusuf dreams that a sun, a moon and eleven stars are bowing to him, Yacub interprets it as a prophecy that his youngest is destined to be a king. A few days later, Yacub's sons return home without Yusuf. They lie. Smearing Yusuf's shirt with sheep's blood, they present it to their father saying that a tiger devoured their brother in the forests. Yacub knows in his heart that his son is alive. Yet, clutching the stained shirt he begins to grieve, his tears destroying his sight in both his eyes. Eventually, news of Yacub's blindness travels to Cairo, where Yusuf is a king and is married to Zelekha – his once illicit lover. When Yusuf hears the story of his father's blinding grief, he takes off the *kurta* that he is wearing and dispatches it to Yacub, with a message to his father to hold the garment close to his face. On receiving the shirt, Yacub inhales the scent of his son, and his eyes light up. When his inner knowledge that his son is alive is confirmed to be true, Yacub's vision is restored and his eyes open.

Could *Kasasol Ambia* have arrived in Broken Hill with someone who heard the book of Yusuf? Disciplining *Kasasol Ambia* into an English-language progress narrative in 1864 in Calcutta, Sanskritist Rajendralal Mitra was perhaps the first historian to step into an orientalist knowledge relation to the text. Since then many historians have consigned its stories to a much larger museum of dead artefacts incapable of living on in the modern world. For as legal theorist Wael Hallaq observes, by the close of the nineteenth century Muslim historiographical traditions had become 'nearly overnight, paradigmatic expressions of a dead past.'[2]

In his most recent book, *Restating Orientalism*, published in 2018, Hallaq extends Edward Said's criticism of orientalist interpretive methods in particular to modern paradigms of knowledge production in general. Pointing out that 'orientalism is a microcosm of the macrocosmic modern structure', he insists that 'whatever charge the Orientalist may be made to bear ... equally attaches to his or her cognates' – the modern 'scientist, journalist, historian, philosopher, or economist, among academic others.'[3] Drawing an analogy between orientalist knowledge relations and the anthropocentric subjugation of non-human beings, Hallaq proposes that endemic to contemporary ecological crisis is an epistemology – a way of understanding, interpreting and being in the world – where the only living being who flourishes is the Enlightened knower who 'lives over the world, not in the world.'[4]

To critique the type of encounters that take place on modern epistemic grounds between historians and the texts of 'others', I have been using the term 'knowledge relation' – an elusive concept for which I never quite found a satisfying English epithet. Nevertheless, in rephrasing epistemology in this way I have argued throughout this book that analyses of knowledge relations must accompany investigations of race relations, gender relations and class relations so integral to the project of history from below. For central to envisioning futures where life flourishes is the urgent need not just to acknowledge but to nurture and cultivate the exhilarating plurality of human ontology that continues to live despite the 'deathscapes' of modernity.[5]

When arguing that racist logics are inherent to Western modernity, many scholars have long critiqued 'the imperial belief that the rest of the world shall submit to its cosmology.'[6] However, as Hallaq observes, it is within the contemporary context of 'a scientific consensus on climate and ecological crisis' that the 'increasingly proliferating and widespread understanding that the modern project, together with its knowledge system, is unsustainable ... is in the process of taking over centre stage.'[7] Joining a growing chorus of activists and writers at a moment when planetary destruction appears imminent, he argues that 'a major restructuring, if not overhauling, of the paradigmatic systems of modernity is now in order.'[8] While many have argued for decades that the tools of modernist critique cannot respond to crises that those tools themselves produce, the bind has long been: to declare modern knowledges as part of a dead past would comprise a profoundly modern act.

Non-Enlightenment historiographical traditions offer ways out of this bind. As we have seen, they can show us how to step into knowledge relations that can enliven knowledges rather then deaden them. For example, stepping past Mitra's tabulation of *Kasasol Ambia* and actually reading the lines of poetry he carved into 'Bengali' and 'Foreign' components reveals a couplet that begins with the directive 'listen (*shuna*) ...'.[9] It is an instruction that invites audiences to enter a knowledge relation quite distinct from orientalist epistemology. Throughout *Kasasol Ambia* directives to 'hear' and 'listen' open episodes of historical storytelling, and listening systematically signals the beginning of narrative cycles that culminate in seeing, attaining consciousness and awakening.

While the tale of 'Adam Sufi' is the story in *Kasasol Ambia* that theorises a form of human consciousness most extensively, the poetic imagery only hints at the relationship between 'hearing' and becoming conscious.[10] Firstly, for example, the instruction '*shuna*' (hear) and its partner '*shune*' (having heard) signpost the transmission and reception of spoken dialogue between Allah and the angels who mould a clay statue enacting creation stories from many intellectual traditions. 'Hear' also commences Allah's instructions to the spirit (*ruh*) to enter the inanimate statue. After entering and leaving it seven times, when the *ruh* is unimpressed with the dark, unlit interiors it must inhabit, Allah gives more directions beginning with '*shuna*'. On entering the statue an eighth time through the statue's nose, the *ruh* travels through four distinct parts of the statue's mind, and we can infer that along with taste, touch and smell, hearing comprises one of the senses that must be roused, before the fifth and final sense – sight – will awaken. While the poet tells his audience that only when the statue opened its eyes did life course through Adam, he does not offer precise details of how listening to this tale would awaken listeners.

Undoubtedly, the first encounter nineteenth-century audiences had with this particular theorisation of human subjectivity narrated in

Kasasol Ambia was aural. As colonial institutions – courts of law, schools, universities, the English novel – were training increasing numbers of South Asians in silent, modern reading methods, audiences continued to gather at Bengali book recitations which were 'always rapid, sonorous, and musical ... accompanied with rapid motions of the head and body,' as one British officer observed.[11] In such spaces, audiences cultivated highly structured, embodied listening practices that have long transmitted knowledges to new generations of book listeners, intricately threading together a multiplicity of old intellectual traditions in new patterns.[12] As cultural historians have shown, it wasn't just stories that were transmitted at these spaces, but also a 'sense of hearing' – a knowledge relation.[13] So how did hearing its stories and seeing its multilayered metaphors actually lead audiences to embody the forms of consciousness that *Kasasol Ambia* theorised?

It was these questions about the particular knowledge relation that *Kasasol Ambia* was embedded in that saw me return again and again to archival records in search of people who might have heard its stories. For just as orientalist institutions were cultivating one type of knowledge relation by the late nineteenth century, gatherings around oral performances of some South Asian texts comprised an epistemic space that sustained another type of knowledge relation. What did it mean to hear its tales of composite human subjectivities indivisible into Hindu, Buddhist and Muslim in a colonial Australian context? While many South Asians began scripting themselves into the settler narrative of the 'pioneer' as the so-called 'alien' was increasingly demonised, did the motifs in *Kasasol Ambia* offer listeners alternative subjectivities to inhabit? How did listeners use the stories of the prophets? What precisely did it mean to hear books?

* * *

It was when my language skills had improved sufficiently to understand contemporary Bengali prose that I came across an account of a gathering of listeners captivated by a performance of *Kasasol Ambia*. It detailed how tales moved from the printed page and into the imaginations of listeners, ordering reality and lived experiences. The account appears in the memoirs of Kazi Motahar Hossain (b. 1897).[14] He was my great-grandfather. Motahar wrote that growing up in a village of what is today the

Faridpur district of Bangladesh, he often heard his genealogy recited. He was the son of Kazi Gouharuddin, son of Naimuddin, son of Koresh, son of Danesh, son of Ataullah.[15] His forefathers were a line of judges (*kazis*) whom some in the family traced from Bengal back to the city of Jaunpur. Others traced them to the Deccan village of Kathipara. Today, both are located within the bounds of contemporary India.

Motahar recalls that when he was four or five years old, on some afternoons his father Gouharuddin would recite stories from a printed copy of *Kasasol Ambia* on the verandah. These were occasions that gathered a crowd. 'Many people from surrounding areas would travel great distances to hear the stories,' writes Motahar.[16] Having memorised the poems that the printed book contained, Gouharuddin would 'freely recite old (*puranic*) stories and historical episodes (*itihasa*) stretching from Adam to Prophet Muhammad without even looking at the book.' Listening to these performances on the verandah first stirred in him the desire to read, inspiring in Motahar a hunger for 'books about Adam-Nuh-Ibrahim-Musa-Isa-Muhammad.' As he recalled, their stories spurred him to 'quickly learn *a*, *aa*, *ka*, *kha* and *alif, ba ta sa*' – the letters of the Bengali alphabet and Arabic-Persian-Urdu scripts respectively.[17]

Throughout his memoirs Motahar highlights that books, and in particular history books, were present at some of the most important junctures of his life. When he travelled to Hugli at the age of twenty-two, his recitation of a part of the Persian historical epic *Shahnama* caught the attention of an older listener. So began negotiations for Motahar's marriage into that Hugli household.[18] The first prospective bride, as rumours informed Motahar, was renowned for her beauty. The second woman, goes family lore, was renowned for her love of books. By the age of nineteen, she had published Urdu translations of the first two Bengali romances penned by modernist writer Bankimchandra Chattopadhay (d. 1894).[19] In 1920, Motahar married book-loving Sajeda Khatun of Hugli, daughter of Moslema Khatun, daughter of Karimunessa. Beginning with the birth of their daughter Zobaida in 1923, Sajeda Khatun gave birth to their eleven children over the next two decades – seven daughters and four sons (Fig. 29).

The role that the motifs from *Kasasol Ambia* played in the lives of Sajeda and Motahar can be glimpsed in the oral archives of their descendants. Today their grandchildren and great-grandchildren live in

London, Newcastle and Cambridge in Britain, Boston, Sydney, Toronto, Stockholm, Vienna, San Francisco, Kiev, Moscow, New York, Philadelphia, New Jersey, and, of course, Dhaka and throughout Bangladesh. Many of us left South Asia from the 1980s and 1990s as newly articulated visa regimes interlocked with various multicultural policies in Western nation-states, rerouting the global terrain of South Asian movement.[20] Today we are technocrats, undocumented workers, writers, historians, unemployed bottle collectors, physicians, refugees, public servants, unpaid caregivers, school students, sailors in the Russian navy, biochemists, chief executive officers and minimum-wage workers scattered across the world, as different as the shattered parts of a coherent whole.

As I have heard recounted many times in Sydney, Dhaka and New York, after Motahar and Sajeda had raised eleven children, and after they had buried one daughter and two sons, one day aged Sajeda took off the single gold bangle she always wore. Before she left her family home for a gallstone operation at PG Hospital in Dhaka, she said to her eldest daughter Zobaida, 'My work here is complete.' She did not open her eyes after surgery. When Motahar arrived to her bedside, Sajeda was in a coma. He took off his shirt and draped it over the face of the woman he affectionately called 'Sheju bibi'. Just as Yusuf's shirt had once awakened Yacub, Motahar insisted that his scent too would awaken sleeping Sajeda.

Sajeda's loved ones waited for days, Zobaida arriving each evening after work to sit by her bedside. But Sheju bibi did not open her eyes. In June 1975, Sajeda Khatun was buried in Banani in Dhaka. Day after day following the funeral, out of habit Zobaida would travel to PG Hospital after work and wait, as her daughter Eshrat would later recall. Motahar, on the other hand, spent night after night holding Sheju bibi's garments to his face, seeking out her most worn saris in particular. As Motahar's use of these narrative motifs confirms, the stories contained in *Kasasol Ambia* accompanied listeners through some of the most difficult junctures of their lives, operating as precedents which people stepped into at moments of rupture, crisis and uncertainty.

Listening to *Kasasol Ambia*, then, began the process by which motifs from the printed book travelled from its pages and into human interiorities, its stories becoming part of an inner library of narratives, the dynamic motifs continuing to travel each time they were used, performed, retold, recalled and enacted. When Kazi Gouharuddin recited *Kasasol Ambia* on a verandah in Bengal, his young son 'took special care to commit these stories to memory.'[21] Hearing the stories imprinted the imagery of the poetry in his imagination, the scenes returning to Motahar on some of the loneliest nights of his life. Years later, having crossed an ocean with the scenes she witnessed imprinted on her memory, my mother told me Sajeda and Motahar's tale many times in South Western Sydney.

It was one of many episodes from family history that Eshrat first began telling me when I was about twelve or thirteen years old. After the 1994 bushfires that ravaged bushlands and homes across the eastern Australian coastline, for the two summers that followed, the fear of fire hung over our street, from which you could always smell the distant scent of burning eucalypts. For the horizon of nearby trees marked the beginning of Holsworthy Army Barracks, comprising of thousands of acres of dry bushland. After sunset my mother and I would venture out to the front verandah and inspect the horizon for smoke. Lying on the warm concrete, as the crimson faded from the sky, Eshrat would begin telling stories about Dhaka. As she had narrated countless times, years ago her grandfather Motahar clung to Sajeda's saris every night following her death. Night after night, he would fall asleep inhaling the aroma of her sweat and the fading scent of her hair.

Years later I realised that when I had listened to Eshrat's tale, I had also heard how Motahar scripted himself into a motif from *Kasasol Ambia* that he too had first heard on a verandah. For these were narratives deeply embedded within the connective tissue of intimate family relations. With these vivid scenes imprinted in my inherited memory, in the winter of July 2009 when I travelled over 1,000 kilometres inland from Sydney, it turns out that I too brought Bengali stories of the prophets (*kasasol ambia*) to Broken Hill.

For when I began reading the aged copy of *Kasasol Ambia* in that mosque, I had already heard the stories it contained – I knew them according to a very different schema of knowledge to Enlightenment modes of historical storytelling. At least since the writings of Buddhist philosopher Dignaga (d. 540), inwardly known models of truth (*antarjñeya-rupa*) have featured at the foundations of many South Asian theories of knowledge. As the work of literary scholar A. K. Ramanujan highlights, these are knowledge systems that have continued to operate long after European imperialism across the Indian Ocean world left in its aftermath a jigsaw of nation-states. As Ramanujan wrote in 1987, 'in India and in Southeast Asia, no one ever reads the *Ramayana* or the *Mahabharata* for the first time. The stories are there, "always already."'[22]

From 1860, these were stories that enjoyed a renewed circulation following the growth of the Bengali-language printing industry in the Calcutta neighbourhood of Battala – the cheap book market that perhaps began in the cool shade of a sprawling Banyan tree (*battala*). As the catalogues of books bearing Kazi Sofiuddin's seal confirm, alongside edition after edition of *Kasasol Ambia*, the most successful entrepreneur operating in the Battala book industry published the *Mahabharata* and the *Ramayana*, adding many titles to the already vast library of historiographical storytelling known as the *itihasa-puranas* discourse. With what Motahar called 'old (*puranic*) stories and historical episodes (*itihasa*) stretching from Adam to Prophet Muhammad' circulated a knowledge relation that South Asian audiences began to access, embody and cultivate from their earliest years through the deceptively simple act of listening.

According to this schema of knowing, if I 'always, already' knew the narratives in *Kasasol Ambia*, what else do I 'always, already' know? Given that I had heard echoes of tales transmitted from Gouharuddin to Motahar over three generations ago, had they in turn heard echoes of tales transmitted over three generations before them by Ataullah to his son Danesh? By this logic, do I too 'know' the books Danesh/Ataulla knew? Do I already know motifs from the historical epic *Shahnama* that Motahar recited in Hugli? Had this Persian history book too become as diffusely distributed in oral archives and everyday meaning-making practices across the Indian Ocean world as titles like *Kasasol Ambia*, the *Mahabharata* and the *Ramayana*? What about the modernist romances written by Bankimchandra Chattopadhyay that Sajeda Khatun translated into Urdu as a young woman? Or does this schema only operate for non-modernist knowledges?

What is obvious is that it is not through men's knowledge transmission, but rather women's, that I have heard the stories that circulate in the family archive. Patrilineal genealogies were by no means the only routes that stories travelled and Motahar's memoirs draw attention to women's participation in the systematic concealment of women's knowledge. While his father's genealogy was cited and debated, his mother's was not. As Motahar writes, he only found out his mother's name when he was fourteen years old. After Tasirunessa told Motahar her name after much coaxing by her son, she covered her face as if she had revealed too much. Noticeably, Motahar's printed memoirs, like those of his daughters, only incidentally gesture at the retinue of servants that were part of their households. That they never delve into their stories draws attention to one of the most powerful set of relations ordering knowledge production: class. And yet, oral family archives as well my own childhood experience confirm a recurring motif in the most popular Sufi romances penned in South Asia: the ayahs who fed, clothed and cleaned the children of their employers were seasoned storytellers and key figures in the ongoing circulation of stories.

As ayahs' stories in the oral archives of my family make clear, knowledge has never only been passed between blood relations, nor solely along the zealously guarded lines of property transmission. Every dialogue between familiar people, every exchange beyond the verandahs marking the edges of the home, and each encounter with a new or old text comprise instances when stories might move from one site to another. The pages of written books are simply sites where circulating stories leave traces particularly legible to modern eyes. What if seven or seventy or 700 generations of knowledge could reach us, along the many axes of transmission that converge upon us at any place? What would be the implications for history writing?

Approaching the past as a conjuncture of historiographical traditions offers the most promising standpoint from which activists and historians alike can hope to glimpse better futures from our contemporary, horrifying moment of escalating racism and intensifying state violence. For it is from such a conjuncture that we can address the colonisation of hope itself by the Enlightenment story of progress – only one of the many philosophies of history that converge upon every site. For over two centuries, while a variety of progress narratives have charted routes forward to different imagined destinations on a left–right political spectrum, what they have in common is that they relegate others' philosophies of history to dead pasts, constructing the illusion that progress alone can structure the pathways that social movements plot to better futures. If 'another world is possible', as Walter Mignolo and Catherine Walsh reiterate in 2018, extending a long legacy of activist-scholarship by modernity's many others, 'it cannot be built with the conceptual tools inherited from the Renaissance and the Enlightenment.'[23]

Envisioning the self and others as always located at the conjuncture of numerous knowledge traditions allows us to reimagine human subjectivities beyond the suffocating oppositional binaries that structure modernist paradigms of historical storytelling. It is an always-subjective perspective from which it is possible to cultivate and extend what historian W. E. B. Du Bois once described as 'the gift of second sight' in his foundational work in African-American literature.[24] As Du Bois wrote in 1903, 'It is a peculiar sensation, this double-consciousness, this sense of always looking at one's self through the eyes of others, of measuring one's soul by the tape of a world that looks on in amused contempt and pity.'[25] Du Bois' much-quoted statement is one of the most lucid articulations of a trope that pervades the work of many non-white thinkers writing in European languages: the recognition that a white self resides within the psyches of those who are not.

That this twin gift and curse of double consciousness is at once a psychic and political condition is something I myself first became conscious of ten years ago, when, sitting on a wooden bench in Sydney, I listened to Eshrat's account of her confinement each night in a hospital ward. The image of the confrontation night after night between the uniformed white soldier returned from Afghanistan and my mother whose Quran was melting did not just dramatise the geopolitical reality of Australian involvement in US-led warfare across Indian Ocean lands. It also imaged a confrontation underway within the psyches of all modern subjects: the perpetual interior war between white selves and non-modern knowledges.

As we have seen, different conceptions of human existence do not have to be at war with each other within psyches. There are theorisations of being that thread together forms of selfhood from different knowledge traditions at the sites upon which they converge – the sea of stories that poet Munshi Rezaulla leapt into, simultaneously searching for the form (*rupa*) of a new book and a new self. In weaving together different stories, he threaded together a garland. Writing 'I name (*nama*) this chain *Kasasol Ambia*', Rezaulla gave his audience a multilayered dream-like metaphor for how he came to embody his name *munshi* (writer). Stepping into a 'pool of stories' just like every author of the *Ramayana*, Rezaulla animated the pair of terms *rupa* and *nama* from Buddhist tools for theorising self, extending the imagery of strings of pearls in Perso-Arabic poetry, and emerged with a new composite narrative and a new form of human subjectivity.[26] As narrative cycles from many South Asian historiographical traditions repeatedly hint, when authors stepped into rich repositories of past stories, they emerged with three novel forms: a fresh story, a new self, and a knowledge relation connecting the two. As *Kasasol Ambia* illustrates, weaving together intellectual traditions comprised one history-writing methodology for producing human subjectivities within which parts are not at perpetual war.

Using these techniques to craft new historical narratives and new selves at the conjunctures of knowledge traditions, historians writing in English today can begin to address the ongoing legacies of the racist, epistemic violence enacted by modernist historiographical traditions. For as Thomas Macaulay wrote after the publication of his influential *History of England*, which laid out a template of progress for others to follow to the Western nation-state, 'I have had the year 2000, and even the year 3000, often in my mind.'[27] Extending what Du Bois called 'double consciousness', approaching every moment in time and place as an intersection of as many intellectual trajectories as living beings that converge there, we can cultivate not just 'second sight', but nurture third ways of seeing and hope to glimpse something of fourth, fifth, sixth and seventh ways forward that have long coexisted alongside the 'theology of progress'.[28] For one key to finding a way out of the prison house of colonial-modernist thought is refusing to interpret the world through the mutually exclusive antagonistic binaries that structure modernist analysis.

It is true that singing about Radha and Krishna at Liverpool Hospital did not actually challenge the Anglo military-industrial complex spanning the Indian Ocean world that produced the Islam versus the West dichotomy playing out each night inside one locked room. Likewise, when I first met Reg Dodd at Marree, neither telling him about the

Bengali book at Broken Hill nor singing about Radha's search dismantled the ongoing structures of invasion that produce the terrain of settler colonialism on which non-Aboriginal people necessarily meet Aboriginal people today. However, at both these junctures, it was cultivating the gift of third and fourth vision, to extend Du Bois' metaphor, that offered a way forward.

Cultivating non-Enlightenment epistemes not only comprises an extraordinary strategy for survival on encounter with the violence of modern institutions; it is also a tactic that has long been at the heart of many Aboriginal movements for land. For example, it was at a protest against uranium mining by Western Mining Corporation (WMC) on Arabunna lands that Kevin Buzzacott declared in 1998 'anthropologists and all that mob – they're trying to tell us who we are, and what we are and what we think. I'm saying "No you can't tell us that." … we *know* the country.'[29] His assertion that Aboriginal peoples' knowledge relations to country cannot ever be displaced was part of a piece of prose poetry inviting outsiders to Arabunna country to join a protest against WMC. Titled *Lake Eyre is Calling*, it summoned travellers to Arabunna lands to build a knowledge relation to country while participating in a political project with Arabunna families and imagining shared futures. As Aboriginal legal theorist Irene Watson showed, their movement reached a crescendo when the protestors walked from Lake Eyre to the site of the Sydney Olympics, traversing over 5,000 kilometres on foot to reach a global audience.[30] As Kevin Buzzacott commented from Broken Hill, 'we are walking along these really old tracks … its like adding on a new chapter, of the old Dreamtime – we are using that old foundation.'[31]

* * *

From March 2018, I began calling remote Australia to speak to Reg Dodd to discuss what I had written about Arabunna country and people. By then I had left Australia and was living in Dhaka, teaching history. It was spring and early mornings before my classes were the best time to call Australia – where it would then be around midday. In Bangladesh, spectacular downpours each morning were bringing the green corridor around Dhanmondi Lake to life, transforming the trees into luminous shades I'd simply never seen before in the concrete mega-city of over 18 million people. When I finally reached Reg one morning, he recognised my voice immediately. It had been about eighteen months since I had last seen him at the 2016 Camel Cup in tiny Marree, population 150. 'Bangladesh?' he chuckled down the line. 'What are you doing all the way over there?'

Resuming the dialogue with Reg that had continued each time I returned to Marree, I sent him the chapter I had written about the two Arabunna girls who feared that the two South Asians would eat them. From Dhaka, a printed copy of 'The Book of Sand' took ten days to reach the Arabunna People's Community Centre in Marree by express courier. Over the phone, Reg talked me through a few re-drafts over the next months. I had misunderstood some things, and got other things wrong.

When I rang Marree most recently, Reg said, 'Well what you have is a good start.' As he explained, 'You have to realise you are just beginning to understand these stories. You have to get very close to really understand how they work.' Arabunna stories, Reg emphasised, were ultimately told for the purpose of caring for the listener and caring for country – their inner logic often hidden. 'You are just beginning to understand and you should come back and sit down around the campfire again!' Describing a harsh winter in Marree, Reg said there were far too many kangaroos around because it was too dry – there were hundreds of them each evening searching for water. While monsoon rains had arrived on the Northern Australian coast, the waters might not reach Lake Eyre, he said, because of the diversions to farmlands. Observing that 'some sort of change is happening,' he said that there hadn't been any snakes that year, and not nearly as many birds as there should have been. He said to me, 'I'll tell you some more stories and you can listen while looking really closely at the places they were told.' It was an invitation back to Arabunna country in spring for another camping trip, another lesson.

For many years, after the migrant tale of Western multiculturalism buckled and collapsed in a hospital garden in Sydney, I travelled back and forth across the Indian Ocean searching ceaselessly for a new story. After ten years, browsing a bookshop one day, I came across a newly published history book that told a tale that was quite different to 'Destination: West'. Titled *Australianama* (The Book of Australia), it was unlike many of the other volumes shelved in the history section. Though it was in English, its pages bore testament to the ongoing circulation of stories according to the logic of colonised epistemes. While at first glance the book appeared to be about Australia and South Asia, it told a larger tale about the exhilarating multiplicity of temporal pathways people can travel between yesterday, today and tomorrow as they envision ways forward toward better futures.

As I read *Australianama*, transported to another realm by what Borges once described as the 'waking dream' of reading, I followed the author along route after route to the interior libraries that remain alive within the colonised.[32] The history books that await in these libraries of knowledge are thrilling. Stories jump from pages and into human imaginations, their motifs finding new expression when audiences step into their plots. They are stories that can cross the partitions between sleep and waking, rousing the wild, spectacular possibilities for all else that human existence is – beyond the narrow forms of life cultivated by the matrix of colonial-modern institutions.

At the very end of the book, the author narrates an intricate dream in which she is sitting in Dhaka entirely immersed in reading a book. She had the dream on a hot spring night in Melbourne after a day spent writing and rewriting a difficult chapter of *Australianama*. With an author absorbed in the act of reading at the centre of its imagery, it is a dream that resonates with Toni Morrison's observation that 'writing and reading are not all that distinct for a writer. Both exercises require being alert and ready for unaccountable beauty.'[33] In her landmark analysis of whiteness and writer's subjectivities, Morrison approaches American literary imagination and its depiction of an African other as a 'dream'. She recounts that 'as a writer reading, I came to realize the obvious: the subject of the dream is the dreamer' – the author.[34] Reading her own dream through Morrison's insights, the author intimates that while writing *Australianama*, her interiority came to be transformed.

'Crossing an ocean in my sleep,' writes the author, 'in the dream I am in the living room of a house in Dhaka, with a book open on my lap. It is the flat downstairs from my childhood home and I am sitting on a wooden bench, carefully balancing there with a man who sits at the other end. A white woman sits on an attached couch, looking out through the two large windows that open onto road 8/A in

Dhanmondi. My two friends, both my own age, are visitors to Dhaka, and while they banter with each other, I am entirely absorbed in the book on my lap.

'In its narrative plot, there are three children: two girls and one boy. They are all ten years old. The leader of the trio is confident, charismatic and likeable, if a little loud. I am devastated when she dies very early in the plot. For the boy was in love with her. In her absence, slowly the boy gets to know the other girl. She is shy and almost never speaks. They become a duo and embark on adventures through a thick, green forest, where the girl finds a flute. Recalling an old song about a flute playing in a forest, she begins to hum its tune. Soon after, under a banyan tree (*battala*), the boy finds a book. It is very old. As they continue exploring the forest, the boy recites the words written in the old book, while the shy girl sings the melody that echoes in her memory.

'One day, they rediscover the grave where their friend is buried. Beneath the trees, below the dirt, she lies motionless in the form of a clay statue "as white as a hospital sheet". It so happens that precisely as the shy girl sings the notes that were once played by a flute, the boy recites out loud the story told in the book. Together, her melody and his words reach the cold statue buried deep in the earth. The eyes of the earthen form suddenly open wide. Both children, as the dream book narrates, are "stunned when the dead girl wakes up."

'Overjoyed yet startled by the striking symbolism of the narrative,' writes the author of *Australianama*, 'I stop reading the book to savour its imagery. With a jolt I am transported from the forest in my imagination back to the living room in Dhaka and back into my body. The wooden bench tips forwards, but my friend on the other end rebalances himself so that neither of us falls. As I read and reread the line "... the dead girl wakes up", I begin to understand that the three children were showing me that enlivening and animating old knowledges is a means of awakening beings that may appear to be dead. The two children who explore the forest, I begin to comprehend, do not just give voice to the book and the flute they find; they become new forms of these old things. For, like the book, the boy begins telling stories; like the flute, the shy girl begins singing a tune. It is as if the children in the forest are mediums through whom knowledges continue to travel, altering the *rupa* (form) of both the narratives and their vessels.

'While I am sitting in Dhaka in my dream, relishing, comprehending and appreciating the imagery in the book that I have just read,' the author continues, 'the white woman on the attached couch suddenly laughs out loud at the scene outside. Through the two windows facing out to the street, she had glimpsed two men. They are the two beggars who wander the streets of Dhanmondi singing Allah's name in call and response. When the first beggar passed the first window of the house on road 8/A, from the couch the woman overheard a snippet of his dialogue with his friend. It is on hearing the second man's witty response when he walked past the second window that she burst into peals of laughter. While neither of us balancing on the wooden bench caught the banter outside, we are delighted at our friend's mirth. Realising that it means that she can now hear and understand Bengali dialogue, I wake up.'[35]

Overjoyed yet startled by the striking symbolism of the dream narrative, I stopped reading *Australianama* to savour its imagery. As I read and reread the line 'she can now hear and understand Bengali dialogue', I began to undertand that female characters in the dream dramatise some of the many things it can mean 'to hear' stories and awaken. In the forest, listening for a tune she remembers, straining to inwardly hear its melody as all singers must, the shy girl awakens her voice. Just as the statue opens its eyes when it hears a tune interwoven with a story, the woman on the couch too experiences awakening when she hears. As the woman looks out to road 8/A, it is on 'hearing' – in the sense of 'comprehending' – the words exchanged between the two beggars that she actually glimpses their interiority, seeing them through the two windows. Freed from the deafening silence of Anglo linguistic monolingualism, emancipated from the epistemic arrogance of modernist paradigms of thought, released from the continuous work of not seeing the poorest of the world, she becomes conscious of others outside – the house and its windows long operating as archetypal motifs for human subjectivity and consciousness in many knowledge traditions.

As the imagery of the dream text suggests, the subjectivity the author began to inhabit as she was writing *Australiamana* was quite different from that of the Enlightened scientist standing over his dead specimens, unlike the modern subject at perpetual war with non-modern knowledges and dissimilar to the colonial-modern historian disciplining archives into tales of progress. The crucial point of distinction is another knowledge relation between people and stories – a dance that is repeatedly and elaborately detailed in the dream as a sense of hearing.

While in written English today, the verb 'to hear' evokes a somewhat muted range of meanings associated with becoming aware, comprehension and perception, far more extensive meanings are fleshed out in the imagery of aural discursive traditions. For example, in the Quran, a heard book, hearing is repeatedly related not just to revelation and seeing, but also to the reception and transmission of knowledge.[36] Unsurprisingly, aural transmission is elaborately theorised through signature narrative cycles in many heard books across the Indian Ocean world. Within the pan-South Asian *bhakti* tradition for example, mystic figure Chaitanya hears a recitation of a Sanskrit book titled *Kṛṣṇakarṇamṛta* (Ambrosia for Krishna's Ears) in the year 1510 CE. Captivated by the poetry, he has his followers pen the verses, ultimately producing a Bengali text that transmits its narrative to new audiences, inaugurating another variety of the *bhakti* discursive tradition.[37]

Usefully interpreted as a theorisation of the knowledge relation that underpinned the writing of *Australianama*, the dream text in its final pages depicts the author as one node in a chain of knowledge transmission, a medium by which stories can move from book to book. This is clearest if we follow the trajectory of a story from the old book the boy finds under a tree. The boy's recitation propels the story from the page and into the statue and the account of its transformative effect on both the boy and the dead girl leaves a trace on the pages of a book in Dhanmondi. Yet the story does not end there. For the author's act of reading the book open on her lap propels the story from the page and into her imagination. When she awakens from slumber to continue writing, the tale leaves a trace on the pages of *Australianama*. As I read *Australianama* and saw its imagery, I realised that just like the author, I too had become a node in the chain of knowledge transmission, a vessel harnessed by motifs to move from book to book and into the imagination of audiences.

It was when I finally recognised the author's name that I understood that *Australianama* was a record of the shimmering multiplicity of things it can mean to hear books. For in Arabic, the range of semantic meanings of the verb 'to hear' – 'to give an ear to', 'to understand', 'to comprehend,' and even 'to learn' – is evoked by the word *Sami'a*.

NOTES

PROLOGUE: THE MELTING QURAN

1. Joachim Guilliard et al., *Body Count: Casualty Figures after 10 Years of the 'War on Terror'* (Washington, DC: International Physicians for the Prevention of Nuclear War, 2015), 15, http://www.psr.org/assets/pdfs/body-count.pdf, last accessed 12 September 2016.
2. Kei Miller, 'The Texture of Fiction', *The Edinburgh Review*, no. 123 (2008).
3. Kei Miller, 'Imaging Nations', *Moving Worlds: A Journal of Transcultural Writings* 11, no. 1 (2011).
4. Christine Stevens, *Tin Mosques & Ghantowns: A History of Afghan Cameldrivers in Australia* (Melbourne: Oxford University Press, 1989), 100a.

1. THE BOOK OF BOOKS

1. 'The Barrier Ranges Silver Mines', *The Argus*, 1 December 1885, 4.
2. Ibid.
3. T. A. Coghlan, 'A Statistical Account of the Seven Colonies of Australasia, 1901–02' (Sydney: Government Printer, 3 December 1902), 839. Gunny Khan, 'The Camel Nuisance', *Barrier Miner*, 23 May 1904, 2.
4. Christine Stevens, *Tin Mosques & Ghantowns: A History of Afghan Cameldrivers in Australia* (Melbourne: Oxford University Press, 1989), 100a.
5. Kazi Sofiuddin, *Kasasol Ambia* (Calcutta: Hanifia Press, 1895), 2.
6. Stevens, *Tin Mosques & Ghantowns*, 12.
7. Basil Fuller, *The Ghan: The Story of the Alice Springs Railway* (Adelaide: Rigby, 1975), 11.

8. The most sustained engagement with non-English-language sources in Australian historiography can be found within the subfield of Aboriginal history. I build on an earlier series of collaborations between linguists, speakers of Aboriginal languages and sometimes historians, which saw the publication of Aboriginal-language stories in the journal *Aboriginal History* from the 1980s. While this scholarship tended to map Aboriginal-language materials into settler temporal frameworks, Minoru Hokari's exploration of Gurindji historical consciousness published in 2011 offered an exciting methodological intervention into the field. More recently, in 2017 Sophie Loy-Wilson has utilised texts in Mandarin in her monograph on Chinese traders in Australia and Laura Rademaker has examined the politics of language on the Groote Eylandt archipelago. See Minoru Hokari, *Gurindji Journey: A Japanese Historian in the Outback* (Sydney: UNSW Press, 2011); Sophie Loy-Wilson, *Australians in Shanghai: Race, Rights and Nation in Treaty Port China* (Abingdon and New York: Routledge, 2017); Laura Rademaker, *Found in Translation: Many Meanings on a North Australian Mission* (Honolulu: University of Hawaii Press, 2018).
9. Balachandra Rajan, *Under Western Eyes: India from Milton to Macaulay, Post-Contemporary Interventions* (Durham, NC: Duke University Press, 1999), 94.
10. James Cook and W. J. L. Wharton, *Captain Cook's Journal During His First Voyage Round the World Made in H. M. Bark Endeavour, 1768–71* (London: Elliot Stock, 1893), 237.
11. J. C. Beaglehole, ed., *The Voyage of the Endeavour, 1768–1771* (Cambridge, UK: Cambridge University Press, 1955), cxxxvi.
12. Joseph Banks and J. C. Beaglehole, *The Endeavour Journal of Joseph Banks: 1768–1771*, vol. 2 (Sydney: The Trustees of the Public Library of New South Wales in association with Angus and Robertson, 1962), 111.
13. Ibid., 58.
14. Historian David Arnold memorably called this formulation the 'Orientalist "triptych" of Indian history' in David Arnold, *The New Cambridge History of India*, III, 5, *Science, Technology and Medicine in Colonial India*, 1st paperback edition (Cambridge, UK and New York: Cambridge University Press, 2004), 4.
15. William Jones cited in Julie Scott Meisami, *Structure and Meaning in Medieval Arabic and Persian Poetry: Orient Pearls* (London: RoutledgeCurzon, 2003), 1.
16. William Jones, *A Grammar of the Persian Language*, 5th edition (London: Printed for J. Murray, 1801), 130.
17. Ibid., 134.

18. That linguistic analysis cannot fully account for the lack of analysis of non-English-language texts is also evident if we consider that the Bengali book in Broken Hill was most recently mislabelled by Nahid Kabir, a Bangladeshi-born historian part of the Bangladeshi diaspora in Australia. Writing in 2007 for a magazine supplement issued by a major English-language newspaper published in Dhaka, Kabir mislabelled the *Kasasol Ambia* as a 'Bangla translation of the Quran'. Nahid Kabir, 'A History of Muslims in Australia', *Star Weekend Magazine* (Supplement to Bangladeshi newspaper *Daily Star*), 7 September 2007.
19. Bernard Cohn, *Colonialism and Its Forms of Knowledge: The British in India* (Princeton: Princeton University Press, 1996), 97.
20. Rajendralal Mitra, 'On the Origin of the Hindvi Language and Its Relation to the Urdu Dialect', *Journal of the Asiatic Society of Bengal* 33, no. 5 (1864), 518.
21. Michel Foucault, *The Order of Things: Archaeology of the Human Sciences*, 2nd edition (London and New York: Routledge, 2001), xviii.
22. Wendy Doniger, ed., *The Magic Doe: Qutban Suhravardī's Mirigāvatī, A New Translation*, trans. Aditya Behl (New York: Oxford University Press, 2012), 26.
23. Reinhart Koselleck, *Futures Past: On the Semantics of Historical Time*, Studies in Contemporary German Social Thought (Cambridge, MA: MIT Press, 1985).
24. Dipesh Chakrabarty, *Provincializing Europe: Postcolonial Thought and Historical Difference* (Princeton: Princeton University Press, 2000), 72–96.
25. One of the key monographs in South Asian historiography to directly engage with Hayden White's insights was *Textures of Time*, published in 2003, which examined sixteenth-century South Indian historical storytelling to develop methodologies for drawing the line between 'myth' and 'history'. The scholarship on Bengali-language historiographical traditions is most voluminous for the pre-British period, with Kumkum Chatterjee, Thibaut D'Hubert and Ayesha Irani plotting how non-modern strategies for narrating the past braided together various Sanskritic and Persianate techniques. Fewer historians have undertaken methodological analyses of the ongoing use of non-Enlightenment strategies of historical storytelling in Bengali-language scholarship in the modern era, though Layli Uddin and Neilesh Bose recently addressed these issues in their research on East Bengal. Explicitly shifting the focus to what I describe in this book as knowledge relations, Varuni Bhatia has plotted the nineteenth-century emergence of a new, anxious reading technique that she calls 'unforgetting' between Bengali speakers and texts from non-modern historiographical traditions.

Velchuru Narayana Rao et. al., *Textures of Time: Writing History in South India* (New York: Other Press, 2003); Sheldon Pollock, 'Forum: Textures of Time', *History and Theory* 46 (October 2007), 364–81; Kumkum Chatterjee, *The Cultures of History in Early Modern India: Persianization and Mughal Culture in Bengal* (New Delhi: Oxford University Press, 2009); Thibaut d'Hubert, *In the Shade of the Golden Palace: Ālāol and Middle Bengali Poetics in Arakan*, South Asia Research (New York: Oxford University Press, 2018); Ayesha A. Irani, 'Sacred Biography, Translation, and Conversion: The "Nabivamsa" of Saiyad Sultan and the Making of Bengali Islam, 1600–Present' (PhD Thesis, University of Pennsylvania, 2011); Layli Uddin, 'In The Land of Eternal Eid: Maulana Bhashani and the Political Mobilisation of Peasants and Lower-Class Urban Workers in East Pakistan, c.1930s–1971' (PhD Thesis, Royal Holloway, University of London, 2015); Neilesh Bose, 'Purba Pakistan Zindabad: Bengali Visions of Pakistan, 1940–1947'. *Modern Asian Studies* 48, no. 1 (January 2014), 1–36; Varuni Bhatia, *Unforgetting Chaitanya: Vaishnavism and Cultures of Devotion in Colonial Bengal* (Oxford and New York: Oxford University Press, 2017).

26. For example, Anand Vivek Taneja's *Jinnealogy* (2017) examines *jinns* in Delhi as ongoing transmitters of knowledges erased by modern nation-states and Indrani Chatterjee's *Forgotten Friends* (2013) places woman-centred chains of knowledge transmission at the heart of non-modern South Asian govermentalities. Examining Punjabi-language love stories, Farina Mir's *The Social Space of Language* (2010) demonstrates the ongoing resilience of some forms of popular knowledges to the twin onslaught of British colonial reform and modernist Islamic reform. Revisiting the thirteenth-century *Chachnama*, a Persian text long 'mislabelled, miscategorised, misinterpreted' by British orientalists, Manan Ahmed Asif's *Book of Conquest* (2016) highlights the contemporary oral circulation of its metaphors, taking the cue from popular understandings of the text to construct new interpretive methods. Anand Vivek Taneja, *Jinnealogy: Time, Islam, and Ecological Thought in the Medieval Ruins of Delhi*, 1st edition (Stanford: Stanford University Press, 2017); Indrani Chatterjee, *Forgotten Friends: Monks, Marriages, and Memories of Northeast India* (New Delhi: Oxford University Press, 2013); Farina Mir, *The Social Space of Language: Vernacular Culture in British Colonial Punjab*, South Asia Across the Disciplines 2 (Berkeley: University of California Press, 2010); Manan Ahmed Asif, *A Book of Conquest: The Chachnama and Muslim Origins in South Asia* (Cambridge, MA: Harvard University Press, 2016).
27. Aditya Behl, 'Qutban from Mrigavati: Translated from the Hindavi', *Calque* 5 (February 2009), 68, fn. 1.
28. Ibid., 78.

29. Sukumar Sen, *Battalar Chappa O Chobi* (Kolkata: Ananda Publishers, 2008).
30. Gautam Bhadra, 'Rashbhab Manoharini', *Robbar* (Supplement to Newspaper *Sambaad Protidin*), 12 December 2010, 12–16. Bhadra discusses Kazi Sofiuddin at some length in Gautam Bhadra. *Nyera Battalae Jae Kaubar* (Kolkata: Chatim Books, 2011).
31. I am indebted to Partha Chatterjee for providing me with Gautam Bhadra's phone number.
32. 'Minute on Education by Thomas Macaulay' (1835), reproduced in Martin Moir and Lynn Zastoupil, eds, *The Great Indian Education Debate: Documents Relating To the Orientalist-Anglicist Controversy, 1781–1843* (Richmond, Surrey: Curzon, 1999), 162–73: 65.
33. Ibid., 166.
34. Ibid., 171.
35. Shaikh Ghulam Maqsud Hilali, *Perso-Arabic Elements in Bengali*, ed. Muhammad Enamul Huq (Rajshahi: Hilali Foundation, 2005), 56.
36. Carlo Ginzburg, 'Morelli, Freud and Sherlock Holmes: Clues and Scientific Method', trans. Anna Davin, *History Workshop* 9 (1 April 1980), 5–36: 7.
37. Ibid., 28.
38. Ibid.
39. Ibid., 27, 29.
40. Michel Foucault, *Power/Knowledge: Selected Interviews and Other Writings, 1972–1977* (Brighton, Sussex: Harvester Press, 1980), 82.
41. Vivek Bald et al., 'Introduction', in *The Sun Never Sets: South Asian Migrants in an Age of U.S. Power* (New York: New York University Press, 2013), 3. Shifting the focus away from examinations of the 'model minority', North American writers have focused on histories of politically active South Asians involved in anti-colonial projects such as the Ghadar movement, and Britain-based writers have explored the long history of political alliances between South Asians and socialist movements. In addition to historians excavating the 'lost histories' of labouring South Asians who have long been 'jumping ship and skirting empire', writers such as Jane McCabe and Gaiutra Bahadur have innovated new forms of historical storytelling in tracing the trajectories that their South Asian ancestors travelled across Anglo imperial terrains. Farzana Shain, 'Uneasy Alliances: British Muslims and Socialists since the 1950s', *Journal of Communist Studies and Transition Politics* 25, no. 1 (1 March 2009), 95–109. Vivek Bald, *Bengali Harlem and the Lost Histories of South Asian America* (Cambridge, MA: Harvard University Press, 2013). There have also been some extraordinary accounts of the 'lost histories' of South Asian labourers in Australian and New Zealand scholarship, which has for the most part not connected with

the debates on South Asian labour and identity recently to have emerged from the US and Canada. See Mark McKenna, *From the Edge: Australia's Lost Histories* (Carlton, Victoria: Melbourne University Publishing, 2016); Tony Ballantyne, 'Te Anu's Story: A Fragmentary History of Difference and Racialisation in Southern New Zealand', in Alison Holland and Barbara Brooks, eds, *Rethinking the Racial Moment: Essays on the Colonial Encounter* (Newcastle: Cambridge Scholars Publishing, 2011), 49–74.

42. Vivek Bald, 'American Orientalism', *Dissent Magazine*, Spring 2015, http://www.dissentmagazine.org/article/american-orientalism, last accessed 8 April 2012.
43. Philip Jones and Anna Kenny, *Australia's Muslim Cameleers: Pioneers of the Inland, 1860s–1930s* (Adelaide: South Australian Museum, 2007), 132.
44. Hsu-Ming Teo, 'Multiculturalism and the Problem of Multicultural Histories: An Overview of Ethnic Historiography', in Richard White and Hsu-Ming Teo, eds, *Cultural History in Australia* (Sydney: UNSW Press, 2003), 150.
45. Marilyn Lake and Henry Reynolds, *Drawing the Global Colour Line: White Men's Countries and the International Challenge of Racial Equality* (Cambridge, UK: Cambridge University Press, 2008), 4.
46. For example, see the work of Ali Cobby Eckermann, *Inside My Mother* (Artamon: Giramondo Publishing, 2015); Ali Cobby Eckermann, *Too Afraid to Cry* (Elsternwick: Ilura Press, 2012).
47. Bald et al., 'Introduction', in *The Sun Never Sets*, 7.
48. Shahid Amin, *Conquest and Community: The Afterlife of Warrior Saint Ghazi Miyan* (New Delhi: Orient BlackSwan, 2015), 190.
49. For an account of elite South Asians' active participation in the production of the 'Aryan' idea, see Tony Ballantyne, *Orientalism and Race: Aryanism in the British Empire*, Cambridge Imperial and Post-Colonial Studies Series (Basingstoke: Palgrave, 2002).
50. Marcia Langton, 'Out From the Shadows: The Development of the Aboriginal Tracker Figure in Australian Film', *Meanjin* 65, no. 1 (2006), 54–64.
51. For accounts of these encounters, see Ann Curthoys, *Freedom Ride: A Freedom Rider Remembers* (Crows Nest: Allen & Unwin, 2002); Heather Goodall and Kevin Cook, *Making Change Happen* (Canberra: ANU Press, 2013).
52. Kevin Buzzacott, *Lake Eyre is Calling* (Murray Bridge: Nyiri Publications, 1998), 7.
53. Deborah Bird Rose, 'Writing Place', in Ann Curthoys and Ann McGrath, eds, *Writing Histories: Imagination and Narration* (Clayton: Monash University ePress, 2009), 117.

54. In 2004, I co-organised a public history project interrogating contemporary race relations between non-Aboriginal and Aboriginal people in response to a race riot in Sydney. For further information, see the documentary that arose from this project: Oliver Lawrance and Melissa Abraham, *Freedom Rides: 40 Years On* (DVD) (Sydney: Australians for Native Title and Reconciliation, 2012), 50 mins.
55. I am greatly indebted to Nat Wasley and Paddy Gibson for delivering my letter to Kevin Buzzacott.
56. See Heather Goodall and Allison Cadzow, *Rivers and Resilience: Aboriginal People on Sydney's Georges River* (Sydney: UNSW Press, 2009); Hokari, *Gurindji Journey*; Deborah Bird Rose, *Nourishing Terrains: Australian Aboriginal Views of Landscape and Wilderness* (Canberra: Australian Heritage Commission, 1996); Ingereth Macfarlane, 'A Water History of the Western Simpson Desert, South Australia', in M. A. Smith and P. Hesse, eds, *23°S: Archaeology and Environmental History of Southern Deserts* (Canberra: National Museum of Australia, 2005); Ingereth MacFarlane, 'Entangled Places: Interactive Histories in the Western Simpson Desert, Central Australia' (PhD Thesis, Australian National University, 2010).
57. Rose, 'Writing Place', 123.
58. See Michael Walsh, 'Languages and their Status in Aboriginal Australia', in Colin Yallop and Michael Walsh, eds, *Language and Culture in Aboriginal Australia* (Canberra: Aboriginal Studies Press, 1993), 6; Alan Walker and R. David Zorc, 'Austronesian Loanwords in Yolngu-Matha of Northeast Arnhem Land', *Aboriginal History* 5 (1981), 109–34: 156. On the influence of Islam on Aboriginal people on the northern coast of Australia, see Peta Stephenson, *Islam Dreaming: Indigenous Muslims in Australia* (Sydney: UNSW Press, 2010), 297.
59. Pamila Gupta, 'Prologue', in Pamila Gupta, Isabel Hofmeyr and Michael Pearson, *Eyes Across the Water: Navigating the Indian Ocean* (Pretoria: Unisa Press; Delhi: Penguin India, 2010), 4. See Devleena Ghosh and Stephen Muecke, eds, *Cultures of Trade: Indian Ocean Exchanges* (Newcastle: Cambridge Scholars Publishing, 2007); Sugata Bose, *A Hundred Horizons: The Indian Ocean in the Age of Global Empire* (Cambridge, MA: Harvard University Press, 2006); Engseng Ho, *The Graves of Tarim: Genealogy and Mobility Across the Indian Ocean* (Berkeley and London: University of California Press, 2006); Nile Green, *Bombay Islam: The Religious Economy of the West Indian Ocean, 1840–1915* (New York: Cambridge University Press, 2011); Kai Kresse and Edward Simpson, eds, *Struggling With History: Islam and Cosmopolitanism in the Western Indian Ocean* (New York: Columbia University Press, 2008); Shanty Moorthy and Ashraf Jamal, eds, *Indian Ocean Studies:*

Cultural, Social and Political Perspectives (New York and London: Routledge, 2010).

60. Manan Ahmed, 'A New Cartography of Imperial Power', *The National* (Abu Dhabi), 17 December 2010, 4–7. For example, see the review essay by Claire Anderson, '"Process Geographies" of Mobility and Movement in the Indian Ocean: A Review Essay', *Journal of Colonialism and Colonial History* 8 (2007). For more information on the Five Eyes alliance, see 'Snowden Digital Surveillance Archive', https://snowdenarchive.cjfe.org/, last accessed 4 March 2015.
61. A number of Australian writers over the last decade have considered the 'view from within the Indian Archipelago' to connect to histories across the Indian Ocean rim, and I build here on their path-breaking scholarship. See Heather Goodall, Devleena Ghosh and Lindi Todd, 'Jumping Ship – Skirting Empire: Indians, Aborigines and Australians Across the Indian Ocean', *Transforming Cultures EJournal* 3 (2008), 44–74; Heather Goodall, 'Port Politics: Indian Seamen, Australian Unions and Indonesian Independence', *Labour History* 94 (2008), 43–68; Heather Goodall, 'Landscapes of Meaning: Views from Within the Indian Archipelago', *Transforming Cultures EJournal* 3 (2008), i–xiii; Haripriya Rangan and Christian Kull, 'The Indian Ocean and the Making of Outback Australia: An Ecocultural Odyssey', in *Indian Ocean Studies: Cultural, Social, and Political Perspectives* (New York and London: Routledge, 2010), 45–72.
62. Richard Tanter, 'The "Joint Facilities" Revisited: Desmond Ball, Democratic Debate on Security, and the Human Interest', NAPSNet Special Reports (Nautilus Institute for Security and Sustainability Special Report, 11 December 2012), 34.
63. Phillip Dorling, 'Pine Gap Drives US Drone Kills', *Sydney Morning Herald*, 21 July 2013, http://www.smh.com.au/national/pine-gap-drives-us-drone-kills-20130720–2qbsa.html, last accessed 2 June 2016.
64. Edward Said, *Orientalism* (London: Penguin, 2003 [1979]), 24.
65. Ibid.
66. Catherine Hall, *Macaulay and Son: Architects of Imperial Britain* (New Haven: Yale University Press, 2012), 320.
67. Dipesh Chakrabarty, 'Aboriginal and Subaltern Histories', in Bain Attwood and Tom Griffith, eds, *Frontier, Race, Nation: Henry Reynolds and Australian History* (Melbourne: Australian Scholarly Publishing, 2009), 55–70: 56.
68. C. L. R. James, *The Black Jacobins; Toussaint L'Ouverture and the San Domingo Revolution*, 2nd edition, rev. (New York: Vintage Books, 1963), 24–5.
69. Ibid., 18, fn. 12.

70. David Scott, *Conscripts of Modernity: The Tragedy of Colonial Enlightenment* (Durham, NC: Duke University Press, 2004), 52.
71. Ibid., 51.
72. Crystal McKinnon, 'Indigenous Music as a Space of Resistance', in Tracy Banivanua-Mar and Penelope Edmonds, eds, *Making Settler Colonial Space: Perspectives on Race, Place and Identity* (New York: Palgrave Macmillan, 2010), 264.
73. McKinnon citing Ronald Wendt in ibid., 269.

2. STORIES OF THE PROPHETS

1. Linguist Sukumar Sen gives 1861 as the date of first publication of Kazi Sofiuddin's *Kasasol Ambia* and, as far as I am aware, the earliest mention of the book was by Rajendralal Mitra in 1864. However, the first book itself carries no mention of its date. With Sofiuddin publishing books from 1855, Munshi Rezaulla may have actually authored the poetry before the events of 1857. Sukumar Sen, *Battalar Chappa O Chobi* (Kolkata: Ananda Publishers, 2008), 50.
2. Marilyn Lake and Henry Reynolds, *Drawing the Global Colour Line: White Men's Countries and the International Challenge of Racial Equality* (Cambridge, UK: Cambridge University Press, 2008), 8.
3. Kazi Sofiuddin, *Kasasol Ambia* (Calcutta: Hanifia Press, 1895), 3.
4. Ibid.
5. Ronald Inden, 'Orientalist Constructions of India', *Modern Asian Studies* 20, no. 3 (1986), 401–46.
6. Ibid., 444.
7. Ibid., 445.
8. Linda Tuhiwai Smith, *Decolonizing Methodologies: Research and Indigenous Peoples* (Dunedin: University of Otago Press, 1999), 59.
9. Sofiuddin, *Kasasol Ambia*, 5–6.
10. Ibid., 6.
11. Ibid.
12. Ibid.
13. Ibid.
14. Wendy Doniger, ed., *The Magic Doe: Qutban Suhravardī's Mirigāvatī, A New Translation*, trans. Aditya Behl (New York: Oxford University Press, 2012), 31.
15. Ibid., 30.
16. Darrin Manuel, 'Student Pursues Ancient Book's Origin', *Barrier Daily Truth*, 21 July 2009, 1.
17. C. W. Bolton, Government of Bengal, Undersecretary to the Secretary, Government of India, Home Department, 29 April 1879, cited in

Tapti Roy, 'Disciplining the Printed Text: Colonial and Nationalist Surveillance of Bengali Literature', in *Texts of Power: Emerging Disciplines in Colonial Bengal* (Minneapolis: University of Minnesota Press, 1995), 47–8.

18. Ibid.
19. J. Long, *Returns Relating to Publications in the Bengali Language, in 1857*, Selections from the Records of the Bengal Government, XXXII (Calcutta: John Gray, General Printing Department, 1859), xxii–xxx; Anindita Ghosh, *Power in Print: Popular Publishing and the Politics of Language and Culture in a Colonial Society* (Delhi: Oxford University Press, 2006), 259–84.
20. The *payar* metre consists of couplets of twenty-eight syllables arranged as 4–4–6 and 4–4–6.
21. Sofiuddin, *Kasasol Ambia*, 4.
22. Ibid., 10.
23. Ibid.
24. Ibid., 18–20.
25. Ibid., 21–2.
26. Sheldon I. Pollock, *The Language of the Gods in the World of Men: Sanskrit, Culture, and Power in Premodern India* (Berkeley: University of California Press, 2006).
27. Ronald Inden, *Imagining India* (Oxford and Cambridge, MA: Basil Blackwell, 1990), 49–84; Nicholas B. Dirks, *Castes of Mind: Colonialism and the Making of Modern India* (Princeton: Princeton University Press, 2001), 19–42.
28. Book X, verse 90 in Stephanie W. Jamison and Joel P. Brereton, eds, *The Rigveda: The Earliest Religious Poetry of India*, South Asia Research (Oxford: Oxford University Press, 2014), 1540.
29. Bernard Cohn, *Colonialism and Its Forms of Knowledge: The British in India* (Princeton: Princeton University Press, 1996), 28.
30. Andre Couture, 'From Viṣṇu's Deeds to Viṣṇu's Play, or Observations on the Word Avatāra as a Designation for the Manifestations of Viṣṇu', *Journal of Indian Philosophy* 29, no. 3 (2001), 314–15; Ayesha A. Irani, 'Sacred Biography, Translation, and Conversion: The "Nabivamsa" of Saiyad Sultan and the Making of Bengali Islam, 1600–Present' (PhD Thesis, University of Pennsylvania, 2011), 260.
31. Bernard Cohn, 'The Census, Social Structure and Objectification in South Asia', in Bernard Cohn, ed., *An Anthropologist Among the Historians and Other Essays* (Delhi: Oxford University Press, 1987), 224–54.
32. Bernard Cohn, 'Representing Authority in Victorian India', in E. J. Hobsbawm and T. O. Ranger, eds, *The Invention of Tradition*, Past and

Present Publications (Cambridge, UK and New York: Cambridge University Press, 1983), 182.

33. Syed Mustafa Siraj, *Aleek Manush* (Kolkata: Sahitya Akademi, 2005), 25–6.
34. Sofiuddin, *Kasasol Ambia*, 61–8.
35. Ibid., 75.
36. Port Augusta Public Library, Local History File Anderson 37, Extract from Diary of Samuel J. Stuckey, 1862–1866.
37. Hasan Musakhan, 'First Mosque Built in Australasia', *Mirror*, 16 August 1924, 8.
38. 'More Camels for the Interior', *Evening Journal*, 25 April 1885, 4.
39. '320 Camels', *Daily News*, 17 January 1895, 2.
40. 'Advertising: Mirza Khan, Bookbinder', *Daily News*, 17 July 1888, 2.
41. Western Australian Registry of Births, Deaths and Marriages, Marriages, 000049W/1890, Marriage Certificate of Julia Thorne and Mirza Khan, 9 March 1890.
42. State Records Office of Western Australia: Colonial Secretary's Office, Passenger Lists and Immigration Records; Accession 108, Albany Inwards from Eastern States 1873–1930; Item 6, Roll 43, Incoming Passengers to Albany, *Bullara* arrived 17 July 1894.
43. Fayz Muhammad Katib Hazarah, *The History of Afghanistan*, trans. R. D. McChesney, annotated edition, vol. 3 (Leiden and Boston: Brill Academic Publishers, 2012), 1272.
44. 'Messrs. E. Laughton and Co.', *Barrier Miner*, 22 February 1895, 3.
45. Gunny Khan, 'The Camel Nuisance', *Barrier Miner*, 23 May 1904, 2.
46. Hazarah, *The History of Afghanistan*, vol. 3, 1272.
47. Gunny Khan, 'Afghan National Character', *Western Herald*, 13 December 1893, 2.
48. Gunny Khan, 'Mohammedanism in Perth', *West Australian*, 13 April 1896, 3. 'News of the Week', *Western Mail*, 27 December 1895, 32.
49. Khan, 'Mohammedanism in Perth', 3.
50. Roberta J. Drewery, *Treks, Camps, & Camels: Afghan Cameleers Their Contribution to Australia* (Broken Hill: Published by Author, 2008), 90.
51. Sofiuddin, *Kasasol Ambia*, 89–90.
52. Ibid., 230.
53. Ibid., 230–3.
54. Ibid., 2.
55. I am indebted to Heather Goodall for sharing her research data that confirms that many sailors had 'Kidderpore' addresses in Calcutta. See Heather Goodall, 'Port Politics: Indian Seamen, Australian Unions and Indonesian Independence', *Labour History* 94 (2008), 43–68.
56. Here I have determined the names of these two men by comparing the entries in the 'Register of Deserters' from the *Darius* on 2 May

1895 at Adelaide with the Incoming Passenger list of *Darius* on 17 May 1895 at Sydney. Public Record Office Victoria, VA 606, Department of Trade and Customs; VPRS 946, Registers of Deserters and Discharged Seamen, 1888–1895; Consignment P0000, unit 5; Page 60, Deserters from the *Darius* at Adelaide, 2 May 1895. NSW State Archives: Shipping Master's Office; NRS 13278, Inward Passengers Lists, 1855–1922; Reel 527, Incoming passengers to Sydney, SS *Darius* arrived 17 May 1895.

57. Janet J. Ewald, 'Crossers of the Sea: Slaves, Freedmen, and Other Migrants in the Northwestern Indian Ocean, c. 1750–1914', *The American Historical Review* 105, no. 1 (2000), 76.
58. 'Imports May 4 *Darius*', *The Age*, 7 May 1895, 4.
59. 'The Steamer *Darius*', *South Australian Register*, 3 May 1895, 5.
60. 'Maritime Record', *Australian Star*, 7 May 1895, 4.
61. Herman Melville, *Redburn, His First Voyage, A Novel* (New York: Anchor Books, 1957), 165.
62. M. Watkins-Thomas, 'Our Asian Crews', *About Ourselves: (P & O Staff Journal)* (September 1955), no page.
63. 'Loss of Maloja', *The Argus*, 1 March 1916, 9.
64. 'Maritime Record', 4.
65. Ibid.
66. Gopalan Balachandran, 'Cultures of Protest in Transnational Contexts: Indian Seamen Abroad, 1886–1945', *Transforming Cultures EJournal* 3 (2008), 46.
67. 'The Steamer *Darius*', 5.
68. 'Asiatic Immigrants', *The Express and Telegraph*, 3 May 1895, 2.
69. Ibid.
70. 'Lascars on Strike', *Newcastle Morning Herald and Miners' Advocate*, 22 October 1888, 3. 'Lascars on Strike', *Newcastle Morning Herald and Miners' Advocate*, 26 November 1888, 5.
71. John Maynard, '"In the Interests of Our People": The Influence of Garveyism on the Rise of Australian Aboriginal Political Activism', *Aboriginal History* 29 (2005), 3.
72. 'Lascars on Strike the *Aparima*'s Crew Put on Board by Police', *Williamstown Chronicle*, 11 February 1911, 3.
73. 'Southern News', *Daily Standard*, 21 June 1922, 6.
74. Heather Goodall, Devleena Ghosh and Lindi Todd, 'Jumping Ship – Skirting Empire: Indians, Aborigines and Australians Across the Indian Ocean', *Transforming Cultures EJournal* 3 (2008), 44–74.
75. Cited in Jane Simpson, 'Camels as Pidgin-Carriers: Afghan Cameleers as a Vector for the Spread of Features of Australian Aboriginal Pidgins and Creoles', in Jeff Siegel, ed., *Processes of Language Contact: Studies*

from Australia and the South Pacific (Fides: Champs Linguistiques, 2000), 207.

76. Maynard, 'In the Interests of Our People', 2–4.
77. Sofiuddin, *Kasasol Ambia*, 150–2.
78. For example, Mrigavati, cited in Aditya Behl, 'The Magic Doe: Desire and Narrative in a Hindavi Sufi Romance, circa 1503', in Richard Maxwell Eaton, ed., *India's Islamic Traditions, 711–1750*, Oxford in India Readings (New Delhi and New York: Oxford University Press, 2003), 191.
79. 'Ben Murray to Philip Jones, 3.11.83' in Peter Austin, Luise Hercus and Philip Jones, 'Ben Murray (Parlku-Nguyu-Thangknyiwarna)', *Aboriginal History* 12 (1988), 128.
80. Violet Turner, *Pearls from the Deep: The Story of Colebrook Home for Aboriginal Children* (Adelaide: United Aborigines Mission, 1936), 8.
81. Khan, 'The Camel Nuisance', 2.
82. For the role of creeks and riverbeds in Aboriginal communities' resistance and resilience, see Heather Goodall and Allison Cadzow, *Rivers and Resilience: Aboriginal People on Sydney's Georges River* (Sydney: UNSW Press, 2009).
83. 'Ben Murray to Philip Jones, 3.11.83' in Austin, Hercus and Jones, 'Ben Murray (Parlku-Nguyu-Thangknyiwarna)', 154.
84. Rabindranath Tagore, 'Kabuliwallah', in *Galpa Guchcha* (Dhaka: Nouroj Sahitya Sangsad, 1990), 84–9.
85. The details given by Sher Khan of his age and date of arrival in the Australian colonies in Yatala prison records match those of 'Sheramul Khan' in the passenger list of a ship travelling from Calcutta to Melbourne in 1900, which saw the arrival of thirty-one South Asian men contracted to the businessman Abdul Wade, also on board that vessel. State Records of South Australia, GRG 54/41, Register of prisoners, Yatala Labour Prison; Consignment 00000, unit 4, vol. 3, file no. 3952, Sher Khan, 2 August 1904. Public Record Office Victoria, VA 606, Department of Trade and Customs; VPRS 947, Inward Overseas Passenger Lists, 1852–1923; Consignment P0000, unit 54, April–Jun 1900; Incoming Passenger List to Melbourne, SS *Argus* arrived 2 May 1900.
86. 'Circuit Court', *Port Augusta Dispatch*, 22 July 1904, 3.
87. 'Was It Marriage or Betrothal?', *Advertiser*, 26 February 1904, 4.
88. 'Police Court', *Port Augusta Dispatch*, 24 June 1904, 2.
89. 'An Afghan Shot', *Register*, 25 May 1904, 5.
90. Charley, cited in 'Police Court', 2.
91. Austin, Hercus and Jones, 'Ben Murray (Parlku-Nguyu-Thangknyiwarna)', 145–56. In addition to the published English translation that I have

cited here, a recording of Ben Murray's Dhirari story about Sher Khan is held today at Australian Institute of Aboriginal and Torres Strait Islander Studies, Audiovisual Archives; Austin P07, Sound recordings collected by Peter Kenneth Austin, 1975–1976; Recording 004002A, timecode 00:52.00–01.00.00, Oral history elicitation in Dhirari with Ben Murray at Farina, 28 November 1975.

92. Austin, Hercus and Jones, 'Ben Murray (Parlku-Nguyu-Thangknyi-warna)', 155.
93. Ibid.
94. Ibid.
95. Ibid.
96. SRSA, GRG54/41/0/4/3/3952.
97. Sofiuddin, *Kasasol Ambia*, 251–4.
98. Ibid., 251.
99. Ibid., 253.
100. Annette Potts, '"I Am a British Subject, and I Can Go Wherever the British Flag Flies": Indians on the Northern Rivers of New South Wales during the Federation Years', *Journal of the Royal Australian Historical Society* 83, no. 2 (1997), 105.
101. Vivek Bald, *Bengali Harlem and the Lost Histories of South Asian America* (Cambridge, MA: Harvard University Press, 2013), 20.
102. 'East Indian Natives in Melbourne', *The Age*, 15 June 1885, 5.
103. National Archives of Australia: Collector of Customs, Western Australia; PP4/2, Applications for certificates of exemption from dictation test with supporting documents, annual single number series; 1931/64, Abdul Sattar [Indian], 1905–1931; Form filled in by Abdul Sattar, 8 July 1903.
104. Ibid.
105. National Archives of Australia: Department of External Affairs, Melbourne; A8, Correspondence files, folio system, 1895–1905; 1902/182/4, Report on the Emigration of Indians from Calcutta to Australia, 1900; List showing the number of passengers who proceeded from Calcutta to the Australian ports.
106. NSW State Archives: Shipping Master's Office; NRS 13278, Inward Passengers Lists, 1855–1922; Reel 542, Incoming passengers to Sydney, SS *Orissa* arrived 22 December 1897.
107. 'Syrian and Indian Hawkers', *Sydney Morning Herald*, 3 January 1896, 3.
108. 'Hawkers' Licenses: The Assyrian Comes Down', *The Australian Star*, 4 January 1895, 3.
109. Ibid.
110. 'Inland River Navigation', *Sydney Morning Herald*, 11 March 1905, 15.

111. 'Fatal Boat Accident at Kotupna – Three Men Drowned', *The Age*, 24 October 1893, 5.
112. Ibid.
113. 'New South Wales', *Brisbane Courier*, 13 December 1898, 5.
114. NAA: PP4/2, 1931/64; Letter from Abdul Sattar in Hooghly to the Hon. Collector of Customs, Fremantle West Australia, 13th April 1911.
115. Ibid.
116. Philip Jones and Anna Kenny, *Australia's Muslim Cameleers: Pioneers of the Inland, 1860s–1930s* (Adelaide: South Australian Museum, 2007).
117. Sofiuddin, *Kasasol Ambia*, 501–2.
118. Ibid., 502.
119. Fatima Mernissi, *Women and Islam: An Historical and Theological Enquiry*, trans. Mary Jo Lakeland (Oxford: Basil Blackwell, 1991), 177.
120. Christine Stevens, *Tin Mosques & Ghantowns: A History of Afghan Cameldrivers in Australia* (Melbourne: Oxford University Press, 1989), 212. Margaret Allen, '"Innocents Abroad" and "Prohibited Immigrants"; Australians in India and Indians in Australia 1890–1910', in Ann Curthoys and Marilyn Lake, eds, *Connected Worlds: History in Transnational Perspective Canberra* (Canberra: ANU E Press, 2005), 81.
121. Allen, '"Innocents Abroad" and "Prohibited Immigrants"', 121.
122. Ho, *The Graves of Tarim*, xxii.
123. Jan Gothard, 'Assisted Female Immigration, 1860–1920', in James Jupp, ed., *The Australian People: An Encyclopedia of the Nation, Its People and Their Origins*, 2nd edition (Cambridge, UK and Oakleigh, Victoria: Cambridge University Press, 2001), 53–7.
124. 'Law Report County Court', *The Argus*, 2 July 1870, 6.
125. Public Record Office Victoria, VA 606, Department of Trade and Customs; VPRS 948, Outward Passengers to Interstate, U.K. and Foreign Ports, 1852–1923; Consignment P0001, unit 33, July–December 1870; Outgoing Passenger List from Melbourne, *Loch Lomond* departed from Melbourne on 26 July 1870.
126. Public Record Office Victoria, VA 606, Department of Trade and Customs; VPRS 947, Inward Overseas Passenger Lists, 1852–1923; Consignment P0000, unit 44, April–June 1891; Incoming Passenger List to Melbourne, SS *Bucephalus* arrived 12 May 1891. Public Record Office Victoria, VA 606, Department of Trade and Customs; VPRS 947, Inward Overseas Passenger Lists, 1852–1923; Consignment P0000, unit 49, January–April 1895; Incoming Passenger List to Melbourne, SS *Argus* arrived 4 March 1895. Public Record Office Victoria, VA 606, Department of Trade and Customs; VPRS 947, Inward Overseas Passenger Lists, 1852–1923; Consignment P0000,

unit 47, Incoming Passenger List to Melbourne, SS *Bhundara* arrived 17 September 1893.

127. Khawajah Muhammad Bux, 'Memoirs of Khawajah Muhammad Bux, Australian Businessman' (Unpublished Manuscript), trans. Syed Haider Hassan (Rawalpindi, Pakistan, 2006), 94.
128. Rokeya Sakhawat Hossein, 'Sultana's Dream', in Firdous Azim and Niaz Zaman, eds, *Galpa: Short Stories by Women from Bangladesh* (London: Stanza, 1905), 17–27.
129. Doniger, *The Magic Doe*, 69–71.
130. Sanjida Khatun, *Atit Diner Smriti* (Dhaka: Prakash, 1993), 40.
131. NSW State Archives: Shipping Master's Office; NRS 13278, Inward Passengers Lists, 1855–1922; Reel 539, Incoming passengers to Sydney, SS *Nuddea* arrived 28 June 1897.
132. This is suggested by a photograph of Mrs Marm Deen in National Archives of Australia: Collector of Customs, Melbourne; B13, General and classified correspondence, annual single number series, 1902–; 1922/7393, Mr & Mrs Marm Deen and Family – Re-admission to Australia, 1913–1922; Photograph of Mr and Mrs Marm Deen and their four daughters.
133. Example: NSW State Archives: Shipping Master's Office; NRS 13278, Inward Passengers Lists, 1855–1922; Reel 535, Incoming passengers to Sydney, SS *Lalpoora* arrived 10 October 1896.
134. Public Record Office Victoria, VA 606, Department of Trade and Customs; VPRS 947, Inward Overseas Passenger Lists, 1852–1923; Consignment P0000, unit 50, September–December 1897; Incoming Passenger List to Melbourne, *Bancoora* arrived 10 September 1895. NSW State Archives: Shipping Master's Office; NRS 13278, Inward Passengers Lists, 1855–1922; Reel 529, Incoming passengers to Sydney, *Bancoora* arrived 14 September 1895.
135. 'Syrians and the Aliens Bill: Female Hawkers', *Sunday Times*, 25 October 1896, 5.
136. Ruby Langford Ginibi, *Real Deadly* (North Ryde: Angus & Robertson, 1992), 75.
137. 'Shipping Notes', *Daily News*, 14 January 1895, 4.
138. See Rajeev Kinra, *Writing Self, Writing Empire: Chandar Bhan Brahman and the Cultural World of the Indo-Persian State Secretary*, South Asia Across the Disciplines (Oakland, CA: University of California Press, 2015), 60–94.
139. Michel Foucault, *The Order of Things: Archaeology of the Human Sciences*, 2nd edition (London and New York: Routledge, 2001), xviii–xix.
140. I am indebted to Taimur Reza at the University of Chicago for drawing my attention to this copy of *Kasasol Ambia*.

141. Franz Rosenthal, *The History of Al-Tabari Vol. 1: General Introduction and From the Creation to the Flood* (Albany: SUNY Press, 1989), 198.
142. Tabari identifies each of these transmitters by placing them within a male lineage in ibid.
143. Ibid., 199.
144. See Andrew Peacock, *Mediaeval Islamic Historiography and Political Legitimacy Bal'ami's Tarikhnamah* (Hoboken: Taylor and Francis, 2013).
145. Janet L. Abu-Lughod, 'The Islamic City – Historic Myth, Islamic Essence, and Contemporary Relevance', *International Journal of Middle East Studies* 19, no. 2 (1 May 1987), 155.
146. Franz Rosenthal, *A History of Muslim Historiography*, 2nd edition (Leiden: Brill, 1968), 74.
147. Kumkum Chatterjee, 'The Persianization of "Itihasa": Performance Narratives and Mughal Political Culture in Eighteenth-Century Bengal', *The Journal of Asian Studies* 67, no. 2 (1 May 2008), 516.

3. SEVEN VOYAGES OF KHAWAJAH MUHAMMAD BUX

1. Husain Haddawy, trans., *Sindbad And Other Stories from the Arabian Nights* (New York: W. W. Norton and Company, 2008), 3.
2. Ibid., 15.
3. 'Sindbad the Wise' appears in *Kitab-al-Fihirist* compiled by Ibn al-Nadim (d. 990). See Aditya Behl, *Love's Subtle Magic: An Indian Islamic Literary Tradition, 1379–1545*, ed. Wendy Doniger (New York: Oxford University Press, 2012), 131. Sindbad's voyages enjoyed enormous popularity with European audiences with the rise of the East India Company in the Indian Ocean. For the extremely complicated history of the translation of these tales into French and English, see Dwight Reynolds, 'A Thousand and One Nights: A History of the Text and Its Reception', in Roger M. A. Allen and D. S. Richards, eds, *Arabic Literature in the Post-Classical Period*, 1st edition, The Cambridge History of Arabic Literature (Cambridge, UK: Cambridge University Press, 2006), 270–91.
4. I am greatly indebted to Professor Gábor Korvin who made available to me the 1944 Urdu edition and 2006 English edition of Bux's travelogue. For reference to the 2006 Urdu edition, see Sarwat Ali, 'Seafarer's Tales', *The News On Sunday*, 22 June 2014, http://tns.thenews.com.pk/seafarers-tales-of-australiawale/, last accessed 7 July 2014; Samina Yasmeen, 'Muslim Australian Contributions: Bux Family as a Case Study' (Unpublished Paper, Centre for Muslim States and Societies, The University of Western Australia, 2009).
5. Kama Maclean, 'Examinations, Access, and Inequity Within the Empire: Britain, Australia and India, 1890–1910', *Postcolonial Studies* 18, no. 2

(3 April 2015), 115–32. For the parallel experiences of the Kwok family from China, see Sophie Loy-Wilson, *Australians in Shanghai: Race, Rights and Nation in Treaty Port China* (New York: Routledge, 2017).

6. 'Rise to Fortune Indian Hawker's Career £40,000 Perth Property', *Daily News*, 9 September 1929, 6. Gábor Korvin, 'Adventures of a Kashmiri Merchant in Australia – An Unknown Urdu Travelogue', *Journal of the Pakistan Historical Society* 52 (2004), 24.
7. T. L. Goodman, '"Australian" Colony In An Indian Bazaar', *Advertiser*, 12 August 1944, 13.
8. Bux mentions his *munshi* in Khawajah Muhammad Bux, 'Memoirs of Khawajah Muhammad Bux, Australian Businessman' (Unpublished Manuscript), ed. Gábor Kovin, trans. Syed Haider Hassan (Rawalpindi, Pakistan, 2006), 136, 138.
9. Yasmeen, 'Muslim Australian Contributions'.
10. The Australasia Bank is the parent company of what are today the Allied Bank in Pakistan and the Rupali Bank in Bangladesh. Rashid Amjad, 'Industrial Concentration and Economic Power in Pakistan', *Pakistan Economic and Social Review* 14, no. 1/4 (1976), 211–61: 235.
11. 'Preface by Mr Khalid Bux, Sydney, March 2004' in Bux, 'Memoirs of Khawajah Muhammad Bux', iii.
12. Ibid.
13. Samina Yasmeen, 'The Bux Family', *History West* 51, no. 3 (April 2012), 1. Korvin, 'Adventures of a Kashmiri Merchant in Australia', 33.
14. Foreword of His Excellency Babar W. Malik in Bux, 'Memoirs of Khawajah Muhammad Bux', i.
15. Vivek Bald, 'American Orientalism', *Dissent Magazine*, http://www.dissentmagazine.org/article/american-orientalism, last accessed 8 April 2012.
16. Vivek Bald et al., 'Introduction', in *The Sun Never Sets: South Asian Migrants in an Age of U.S. Power* (New York: New York University Press, 2013), 3–4. Junaid Akram Rana, *Terrifying Muslims: Race and Labor in the South Asian Diaspora* (Durham, NC: Duke University Press, 2011).
17. 'Bakhtiari Family Arrive in Pakistan', *Sydney Morning Herald*, 3 January 2005.
18. 'Bakhtiyaris Deported to Save Face, Says Centacare Head', *Catholic News*, 4 January 2005, http://cathnews.acu.edu.au/501/4.php, last accessed 25 July 2017.
19. 'Australian Companies Invited to Invest in Pakistan Islamabad', Organization of Asia-Pacific News Agencies, 25 July 2003. Thea Williams, 'Bakhtiyari Family to Be Deported to Pakistan', *The Australian*, 29 July 2003. 'Australia Urged to Liberalise Visa Policy', Pakistan Press International, 25 July 2003.

20. 'Australia to Train Pakistani Immigration Staff Islamabad,' Pakistan Press International, 25 July 2003.
21. Behl, *Love's Subtle Magic*, 119–34. Buzurg ibn Shahriyār, *The Book of the Wonders of India: Mainland, Sea, and Islands*, ed. and trans. G. S. P. Freeman-Grenville (London and The Hague: East-West Publications, 1981).
22. Haddawy, *Sindbad And Other Stories from the Arabian Nights*, 17.
23. Ibid.
24. Bux, 'Memoirs of Khawajah Muhammad Bux', 1.
25. Ibid.
26. Ibid., 2.
27. Ibid., 4.
28. Ibid., 5.
29. Ibid.
30. Ibid.
31. Ibid., 6.
32. Ibid., 152.
33. Ibid., 17.
33. Ibid., 19.
34. Ibid., 17–18.
35. Ibid., 19.
36. Janet J. Ewald, 'Crossers of the Sea: Slaves, Freedmen, and Other Migrants in the Northwestern Indian Ocean, c. 1750–1914', *The American Historical Review* 105, no. 1 (2000), 76.
37. Bux, 'Memoirs of Khawajah Muhammad Bux', 20.
38. Ibid.
39. Ibid.
40. Ibid.
41. For an analysis of rules against desertion in maritime labour law, see Ravi Ahuja, 'Mobility and Containment: The Voyages of South Asian Seamen, c. 1900–1960', *International Review of Social History* 51, (2006), 119.
42. Bux, 'Memoirs of Khawajah Muhammad Bux', 20.
43. Ibid., 21.
44. Ibid.
45. Ibid., 22.
46. Ibid.
47. Ibid.
48. This is a phrase he repeatedly uses when addressing the audience. Bux, 'Memoirs of Khawajah Muhammad Bux', 204.
49. On the *Kathasaritsagara* corpus, see Luther Obrock, 'Translation and History: The Development of a Kashmiri Textual Tradition from ca.

1000–1500' (PhD Thesis, University of California, Berkeley, 2015), 13–30; Somadeva Vasudeva, *The Ocean of the Rivers of Story*, trans. James Mallinson, 1st edition, Clay Sanskrit Library (New York: New York University Press: JJC Foundation, 2007); Budhasvāmin, *The Emperor of the Sorcerers*, trans. James Mallinson, 1st edition, Clay Sanskrit Library (New York: New York University Press: JJC Foundation, 2005).

50. Arshia Sattar, *The Mouse Merchant: Money in Ancient India* (New Delhi: Penguin, 2013), 29–30. Behl, *Love's Subtle Magic*, 132–4.
51. Bux, 'Memoirs of Khawajah Muhammad Bux', 23.
52. Ibid.
53. Ewald, 'Crossers of the Sea', 72.
54. Bux, 'Memoirs of Khawajah Muhammad Bux', 23.
55. Rajat Kanta Ray, 'Asian Capital in the Age of European Domination: The Rise of the Bazaar, 1800–1914', *Modern Asian Studies* 29 (1995), 476.
56. Bux, 'Memoirs of Khawajah Muhammad Bux', 25.
57. Ibid., 28.
58. Ray, 'Asian Capital in the Age of European Domination', 454.
59. Sattar, *The Mouse Merchant: Money in Ancient India*, 135–6.
60. Bux, 'Memoirs of Khawajah Muhammad Bux', 28.
61. Ibid.
62. Ibid., 17.
63. Sarah Waheed, 'Women of "Ill Repute": Ethics and Urdu Literature in Colonial India', *Modern Asian Studies* 48, no. 4 (July 2014), 986–1023: 993.
64. Budhasvāmin, *The Emperor of the Sorcerers*, 127–9.
65. Bux, 'Memoirs of Khawajah Muhammad Bux', 55.
66. Ibid., 29–30.
67. Ibid., 30.
68. Ibid.
69. Ibid.
70. Ibid., 31. Michael Christopher Low, '"The Infidel Piloting the True Believer": Thomas Cook and the Business of the Colonial Hajj', 5 October 2016, 67.
71. Bux, 'Memoirs of Khawajah Muhammad Bux', 31.
72. Michael Wolfe, *One Thousand Roads to Mecca: Ten Centuries of Travelers Writing About the Muslim Pilgrimage*, 1st edition (New York: Grove Press, 1997).
73. Richard Francis Burton, *Personal Narrative of a Pilgrimage to El-Medinah and Meccah* (London: Longman, Brown, Green, and Longmans, 1855), 2. Burton disguised himself as South Asian to write narratives on many occasions; see, for example, Indira Ghose, 'Imperial Player: Richard

Burton in Sindh', in Tim Youngs, ed., *Travel Writing in the Nineteenth Century: Filling the Blank Spaces* (London and New York: Anthem Press, 2006), 71–86.

74. Burton, *Personal Narrative of a Pilgrimage to El-Medinah and Meccah*, 2.
75. John Slight, 'British Colonial Knowledge and the Hajj in the Age of Empire', in Umar Ryad, ed., *The Hajj and Europe in the Age of Empire* (Leiden and Boston: Brill, 2016), 81–111: 89.
76. For example, as John Slight shows, from 1878 the British Raj began annually dispatching surgeon Dr Abdur Razzack from the Bengal Medical Service to Mecca to gather insider data about 'pauper pilgrims'. Slight, 'British Colonial Knowledge and the Hajj in the Age of Empire', 90.
77. Wael Hallaq, *Sharī'a: Theory, Practice, Transformations* (Delhi: Cambridge University Press, 2009), 3.
78. Hallaq takes the phrase 'ontological imperialism' from Emmnuel Levinas in Hallaq, *Sharī'a*, 3–4
79. Low, '"The Infidel Piloting the True Believer"', 50.
80. Bux, 'Memoirs of Khawajah Muhammad Bux', 32.
81. Ibid., 33.
82. Ibid., 34, 36.
83. Ibid., 39.
84. Ibid., 40.
85. Ibid., 41.
86. Ibid., 42.
87. Ibid.
88. Ibid., 43.
89. Wolfe, *One Thousand Roads to Mecca*. Barbara Metcalfe, 'The Pilgrimage Remembered: South Asian Accounts of the Hajj', in *Muslim Travellers: Pilgrimage, Migration, and the Religious Imagination* (Berkeley: University of California Press, 1990), 85–107.
90. Eighteenth century Punjabi poet Bulhe Shah cited in fn. 13 in Metcalfe, 'The Pilgrimage Remembered,' 103. Farina Mir's examination of nineteenth-century accounts of the Hir and Ranjha romance also points to a connection to hajj narratives in Farina Mir, 'The Social Space of Language: Punjabi Popular Narrative in Colonial India, c. 1850–1900' (PhD Thesis, Columbia University, 2002), 177.
91. Farina Mir, *The Social Space of Language: Vernacular Culture in British Colonial Punjab*, South Asia Across the Disciplines 2 (Berkeley: University of California Press, 2010), 104. For accounts of listening practices in Muslim knowledge traditions, see bibliography of J. During and R. Sellheim, 'Samāʿ', in P. Bearman, W. P. Heinrichs, C. E. Bosworth, Th. Bianquis, and E. van Donzel, eds, *Encyclopaedia of Islam, Second Edition*, 24 April 2012.

92. Abdul Majid Daryabadi, cited in Homayra Ziad, 'The Return of Gog: Politics and Pan-Islamism in the Hajj Travelogue of Abd Al-Majid Daryabadi', in *Global Muslims in the Age of Steam and Print*, 1st edition (Berkeley: University of California Press, 2014), 227–48: 235.
93. Bux, 'Memoirs of Khawajah Muhammad Bux', 47.
94. Ibid.
95. See, for example, Lionel Casson, *The Periplus Maris Erythraei: Text with Introduction, Translation, and Commentary* (Princeton: Princeton University Press, 1989), 182, 209, 238.
96. Behl, *Love's Subtle Magic*, 133.
97. Shawkat M. Toorawa, 'Wâq Al-Wâq: Fabulous, Fabular, Indian Ocean (?) Island(s) ...', *Emergences: Journal for the Study of Media & Composite Cultures* 10 (2000), 387–402: 391.
98. Bernard Cohn, 'Representing Authority in Victorian India', in E. J. Hobsbawm and T. O. Ranger, eds, *The Invention of Tradition*, Past and Present Publications (Cambridge, UK and New York: Cambridge University Press, 1983), 167.
99. Bux, 'Memoirs of Khawajah Muhammad Bux', 48.
100. I. M. Lewis, *A Modern History of the Somali: Nation and State in the Horn of Africa*, 4th edition, Eastern African Studies (Oxford: James Currey and Athens, OH: Ohio University Press, 2002), 46.
101. Bux, 'Memoirs of Khawajah Muhammad Bux', 50.
102. Ibid.
103. Ibid., 51.
104. Andrew Pope, 'The P&O and the Asian Specie Network, 1850–1920,' *Modern Asian Studies* 30 (1996), 145–72. Andrew Pope, 'Precious Metals Flow in the Indian Ocean in the Colonial Period: Australian Gold to India, 1866–1914', in John McGuire, Patrick Bertola and Peter Reeves, eds, *Evolution of the World Economy, Precious Metals and India* (Oxford: Oxford University Press, 2001).
105. Joseph Conrad, *Heart of Darkness* (London: HarperCollins, 2013 [1899]), 7.
106. Citing the *Northern Territory Times*, 17 December 1875: 2, in C. C. Macknight, *The Voyage to Marege': Macassan Trepangers in Northern Australia* (Carlton, Victoria: Melbourne University Press, 1976), 138. C. C. Macknight, 'Journal of a Voyage Around Arhem Land in 1875,' *Aboriginal History* 5, no. 2 (1981), 144.
107. Ibid., 141.
108. Mary Louise Pratt, *Imperial Eyes: Travel Writing and Transculturation*, 2nd edition (London and New York: Routledge, 2008).
109. Bux, 'Memoirs of Khawajah Muhammad Bux', 51.
110. Ibid., 51.

111. Ibid., 30.
112. Ibid., 56, 64.
113. Ibid., 52.
114. Ibid.
115. See Tony Ballantyne, 'Remaking the Empire from Newgate: Wakefield's A Letter from Sydney', in Antoinette M. Burton and Isabel Hofmeyr, eds, *Ten Books That Shaped the British Empire: Creating an Imperial Commons* (Durham, NC: Duke University Press, 2014).
116. Radhika Viyas Mongia, 'Race, Nationality, Mobility: A History of the Passport', *Public Culture* 11, no. 3 (1999), 532.
117. Bux, 'Memoirs of Khawajah Muhammad Bux', 52.
118. Gopalan Balachandran, 'Circulation through Seafaring: Indian Seamen, 1890–1945', in Claude Markovits, Jaques Pouchepadass and Sanjay Subrahmanyam, eds, *Society and Circulation: Mobile People and Itinerant Cultures in South Asia, 1750–1950* (Delhi: Permanent Black, 2003), 111, fn. 49.
119. Bux, 'Memoirs of Khawajah Muhammad Bux', 61.
120. Ibid., 65.
121. Ibid., 66.
122. Ibid., 69, 68.
123. Ibid., 69.
124. Ibid.
125. Ibid., 52.
126. Ibid., 71. Julia Martínez and Adrian Vickers, *The Pearl Frontier: Indonesian Labor and Indigenous Encounters in Australia's Northern Trading Network* (Honolulu: University of Hawaii Press, 2015).
127. Bux, 'Memoirs of Khawajah Muhammad Bux', 71.
128. This is the approximate date given in the 'Life Summary' written by Bux's grandson, in Bux, 'Memoirs of Khawajah Muhammad Bux', iv.
129. 'Monday', *The Argus*, 20 April 1891, 4, cited in Nadia Rhook, '"Turban-Clad" British Subjects: Tracking the Circuits of Mobility, Visibility, and Sexuality in Settler Nation-Making', *Transfers* 5, no. 3 (1 December 2015), 51.
130. Bux, 'Memoirs of Khawajah Muhammad Bux', 71.
131. Ibid., 72.
132. On South Asians on Young Street in Fitzroy, see 'The Ebony Agony', *Fitzroy City Press*, 7 February 1890, 3.
133. Bux, 'Memoirs of Khawajah Muhammad Bux', 72.
134. Ibid.
135. Ibid., 73.
136. Alick Jackomos, 'Genealogies of Gippsland & Wimmera (Victoria) Families, Includes Lake Tyers, Ebonezer Mission and Former

Coranderrk Families That Moved to Lake Tyers and Descendants Now Living in Melbourne' (Unpublished Manuscript), 1987.

137. Bux, 'Memoirs of Khawajah Muhammad Bux', 73.
138. Ibid., 74.
139. Ibid., 4.
140. Partha Chatterjee, *The Nation and Its Fragments: Colonial and Postcolonial Histories*, Princeton Studies in Culture/Power/History (Princeton: Princeton University Press, 1993), 116–57.
141. Bux, 'Memoirs of Khawajah Muhammad Bux', 83.
142. Ibid., 84.
143. Ibid., 88.
144. Ibid., 92.
145. Ibid., 94.
146. Ibid., 93.
147. Ibid.
148. Ibid., 94.
149. Ibid., 140. Flavia Agnes, 'Economic Rights of Women in Islamic Law', *Economic and Political Weekly* 31, no. 1 (12 October 1996), 2832–8.
150. Bux, 'Memoirs of Khawajah Muhammad Bux', 145.
151. 'Ashraf 'Alī Thānvī, *Perfecting Women: Maulana Ashraf 'Ali Thanawi's Bihishtizewar: A Partial Translation with Commentary*, trans. Barbara Daly Metcalf (Berkeley: University of California Press, 1990).
152. Suneetha Achyutha, 'Deoband Patriarchy', *Economic and Political Weekly* 46, no. 26/27 (2011), 573–4.
153. Bux, 'Memoirs of Khawajah Muhammad Bux', 143.
154. Ibid., 144.
155. Ibid., 207.
156. Ibid., 224.
157. Ibid.
158. Ibid., 141.
159. Ibid., 150.
160. Western Australian Registry of Births, Deaths and Marriages, 1892/1221, Birth Certificate of Mohamed Shareef, 1892.
161. E. Jaggard, 'Vosper, Frederick Charles Burleigh (1869–1901)', in *Australian Dictionary of Biography* (Canberra: National Centre of Biography, Australian National University, 1990), http://adb.anu.edu.au/biography/vosper-frederick-charles-burleigh-8933, last accessed 29 May 2017.
162. Bux, 'Memoirs of Khawajah Muhammad Bux', 99.
163. Ibid., 95.
164. Ibid., 96.
165. Ibid.

166. 'Shipping Notes', *Daily News*, 14 January 1895, 4.
167. Bux, 'Memoirs of Khawajah Muhammad Bux', 125.
168. Ibid.
169. Colonial records confirm that many of the South Asian wives of merchants operating in Australia held substantial property of their own and engaged in various business pursuits. Noorbibi in Karachi, for example, engaged a legal team to track down the estate of her deceased husband Abdul Kader in South Australia, so she could service her loans. Bibi Ismat, likewise, was engaged in business activities in British India, her correspondence to Australian authorities highlighting that she had taken out loans in Karachi that were accruing interest at the rate of 12 per cent annually. State Records of South Australia, GRG 5/2 Police Commissioner's Office, Correspondence Files ('PCO' Files); Box 145, file no. 1148 of 1925, Hiranand & Santdas – Kader Mucher – Whereabouts of, 4 June 1925. Noel Butlin Archives Centre, Australian National University: Elder Smith & Co. Ltd.; 8/68, Correspondence, Documents, Memoranda and Some Accounts and Insurance Papers Relating to Faiz and Tagh Mohamet of Hergott and later of Perth, Merchants, Camel Proprietors and Carriers, Including Some Personal Papers of Faiz Mohamet; Item 25, Letter from M. Crouch (Karachi) to the West Australian Trustee Executor and Agency Company (Perth), 11 September 1903.
170. Bux, 'Memoirs of Khawajah Muhammad Bux', 100.
171. Haddawy, *Sindbad And Other Stories from the Arabian Nights*, 51.
172. Ibid., 53.
173. Ibid.
174. Ibid., 61.
175. Foreword of His Excellency Babar W. Malik in Bux, 'Memoirs of Khawajah Muhammad Bux', i.
176. Bald et al., 'Introduction', in *The Sun Never Sets*, 18.
177. Khawajah Muhammad Bux, 'Sawanih-E-Umri' (Unpublished Manuscript), c. 1944. A 2004 English edition titled *Amazing Migrant* is mentioned in 'Preface by Mr Khalid Bux, Sydney, March 2004' in the front matter of the 2006 unpublished English manuscript titled 'Memoirs of Khawajah Muhammad Bux, Australian Businessman'. An Urdu edition titled *Lahore Ka Sindbad* is mentioned in the newspaper article Sarwat Ali, 'Seafarer's Tales', *News On Sunday*, 22 June 2014, http://tns.thenews.com.pk/seafarers-tales-of-australiawale/. Samina Yasmeen, 'Muslim Australian Contributions: Bux Family as a Case Study' (Unpublished Paper, Centre for Muslim States and Societies, The University of Western

Australia, 2009). Devleena Ghosh, 'Under the Radar of Empire: Unregulated Travel in the Indian Ocean', *Journal of Social History* 45 (2011), 497–514. From 2016 onwards, Bux's travelogue has started to be serialised in the *Journal of the Pakistan Historical Society*. See Gábor Korvin, 'The Memoirs of Khawajah Muhammad Bux, (Australian Businessman): Part I', *Journal of the Pakistan Historical Society (Historicus)* 64, no. 1 (2016), 67–91.

178. Jordana Silverstein, *Anxious Histories: Narrating the Holocaust in Jewish Communities at the Beginning of the Twenty-First Century*, 1st edition (New York: Berghahn Books, 2015), 4.

4. THE TRAIN AT BELTANA

1. Said Mulladad, cited in 'Across Australia', *Register*, 2 August 1924, 13.
2. 'The Great Northern Railway', *South Australian Register*, 8 July 1881, 6.
3. 'Pioneer of Far North', *Mail* (Adelaide), 13 June 1925, 1.
4. Ibid.
5. Ibid.
6. Dale Kerwin, *Aboriginal Dreaming Paths and Trading Routes: The Colonisation of The Australian Economic Landscape* (Brighton: Sussex Academic Press, 2010), 102.
7. Hercus published the song in 1985, accompanied by an English translation in the journal *Aboriginal History*. A recording remains in Australian government archives. Luise Hercus, 'Leaving the Simpson Desert', *Aboriginal History* 9 (1985), 22–43: 32.
8. Lorena Alam. '"In 1788 It Was Nothing but Bush": Tony Abbott on Indigenous Australia', *The Guardian*, 29 August 2018, https://www.theguardian.com/australia-news/2018/aug/29/in-1788-it-was-nothing-but-bush-tony-abbott-on-indigenous-australia, last accessed 14 September 2018.
9. Joel Dry, 'Imagine Having Your Whole History Erased: Indigenous Rights Activists Burn Australian Flag During G20 Protests' (Television Broadcast), *Nine News* (Channel Nine, 16 November 2014).
10. Tracy Banivanua-Mar and Penelope Edmonds, eds, *Making Settler Colonial Space: Perspectives on Race, Place and Identity* (New York: Palgrave Macmillan, 2010), 3.
11. John McLaren, A. R. Buck and Nancy E. Wright, 'Property Rights in the Colonial Imagination and Experience', in John McLaren, A. R. Buck and Nancy E. Wright, eds, *Despotic Dominion: Property Rights in British Settler Societies* (Vancouver: University of British Columbia Press, 2005), 2–3.

12. State Records of South Australia, GRS 3570/1, Surrendered Pastoral Lease of Waste Lands of the Crown; Box 12, file no. 379 of 1855, Lease signed by John Haimes.
13. Simon Ville, *The Rural Entrepreneurs: A History of the Stock and Station Agent Industry in Australia and New Zealand* (Oakleigh: Cambridge University Press, 2000), 28.
14. Christine Macgregor, *A History of the Beltana Pastoral Company Limited* (Adelaide: Gillingham Printers, 1965), 21.
15. 'British Shipping', *South Australian Weekly Chronicle*, 18 July 1863, 2.
16. 'London Wool Sales', *South Australian Register*, 9 October 1863, 4.
17. Karl Marx, *Capital*, vol. 1 (London: Penguin Books, 1990), 579.
18. Cited in Philip Jones, *Ochre and Rust* (Adelaide: Wakefield Press, 2007), 363.
19. 'Letter from Wenowie', *The Argus*, 16 December 1863, 6.
20. Ibid.
21. 'Inquest on Natives Shot in the Far North', *South Australian Register*, 26 January 1864, 6.
22. T. Masey, 'The Red-Ochre Caves of the Blacks', *South Australian Register*, 10 June 1882, 6.
23. 'Inquest on Natives Shot in the Far North', 6.
24. 'Fatal Affray with the Blacks in the North', *The Argus*, 16 December 1863, 6.
25. 'Annual Retrospect', *South Australian Register*, 20 January 1864, 2. 'The Year's Retrospect', *South Australian Advertiser*, 1 January 1881, 6.
26. For example see accounts of massacres in Mick McLean, 'The End of the Mindiri People', in Peter Sutton and Luise Hercus, eds, *This Is What Happened*, trans. Luise Hercus (Canberra: Australian Institute of Aboriginal Studies, 1971), 182–92.
27. Robert Foster, 'Coexistence and Colonisation on Pastoral Leaseholds in South Australia, 1851–99', in John McLaren, A. R. Buck and Nancy E. Wright, eds, *Despotic Dominion: Property Rights in British Settler Societies* (Vancouver: University of British Columbia Press, 2005), 248–65: 255.
28. Luise Hercus, Flavia Hodges and Jane Simpson, *The Land Is a Map* (Canberra: Pandanus Books, 2002), 10. Dorothy Tunbridge, 'Aboriginal Place Names', *Australian Aboriginal Studies* 2 (1987), 2–13.
29. J. Woods et al., *The Native Tribes of South Australia* (Adelaide: E. S. Wigg and Son, 1879), 267.
30. Hercus, Hodges and Simpson, *The Land Is a Map*, 12.
31. Personal Communication with Luise Hercus and Jane Simpson, 7 April 2010. Bernhard Schebeck, 'Some Remarks on Placenames in the Flinders', in Hercus, Hodges and Simpson, *The Land Is a Map*, 146.

32. Macgregor, *A History of the Beltana Pastoral Company Limited*, 19.
33. 'Played with the Blacks', *Register News-Pictorial*, 24 September 1930, 6.
34. 'Letter from "Coollannie"', *Register*, 11 August 1924, 7.
35. Macgregor, *A History of the Beltana Pastoral Company Limited*, 19.
36. Dorothy Tunbridge, *Flinders Ranges Dreaming* (Canberra: Aboriginal Studies Press, 1988), 60, 76.
37. Michael Organ, 'Australian Aboriginal Dreaming Stories: A Chronological Bibliography of Published Works 1789–1991', *Aboriginal History* 18 (1994), 123–44.
38. 'Letter from "Coollannie"'.
39. 'Billy Pondi's Challenge', *Register News-Pictorial*, 29 November 1929, 6.
40. I am indebted to members of the Coulthard family for sharing this story with me in November 2014 at Iga Warta, an Adnyamathanha-owned tourism company in the Flinders Ranges, South Australia.
41. 'The Great Northern Railway', 6.
42. 'Pioneer of Far North', 1.
43. Lorenzo Veracini, 'The Imagined Geographies of Settler Colonialism', in Tracy Banivanua-Mar and Penelope Edmonds, eds, *Making Settler Colonial Space: Perspectives on Race, Place and Identity* (New York: Palgrave Macmillan, 2010), 179.
44. Reinhart Koselleck, '"Progress" and "Decline"', in *The Practice of Conceptual History*, trans. Todd Presner (Stanford: Stanford University Press, 2002), 218–36.
45. 'Water in the North', *South Australian Register*, 7 November 1856, 2.
46. Koselleck, '"Progress" and "Decline"', 225, 221.
47. 'Pioneer of Far North', 1.
48. Ibid.
49. Ibid.
50. Andrew Fitzmaurice, *Sovereignty, Property and Empire 1500–2000* (New York: Cambridge University Press, 2014), 1–33.
51. John Locke, *Two Treatises of Government: A Critical Edition with an Introduction and Apparatus Criticus by Peter Laslett* (Cambridge, UK: Cambridge University Press, 1960), 288–90.
52. Fitzmaurice, *Sovereignty, Property and Empire 1500–2000*, 1–33.
53. Government of South Australia, 'South Australian Act or Foundation Act of 1834', 15 August 1834, http://www.foundingdocs.gov.au/resources/transcripts/sa1_doc_1834.pdf, last accessed 2 July 2015. Edward John Eyre, *Journals of Expeditions of Discovery into Central Australia and Overland from Adelaide to King George's Sound, In the Years 1840–1*, vol. 1, 25 June 1840 (Project Gutenberg, 2004), http://www.gutenberg.org/ebooks/5344, last accessed 7 April 2014.
54. 'Pioneer of Far North', 1.

55. Peggy Brock, *Yura and Udnyu: A History of the Adnyamathanha of the North Flinders Ranges* (Adelaide: Wakefield Press, 1985), 49–50.
56. Ibid., 13–17.
57. 'Billy Pondi's Challenge', 6.
58. Macgregor, *A History of the Beltana Pastoral Company Limited*, 29.
59. Masey, 'The Red-Ochre Caves of the Blacks', 6.
60. 'Water in the North', 2.
61. Kerwin, *Aboriginal Dreaming Paths and Trading Routes*, 102.
62. Hercus, 'Leaving the Simpson Desert', 32.
63. Peter Austin, Luise Hercus and Philip Jones, 'Ben Murray (Parlku-Nguyu-Thangknyiwarna)', *Aboriginal History* 12 (1988), 144.
64. Jones, *Ochre and Rust*, 370.
65. Luise Hercus, 'Singing and Talking about Red Ochre' (Unpublished Manuscript, Australian National University, 2009), 4a.
66. George Horne and George Aiston, *Savage Life in Central Australia* (London: Macmillan, 1924), 128–130. Kerwin, *Aboriginal Dreaming Paths and Trading Routes*, 104.
67. Hercus, 'Leaving the Simpson Desert', 29.
68. Ibid., 31.
69. Ibid., 32.
70. Ibid.

5. THE CAMEL AND THE PROPHECY

1. 'Peace and Prophecy', *Register*, 21 July 1919, 6. 'Fate of Turkey an Indian Prophecy', *Daily News*, 22 December 1917, 8.
2. The figures here have been cited by contemporary historians of India, Australia and Turkey respectively, Reşat Kasaba, ed., *Turkey in the Modern World*, The Cambridge History of Turkey, vol. 4 (Cambridge, UK: Cambridge University Press, 2010), 93; Stuart Macintyre, *The Oxford History of Australia: Volume 4, 1901–1942* (Melbourne: Oxford University Press, 1986), 142–67; Shrabani Basu, *For King and Another Country: Indian Soldiers on the Western Front 1914–18* (New Delhi: Bloomsbury, 2015), xxi.
3. 'Peace and Prophecy', 6.
4. In 1917, an Ahmadiyya scholar based in Sind, British India, sent to Musakhan, who was then living in the town of Bourke, New South Wales, a doctrinal proof of some of the key ideas that underpin Ahmadiyya thought. This sixty-two-page Persian-language document today remains at the State Library of Western Australia, Perth. Abraham Khan Musakhan, 'An Open Letter On a Literary Subject in the Persian Language' (Unpublished Manuscript), c. 1917.

5. Adil Hussain Khan, *From Sufism to Ahmadiyya: A Muslim Minority Movement in South Asia* (Bloomington and Indianapolis: Indiana University Press, 2015), 27.
6. Ghulam Ahmad, *Tadhkirah: English Rendering of the Divine Revelations, Dreams and Visions Vouchsafed to Hadrat Mirza Ghulam Ahmad of Qadian*, ed. Mirza Masroor Ahmad, trans. Chaudhry Muhammad Zafrullah Khan, rev. Munawar Ahmed Saeed (Tilford: Islam International Publications Ltd, 2009), 239.
7. 'Ahmadia News Abroad', *The Moslem Sunrise* 1, no. 6 (October 1922), 113.
8. Manan Ahmed Asif, 'Prophetic Pakistan,' (Unpublished Paper, Columbia University, 2013), 4–5.
9. Denise M. Bostdorff, 'George W. Bush's Post-September 11 Rhetoric of Covenant Renewal: Upholding the Faith of the Greatest Generation', *Quarterly Journal of Speech* 89, no. 4 (November 2003), 293–319.
10. Robert Manne, 'Little America', *The Monthly*, 8 March 2006, https://www.themonthly.com.au/monthly-essays-robert-manne-little-america-how-john-howard-has-changed-australia-184, last accessed 8 May 2017.
11. C. A. Bayly, *Empire and Information: Intelligence Gathering and Social Communication in India, 1780–1870* (Cambridge, UK: Cambridge University Press, 2000), 58.
12. Biswamoy Pati, ed., *The Great Rebellion of 1857 in India: Exploring Transgressions, Contests and Diversities* (London: Routledge, 2012), 5.
13. Bayly, *Empire and Information*, 338.
14. John Martineau, *The Life and Correspondence of Sir Bartle Frere* (London: Murray, 1895), 191–92. Very little has been written about colonial resources funnelled from the Australian colonies to British India during the upheaval of 1857. British military regiments stationed across the colonies were funnelled to Indian ports during the upheaval of 1857, with the governor-general of India requesting troops from the colony of New South Wales in April 1858. In addition, horses were sourced from Australian colonial firms. See 'Parliament of Victoria: Troop Horses For India', *Bendigo Advertiser*, 12 September 1857, 2; 'Legislative Assembly: Troops for India', *Maitland Mercury and Hunter River General Advertiser*, 10 April 1858, 2.
15. Shahid Amin, 'Of Many Pasts: The 1857 Celebrations Raise Questions Indians Must Confront', *The Telegraph* (India), 13 July 2006, https://www.telegraphindia.com/1060713/asp/opinion/story_6461478.asp, last accessed 14 September 2018.
16. Bernard Cohn, 'Representing Authority in Victorian India', in E. J. Hobsbawm and T. O. Ranger, eds, *The Invention of Tradition, Past and Present Publications* (Cambridge, UK and New York: Cambridge University Press, 1983).

17. Ibid., 167.
18. 'Importation of Camels', *The Argus*, 24 March 1862, 6. On George Landells encounter with Moradkhan in 1859, see George Landells, 'The Camels', *The Argus*, 29 March 1862, 5.
19. Simon Ville, *The Rural Entrepreneurs: A History of the Stock and Station Agent Industry in Australia and New Zealand* (Oakleigh: Cambridge University Press, 2000), 18–55.
20. 'Obituary of Mr. Samuel J. Stuckey', *Border Watch*, 14 December 1912, 2.
21. Port Augusta Public Library, Local History File Anderson 37, Extract from Diary of Samuel J. Stuckey, 1862–1866, 2.
22. Western Australian Registry of Births, Deaths and Marriages, 0000920X/1898, Marriage Certificate of Hasan Musa Khan and Sophia Blitz, 10 March 1898.
23. Musakhan's birthdate is cited as '30 May 1863' in Mohamed Hasan Musakhan, *Islam in Australia: 1862–1932* (Adelaide: Mahomet Allum, 1932), 2.
24. PAPL, Anderson 37, Diary of Stuckey, 2.
25. For one of the earliest settler accounts of Pompey, see Thomas Babbage, 'The Gold Search', *South Australian Register*, 27 October 1856, 2.
26. PAPL, Anderson 37, Diary of Stuckey, 4.
27. 'Police Courts', *South Australian Register*, 4 May 1864, 3. Also see Peggy Brock, *Outback Ghettos: Aborigines, Institutionalisation and Survival* (Cambridge, UK and Melbourne: Cambridge University Press, 1993), 128; A. W. Howitt, *Native Tribes of South-East Australia* (London: Macmillan and Co., 1904), 47.
28. 'The Death of Pompey', *Adelaide Observer*, 7 May 1864, 5.
29. 'Police Court – Adelaide', *South Australian Advertiser*, 4 May 1864, 3.
30. PAPL, Anderson 37, Diary of Stuckey, 5.
31. 'The Death of Pompey', 5.
32. 'Pompey's Head', *South Australian Register*, 26 July 1864, 6.
33. Karuna Mantena, *Alibis of Empire: Henry Maine and the Ends of Liberal Imperialism* (Princeton: Princeton University Press, 2010), 2.
34. 'Shipment of Horses By the Kohinoor', *South Australian Register*, 20 February 1868, 3.
35. 'South Australia: The Kohinoor', *Launceston Examiner*, 2 January 1869, 5.
36. 'The Brindisi Route', *South Australian Register*, 1 December 1866, 2.
37. C. M. Naim, '"Prophecies" in South Asian Muslim Political Discourse: The Poems of Shah Ni'matullah Wali', *Economic and Political Weekly*, 9 July 2011.
38. Ibid.

39. Ibid., 52–3.
40. Khan, *From Sufism to Ahmadiyya*, 21–42.
41. Mirza Ghulam Ahmad, *A Brief Sketch of My Life* (Lahore: Ahmadiyya Anjuman Isha'at Islam, 1996), 17, cited in Simon Ross Valentine, *Islam and the Ahmadiyya Jama'at: History, Belief, Practice* (London: Hurst, 2008), 42, fn. 49.
42. See A. Azfar Moin, *The Millennial Sovereign: Sacred Kingship and Sainthood in Islam*, South Asia Across the Disciplines (New York: Columbia University Press, 2012), 56–93.
43. Khan, *From Sufism to Ahmadiyya*, 44. On controversies surrounding Nicolas Notovitch, see Douglas T. McGetchin, *Indology, Indomania, and Orientalism: Ancient India's Rebirth in Modern Germany* (Madison: Fairleigh Dickinson University Press, 2009), 133.
44. Dream published in Arabic in 1891, reproduced in Ahmad, *Tadhkirah*, 593.
45. Dream published in Urdu in 1902, reproduced in Ahmad, *Tadhkirah*, 539.
46. Dream published in Arabic in 1881, reproduced in Ahmad, *Tadhkirah*, 59.
47. Moin, *The Millennial Sovereign*, 10.
48. Ibid.
49. Azfar Moin, 'Akbar's "Jesus" and Marlowe's "Tamburlaine": Strange Parallels of Early Modern Sacredness', *Fragments: Interdisciplinary Approaches to the Study of Ancient and Medieval Pasts* 3 (2013–14).
50. Late-sixteenth-century poet Krsnadasa praises Akbar as the embodiement of Vishnu in Audrey Truschke, *Culture of Encounters: Sanskrit at the Mughal Court*, South Asia Across the Disciplines (New York: Columbia University Press, 2016), 39.
51. From the ESCo camel yard, a separate camel line was dispatched to the Barrier Ranges in the colony of New South Wales. 'South Australia: The Kohinoor', 5.
52. 'Camels at Crystal Brook', *South Australian Register*, 16 July 1884, 5.
53. Musakhan, *Islam in Australia*, 2.
54. Gauri Viswanathan, *Masks of Conquest: Literary Study and British Rule in India*, Social Foundations of Aesthetic Forms Series (New York: Columbia University Press, 1989), 148.
55. Musakhan, *Islam in Australia*, 2.
56. 'Camel Drivers' Differences, *Port Augusta Dispatch, Newcastle and Flinders Chronicle*, 6 October 1893, 3.
57. In 1897 Faiz Mahomet wrote that wages started at £3 per month in Faiz Mahomet, 'Immigration of Aliens: To the Editor', *West Australian*, 2 December 1897, 6.

58. Noel Butlin Archives Centre, Australian National University: Elder, Smith & Co. Ltd.; 8/68, Correspondence, documents, memoranda and some accounts and insurance papers relating to Faiz and Tagh Mohamet of Hergott and later of Perth, Merchants, Camel Proprietors and Carriers, including some personal papers of Faiz Mohamet, 1888–1905; Item 2, Bill of Sale no. 10075 from Gunny Khan to Faiz Mahomet, 3 March 1893.
59. Hasan Musakhan, 'An Asiatic on Coolgardie', *West Australian*, 16 July 1895, 6.
60. 'The Afghans at Hergott', *Port Augusta Dispatch, Newcastle and Flinders Chronicle*, 16 June 1893, 2.
61. Gunny Khan, 'Mohammedanism in Perth', *West Australian*, 13 April 1896, 3.
62. Ibid.
63. Ibid.
64. Barry Chant, 'The Australian Career of John Alexander Dowie', *Centre for the Study of Australian Christianity Working Papers* 1, no. 10 (10 August 1992), 1–26.
65. John Dowie's newspaper, 19 December 1903, cited in K. S. Mian Rahim Bakhsh, *The Debt Forgotten* (Columbus: Ahmadiyya Anjuman Isha'at Islam, 1993), 54–5.
66. Yohanan Friedmann, *Prophecy Continuous: Aspects of Ahmadi Religious Thought and Its Medieval Background*, Comparative Studies on Muslim Societies 3 (Berkeley: University of California Press, 1989), 6–7.
67. This was Ghulam Ahmad's interpretation of a particular *hadith* (or saying of Muhammad [d. 632]) elaborating on a verse in the Quran (75: 9–10) drawing a connection between eclipses and the Day of Resurrection. Ghulam Ahmad's prophecy is reproduced in English in Ahmad, *Tadhkirah,* 324–5.
68. 'Eclipse of the Moon', *Evening Journal*, 22 March 1894, 2.
69. M. Wallace, 'The Camels Came Overland', *Western Mail*, 30 April 1953, 6.
70. M. Wallace, 'The Camels Came Overland (Part 2)', *Western Mail*, 7 May 1953, 8.
71. Hasan Musakhan, 'The Anti-Asiatic Movement: Letter to the Editor', *Daily News*, 16 March 1895, 1.
72. Hamid Snow, '[COPY.] Ludhiana, Punjab, India, January 24, 1895', *Daily News*, 16 March 1895, 1.
73. Musakhan, 'The Anti-Asiatic Movement', 1.
74. For a close examination of the 'Durand Line' see Shah Mahmoud Hanifi, *Connecting Histories in Afghanistan: Market Relations and State Formation on a Colonial Frontier* (Stanford: Stanford University Press, 2011).

75. Musakhan, 'The Anti-Asiatic Movement', 1.
76. Snow, '[COPY.] Ludhiana, Punjab, India, January 24, 1895', 1.
77. Marilyn Lake and Henry Reynolds, *Drawing the Global Colour Line: White Men's Countries and the International Challenge of Racial Equality* (Cambridge, UK: Cambridge University Press, 2008), 62.
78. Hasan Musakhan, 'Indian British Subjects and the Immigration Restriction Act', *West Australian*, May 1898, 6.
79. Ibid.
80. 'Importation of Camels', *Daily News*, 22 March 1901, 3.
81. The administrative history of the Perth Mosque is outlined in Musakhan, *Islam in Australia*.
82. 'Rival Messiahs', *Register*, 8 December 1903, 8.
83. Dowie's newspaper, 19 December 1903, cited in Bakhsh, *The Debt Forgotten*, 54–5.
84. John Dowie, 'Leaves of Healing', 26 September 1900, cited in Bakhsh, 56.
85. 'Dowie in India: A Mohammedan Messiah', *Sunday Times* (Perth), 29 May 1904, 9.
86. Bakhsh, *The Debt Forgotten*, 56.
87. 'Dr. Dowie and an Indian Messiah', *Western Mail*, 1 June 1907, 49.
88. 'Dowie's Double', *The Sunday Sun* (Sydney), 17 April 1904, 5.
89. 'A Mohammedan Prophet', *Register*, 3 June 1907, 6, citing newspaper reports in 1903.
90. 'A Mohammedan Prophet', 6.
91. Muhammad Ali, *The Ahmadiyyah Movement*, trans. S. Muhammad Tufail (Lahore: Ahmadiyya Anjuman, 1973), 4.
92. Naim, '"Prophecies" in South Asian Muslim Political Discourse', 52.
93. Azmi Özcan, *Pan-Islamism: Indian Muslims, the Ottomans and Britain, 1877–1924*, The Ottoman Empire and Its Heritage, vol. 12 (Leiden and New York: Brill, 1997).
94. The collection of Ghulam Ahmad's dreams cites a line from the Quran (30: 2). While the reference in the Quran is to the 'Byzantines' or 'Romans' (*al-Rum*), Ahmadi writers such as Hasan Musakhan reproduced it as a prophecy about Ottoman Turkey, whose capital Constantinople marked where Byzantium once stood at the centre of the Roman empire. Ahmad, *Tadhkirah*, 655. Here I have cited Hasan Musakhan's 1913 rendering of the line in 'A Letter from India Turkey and the Mahommedans', *Sunday Times* (Perth), 16 February 1913, 4.
95. Musakhan, 'Prophets and Prophecies: The Indian Messiah, and Turkey's Fate (to the Editor of "Truth")', *Truth*, 20 May 1916, 3.
96. Musakhan, 'A Letter from India Turkey and the Mahommedans', 4.
97. Musakhan, 'Prophets and Prophecies', 3.

98. Hasan Musakhan, 'Turkey's Fate', *Sydney Morning Herald*, 10 June 1916, 19.
99. Ibid.
100. Ibid.
101. 'Remarkable Prophecies', *Inverell Times*, 25 July 1919, 5.
102. Ibid.
103. 'Peace and Prophecy', 6.
104. Musakhan appears as the Perth representative in this list of 'branches' cited in Abdullah Allahdin, *Claims and Teachings of Ahmad, the Promised Messiah and Mahdi*, 4th edition (Secunderabad: The Universal Press, 1922), ii.
105. 'Ahmadia News Abroad', *The Moslem Sunrise* 2, nos 2–3 (July 1923), 197. The titles of *The Moslem Sunshine* issued in Australia by Musakhan and *The Moslem Sunrise* published in Chicago both referenced Ghulam Ahmad's dream about the white partridges in a pulpit in England. On awakening from this dream in 1891, the founder of the Ahmadiyya movement had interpreted its iconography to articulate a prophecy about 'the West'. According to some Muslim eschatological narratives, one event signposting the approach of Judgement Day will be the rising of the sun from the west rather then the east. Following his dream set in the 'city of London', Ghulam Ahmad produced a new interpretation of this older eschatological narrative. He prophesied, 'the rising of the sun from West means that the Western countries which have been steeped in darkness and infidelity for a long time will be illumined with the sun of truthfulness and they will partake of Islam', Ahmad, *Tadhkirah*, 654.
106. 'Ahmadia News Abroad', October 1922, 113.
107. Khan, *From Sufism to Ahmadiyya*, 128–53.
108. 'Family Notices', *Sunday Times* (Perth), 16 September 1923, 2.
109. Musakhan, *Islam in Australia*.
110. Hasan Musakhan, 'Like Ships in the Night Afghan Life Passes to the Mists', *Mirror* (Perth), 16 August 1924, 8.
111. Ibid.
112. Hasan Musakhan, 'Address of Welcome in "Pushto" Tongue', *Mirror* (Perth), 16 August 1924, 8.

6. THE BOOK OF SAND

1. Arrival time of train from Oodnadatta at Davenport/Alberrie Creek in years spanning 1891–1899 calculated from State Records of South Australia, GRS/2844, Working and Public Timetables; Consignment 00001, Unit 6, 1888–1911.

2. Mona Merrick, cited in Luise Hercus, 'Afghan Stories from the Northeast of South Australia', *Aboriginal History* 5 (1981), 46. All translations I use in this chapter of Mona Merrick's Arabunna story are by Luise Hercus unless otherwise stated.
3. Hercus, 'Afghan Stories from the Northeast of South Australia', 46.
4. Mona Merrick identified these girls as the mothers of Jimmy and Leslie Russell. Hercus' larger body of research indicates that Jimmy Russell was born in c. 1900 and Leslie Russell in c. 1906. Given that the railway tank that features in the story was constructed in 1891 and that by the 1900s the sisters who are featured in this Arabunna tale both had young children of their own, we can date their encounter with the South Asian men at Alberrie Creek to roughly 1895. State Records of South Australia, GRG 42/120, South Australian Railways; Consignment 00001, unit 1, List of Wells, Bores, Dams, &c., prepared for The Royal Commission (to 30 June 1902), 12. L. A. Hercus, *A Grammar of the Arabana-Wangkangurru Language Lake Eyre Basin*, South Australia (Canberra: Dept of Linguistics, Research School of Pacific and Asian Studies, Australian National University, 1994), 3.
5. Hercus, 'Afghan Stories from the Northeast of South Australia', 46.
6. Ibid.
7. Ibid.
8. Ibid.
9. Ibid.
10. Ibid., 47.
11. Ibid.
12. Ibid.
13. See ibid., 40–43.
14. Ibid., 48.
15. Arabunna translations from ibid., 39.
16. Ibid., 47.
17. On the forced removal of Aboriginal children, see Ronald Wilson, *Bringing Them Home: Report of the National Inquiry into the Separation of Aboriginal and Torres Strait Islander Children from Their Families* (Sydney: Human Rights and Equal Opportunity Commission, 1997); Anna Haebich, *Broken Circles: Fragmenting Indigenous Families 1800–2000* (Fremantle: Fremantle Arts Centre Press, 2000); Robert Manne, 'In Denial: The Stolen Generations and the Right', *Quarterly Essay*, no. 1 (2001), 1; Gordon Briscoe, *Racial Folly: A Twentieth-Century Aboriginal Family* (Canberra: ANU E Press, 2010).
18. Violet Turner, *Pearls from the Deep: The Story of Colebrook Home for Aboriginal Children* (Adelaide: United Aborigines Mission, 1936).

19. Isobel White, 'Introduction' in Peter Austin, ed., *Language and History: Essays in Honour of Luise A. Hercus* (Canberra: Dept of Linguistics, Research School of Pacific Studies, Australian National University, 1990), 2.
20. Isobel White, 'Introduction', 3.
21. Reg Dodd has contributed to a number of historical and environmental pieces of research, including: Leah Gibbs, 'Valuing Water: Variability and the Lake Eyre Basin, Central Australia', *Australian Geographer* 37 (2006), 73–85; Leah Gibbs, 'Just Add Water: Colonisation, Water Governance, and the Australian Inland', *Environment and Planning* 41 (2009), 2964–83; G. M. Mudd, 'Mound Springs of the Great Artesian Basin in South Australia: A Case Study from Olympic Dam', *Environmental Geology* 39, no. 5 (2000), 463–76; Gavin Mudd, 'The Sustainability of Mound Springs in South Australia: Implications for Olympic Dam', Commission on Mineral and Thermal Waters Meeting (Paper Presented at the International Association of Hydrogeologists (IAH), Ballarat, Australia, 1998).
22. There is a rich archive of Aboriginal country music that narrates histories of encounter with South Asians. See Central Australian Aboriginal Media Association (CAAMA), *The Last Camel Train* (CD) (Alice Springs: CAAMA Music, 2002).
23. Reg Dodd and Tom Jenkin, 'Aboriginal Tourism and Land Management in the Lake Eyre Basin: Arabunna Aboriginal Tours', in *Lake Eyre Basin – Today And Tomorrow: Place, People, Possibilities* (Renmark: Lake Eyre Conference Steering Committee, 2006), 126–45.
24. On this sculpture, see Graham St John, 'Off Road Show: Techno, Protest and Feral Theatre', *Continuum: Journal of Media and Cultural Studies* 19, no. 1 (2005), 5–20; Esther Lindstrom, 'Sculptures in the Outback' (Television Broadcast), *Stateline* (Australian Broadcasting Corporation, 2004), https://www.youtube.com/watch?v=l53qID5AB0E, last accessed 15 September 2018.
25. Reg Dodd and Jen Gibson, 'Learning Times: An Experience of Arabana Life and Mission Education', *Aboriginal History* 13 (1989), 81–93.
26. 'Home For Aborigines', *Advertiser*, 10 September 1943, 2.
27. During this camping trip, each morning, as soon as it was light enough to see, I wrote down everything I could remember from the previous day's travel. When citing Reg Dodd, I am drawing upon his words as recorded in my own travel diary. I am greatly indebted to Reg for his permission to write about this trip.
28. Kerry Staight, 'Creek Dries Up' (Television Broadcast), *Landline* (Australian Broadcasting Corporation, 7 June 2008).
29. 'Late Mrs. M. Zada', *Barrier Miner*, 13 June 1949, 8.

30. Peter Austin, Luise Hercus and Philip Jones, 'Ben Murray (Parlku-Nguyu-Thangknyiwarna)', *Aboriginal History* 12 (1988), 128.
31. On the system of rations for Aboriginal people in South Australia, see Robert Foster, 'Feasts of the Full-Moon: The Distribution of Rations to Aborigines in South Australia: 1836–1861', *Aboriginal History* 13 (1989), 63–78; Robert Foster, 'Coexistence and Colonisation on Pastoral Leaseholds in South Australia, 1851–99', in John McLaren, A. Buck, and Nancy Wright, eds, *Despotic Dominion: Property Rights in British Settler Societies* (Vancouver: University of British Columbia Press, 2005), 248–65.
32. Dodd and Gibson, 'Learning Times: An Experience of Arabana Life and Mission Education', 86.

7. THE BOOK OF MARRIAGE

1. 'Police Court', *Port Augusta Dispatch*, 24 June 1904, 2.
2. 'Police Court', p. 2.
3. Ibid.
4. Moosha Balooch, cited in ibid. 'An Afghan Shot', *Register*, 25 May 1904, 5.
5. Christine Stevens, *Tin Mosques & Ghantowns: A History of Afghan Cameldrivers in Australia* (Melbourne: Oxford University Press, 1989), 224–5.
6. The term 'brideprice' first appears in Luise Hercus, 'Afghan Stories from the Northeast of South Australia', *Aboriginal History* 5 (1981), 39–70: 39.
7. Georgine Clarsen, 'Gender and Mobility: Historicising the Terms', in Gijs Mom, Gordon Pirie and Laurent Tissot, eds, *Mobility in History* (Neuchâtel: Alphil, 2009), 235–41: 236.
8. Engseng Ho, *The Graves of Tarim: Genealogy and Mobility Across the Indian Ocean* (Berkeley and London: University of California Press, 2006), xxii.
9. Mitra Sharafi, 'The Marital Patchwork of Colonial South Asia: Forum Shopping from Britain to Baroda', *Law and History Review* 28, no. 4 (November 2010), 979–1009: 979.
10. See Peta Stephenson, *Islam Dreaming: Indigenous Muslims in Australia* (Sydney: UNSW Press, 2010), 141.
11. Pamela Rajkowski, *In the Tracks of the Camelmen: Outback Australia's Most Exotic Pioneers* (Sydney: Angus and Robertson, 1987), 175.
12. Edward Said, *Orientalism* (London: Penguin, 2003 [1979]), 23. Stevens, *Tin Mosques & Ghantowns*, 228, fn. 357. On Fredrik Barth, see Magnus Marsden and Benjamin Hopkins, eds, *Beyond Swat: History, Society and Economy Along the Afghanistan-Pakistan Frontier* (London: Hurst, 2013), 1–16.

13. Mountstuart Elphinstone, *An Account of the Kingdom of Caubul* (London: Longman, Hurst, Rees, Orme & Brown, 1815), 179. Benjamin Hopkins, *The Making of Modern Afghanistan* (Basingstoke: Palgrave Macmillan, 2008), 13.
14. Henry Sumner Maine, *Lectures on the Early History of Institutions* (London: J. Murray, 1875), 324. Charles Staniland Wake, *The Development of Marriage and Kinship* (London: George Redway, 1889), 452. William Crooke, *The North-Western Provinces of India* (London: Methuen & Co., 1897), 138, 361. William Francis, *The Nilgiris*, Madras District Gazetteers (New Delhi: Logos Press, 1984 [1908]), 136, 153, 161.
15. Kathleen Wilson, 'Empire, Gender, and Modernity in the Eighteenth Century', in Philippa Levine, ed., *Gender and Empire* (New York: Oxford University Press, 2004), 18–20.
16. Paul McGeough, 'The Face of Fear Hidden Behind a Veil of Tyranny', *Sydney Morning Herald*, 10 September 2001, 10.
17. Lila Abu-Lughod, *Do Muslim Women Need Saving?* (Cambridge, MA: Harvard University Press, 2013), 30–32. Shakira Hussein, *From Victims to Suspects: Muslim Women Since 9/11* (Sydney: Newsouth Books, 2016), 13–39.
18. Abu-Lughod, *Do Muslim Women Need Saving?*, 142.
19. See Antoinette Burton, 'Some Trajectories of "Feminism" and "Imperialism"', *Gender & History* 10, no. 3 (1 November 1998), 558–68.
20. Gayle Rubin, 'The Traffic in Women: Notes on the "Political Economy" of Sex', in Rayna Reiter, ed., *Toward an Anthropology of Women* (New York: Monthly Review Press, 1975), 157–210. See essays in Srimati Basu, ed., *Dowry and Inheritance* (London: Zed Books, 2006).
21. Chandra Talpade Mohanty, 'Under Western Eyes: Feminist Scholarship and Colonial Discourses', *Boundary 2* 12 (1984), 333–58: 334. Lila Abu-Lughod, 'Against Universals: The Dialectics of (Women's) Human Rights and Human Capabilities', in J. Michelle Molina, Donald Swearer and Susan McGarry, eds, *Rethinking the Human* (Cambridge, MA: Harvard University Press, 2010), 69–94: 76. Valerie Amos and Pratibha Parmar, 'Challenging Imperial Feminism', *Feminist Review* 80 (2005), 44–63: 47–8.
22. Flavia Agnes, 'Economic Rights of Women in Islamic Law', *Economic and Political Weekly* 31, no. 1 (12 October 1996), 2832–8: 2833.
23. Abu-Lughod, *Do Muslim Women Need Saving?*, 196.
24. Fatima Mernissi, *Dreams of Trespass: Tales of a Harem Girlhood* (New York: Addison-Wesley Publishing Company, 1994), 12–19.

25. Zakia Pathak, Saswati Sengupta and Sharmila Purkayastha, 'The Prisonhouse of Orientalism', *Textual Practice* 5, no. 2 (1 June 1991), 195–218: 195.
26. Gloria Anzaldúa, *Borderlands/La Frontera: The New Mestiza* (San Francisco: Aunt Lute Books, 2007), 7, 25–40.
27. 'Pack Camel Days Recalled', *Western Herald*, 17 June 1966, 5.
28. National Archives of Australia: Department of External Affairs, Melbourne; A1, Correspondence files, annual single number series, 1890–1969; 1912/6069, Application by an Indian named Perooz for permission for his brother and his nephew to enter the Cmth.; Letter from Biddulph and Salenger Solicitors to the Department of External Affairs, 15 February 1912.
29. National Archives of Australia: Department of Air, Central Office; A9301, RAAF Personnel files of Non-Commissioned Officers (NCOs) and other ranks, 1921–1948; 300184, Perooz James Percy; Record of Service – Airmen (Permanent) RAAF.
30. New South Wales Registry of Births, Deaths and Marriages, 7310/1913, Marriage Certificate of Perooz Khan and Myrtle Mary Dee, 31 March 1913.
31. Wael Hallaq, 'What Is Shari'a', *Yearbook of Islamic and Middle Eastern Law* 12 (2005–6), 151–80: 156.
32. Wael Hallaq, *The Origins and Evolution of Islamic Law* (Cambridge, UK: Cambridge University Press, 2005), 122–49.
33. Zafarul Islam, 'The Fatawa Firuz Shahi as a Source for the Socio-Economic History of the Sultanate Period', *Islamic Culture* 60, no. 2 (1986), 97–117: 108–9.
34. Ibid.
35. Wael Hallaq, 'From Fatwās To Furū: Growth and Change in Islamic Substantive Law', *Islamic Law and Society* 1 (1994), 29–65: 31.
36. Islam, 'The Fatawa Firuz Shahi', 98, fn. 5.
37. Bernard Cohn, *Colonialism and Its Forms of Knowledge: The British in India* (Princeton: Princeton University Press, 1996), 57–75.
38. John Strawson, 'Islamic Law and English Texts', *Law and Critique* 6, no. 1 (1 March 1995), 21–38: 29.
39. Bourke Public Library; Alan Barton Local History Collection, Marriage Contract of Morbine Perooz and Myrtle Mary Dee, 14 January 1917.
40. Kecia Ali, *Marriage and Slavery in Early Islam* (Cambridge, MA: Harvard University Press, 2010), 12.
41. Ibid.
42. John McLaren, A. R. Buck and Nancy E. Wright, 'Property Rights in the Colonial Imagination and Experience', in John McLaren, A. R. Buck, and Nancy E. Wright, eds, *Despotic Dominion: Property Rights in*

British Settler Societies (Vancouver: University of British Columbia Press, 2005), 1–21: 2–3; See also Muhammad Wohidul Islam, 'Al-Mal: The Concept of Property in Islamic Legal Thought', *Arab Law Quarterly* 14 (1 January 1999), 361–8.

43. Ali, *Marriage and Slavery in Early Islam*, 50–2.
44. Commonwealth of Australia, *Parliamentary Debates, House of Representatives: Official Hansard* 1, 24694 (12 February 2004).
45. 'The Great Camel Deal', *Sunday Times* (Perth), 19 April 1908, 3.
46. 'Camels from India', *Evening News*, 8 April 1907, 4.
47. Noel Butlin Archives Centre, Australian National University: Elder Smith & Co. Ltd., 8/68 Correspondence, documents, memoranda and some accounts and insurance papers relating to Faiz and Tagh Mohamet of Hergott and later of Perth, Merchants, Camel Proprietors and Carriers, including some personal papers of Faiz Mohamet, 1888–1905; Item 55, Statutory Declaration by Faiz Mohamed, c. 1898.
48. 'Murder at Coolgardie', *West Australian*, 11 January 1896, 4.
49. 'The Murder of Tagh Mahomet', *Kalgoorlie Miner*, 13 January 1896, 2.
50. 'Astounding Allegations', *Sunday Times* (Perth), 19 May 1907, 13.
51. 'Supreme Court', *West Australian*, 30 July 1897, 3.
52. 'Tagh Mahomet's Will', *Kalgoorlie Miner*, 30 July 1897, 3.
53. 'The Estate of the Late Tagh Mahomet', *The Norseman Pioneer*, 3 October 1896, 1.
54. Ibid.
55. See chapters introduced by Elizabeth Kolsky, 'Maneuvering the Personal Law System in Colonial India', *Law and History Review* 28, no. 4 (1 November 2010), 973–8.
56. 'Importation of Camels', *Daily News*, 22 March 1901, 3.
57. 'Faiz Mahomet vs. The Government', *Daily News*, 14 June 1905, 3.
58. 'Tagh Mahomet's Will', 3. Noel Butlin Archives Centre, Australian National University: Elder Smith & Co. Ltd.; 8/68, Correspondence, documents, memoranda and some accounts and insurance papers relating to Faiz and Tagh Mohamet of Hergott and later of Perth, Merchants, Camel Proprietors and Carriers, including some personal papers of Faiz Mohamet, 1888–1905; Item 79, Transfer of Power of Attorney from Faiz Mahomet to Ghulam Mahomet, 20 April 1904.
59. Gulam Faiz Mahomet, 'Suggested Importation of Camels', *West Australian*, 20 October 1906, 2.
60. National Archives of Australia: Collector of Customs, Western Australia; K1145, Certificates of Exemption from Dictation Test, annual certificate number order 1901–1955; 1907/39, Gulam Faiz Mahomed [Mahomet] [Indian].

61. State Records Office of Western Australia: Colonial Secretary's Office, Passenger Lists and Immigration Records; Accession 457, Arrivals and Departures for Fremantle and Outports, 1898–1915; Item 36, roll 170, Incoming Passenger List to Port Headland, SS *Century* arrived 20 March 1907.
62. Nellie Mahomet, cited in 'Astounding Allegations', 13.
63. Ibid.
64. Ibid.
65. 'The Antics of Abraham', *Sunday Times* (Perth), 16 June 1907, 8.
66. Elizabeth Kolsky, '"The Body Evidencing the Crime": Rape on Trial in Colonial India, 1860–1947', *Gender & History* 22, no. 1 (April 2010), 109–30: 111. Amanda Kaladelfos, 'Crime and Outrage: Sexual Villains and Sexual Violence in New South Wales, 1870–1930' (PhD Thesis, University of Sydney, 2010), 20–47.
67. Pratiksha Baxi, *Public Secrets of Law: Rape Trials in India* (New Delhi: Oxford University Press, 2014), 86.
68. 'The Antics of Abraham', 8.
69. 'Tagh Mahomet's Will', 6.
70. Ibid.
71. 'The Antics of Abraham', 8.
72. Ibid.
73. Ibid.
74. National Archives of Australia: Collector of Customs, Western Australia; K269, Inward passenger manifests for ships and aircraft arriving at Fremantle, Perth Airport and Western Australian outports, chronological series, 1897–1978; 18 JUL 1907 PAROO, Incoming passenger list to Fremantle, *Paroo* arrived 18 July 1907.
75. National Archives of Australia: Department of External Affairs, Melbourne; A1, Correspondence files, annual single number series, 1890–1969; 1907/10940, Abraham Mahomet – Exemption Certificate, 1907; Letter from Clayton Mason, Collector of Customs to the Secretary of External Affairs, Melbourne, 15 November 1907.
76. Ibid.
77. South Australian Registry of Births, Deaths and Marriages, 456/235, Birth Certificate of Adelaide Neackmore Khan, 8 March 1890.
78. Ibid.
79. 'Afghans in Adelaide', *Advertiser*, 13 May 1903, 5.
80. 'Was It Marriage or Betrothal?', *Advertiser*, 26 February 1904, 4–5.
81. Ibid.
82. For Aboriginal-language accounts, see Hercus, 'Afghan Stories from the Northeast of South Australia', 49; Peter Austin, Luise Hercus and Philip Jones, 'Ben Murray (Parlku-Nguyu-Thangknyiwarna)', *Aboriginal History* 12 (1988), 115–88: 145–56.

83. 'Out Among the People', *Advertiser*, 30 June 1937, 25.
84. 'Land Allotments', *Advertiser*, 11 December 1902, 2.
85. State Records of South Australia, GRG 5/2, Police Commissioner's Office, Correspondence Files ('PCO' Files); Box 99, file no. 202 of 1906, Letter from Surwah Khan to Police Commissioner, 8 April 1906.
86. Moosha Balooch, cited in 'Police Court', 2.
87. 'Circuit Court', *Port Augusta Dispatch*, 22 July 1904, 3.
88. Ibid.
89. Ibid.
90. 'Police Court', p. 2.
91. Gunny Khan, 'The Camels', *Western Herald*, 15 October 1890, 2. Philip Jones and Anna Kenny, *Australia's Muslim Cameleers: Pioneers of the Inland, 1860s–1930s* (Adelaide: South Australian Museum, 2007), 84.
92. Mohamed Hasan Musakhan, *Islam in Australia: 1862–1932* (Adelaide: Mahomet Allum, 1932), 28–9.
93. Jawan Shir, 'Nationalism in Afghanistan: Colonial Knowledge, Education, Symbols, and the Junket Tour of Amanullah Khan, 1901–1929' (Master's Thesis, James Madison University, 2012), 34. Shah Mahmoud Hanifi, 'Quandaries of the Afghan Nation', in Shahzad Bashir and Robert Crews, eds, *Under the Drones: Modern Lives in the Afghanistan-Pakistan Borderlands* (Cambridge, MA: Harvard University Press, 2012), 83–101: 93–5.
94. Gunny Khan, 'The Camel Nuisance', *Barrier Miner*, 23 May 1904, 2.
95. Ibid.
96. Ibid.
97. 'Police Court', 2.
98. 'Police Court', 2.
99. 'An Afghan Vendetta', *Advertiser*, 6 January 1905, 7.
100. 'Circuit Court', 3.
101. 'Afghan Shooting Case', *Register*, 20 July 1904, 5.
102. Mohammad Hashim Kamali, *Law in Afghanistan: A Study of the Constitutions, Matrimonial Law and the Judiciary* (Leiden: Brill, 1985), 84–6.
103. 'A Heavy Sentence', *Norseman Times*, 22 July 1904, 3.
104. 'Police Court', 2.
105. South Australian Registry of Births, Deaths and Marriages, 227/102, Marriage Certificate of Adelaide Neackmore Khan and Moosha Balooch, 8 April 1906.
106. Pamela Rajkowski, *Linden Girl: A Story of Outlawed Lives* (Perth: University of Western Australia Press, 1995), 72.
107. On Wongatha history, see Craig Muller, 'The "Allurements of the European Presence": Examining Explanations of Wongatha Behaviour

in the Northern Goldfields of Western Australia', *Aboriginal History* 38 (December 2014), 59–87.

108. South Australian Registry of Births, Deaths and Marriages, 315/707, Marriage Certificate of Jack Akbar and Lali Matber, 23 May 1928.
109. 'Walked 500 Miles to Marry', *Barrier Miner*, 27 November 1928, 3.
110. Ibid.
111. Rajkowski, *Linden Girl*, 72.
112. Government of Western Australia, 'Section 2, Aborigines Act 1905 (WA)'.
113. Government of Western Australia, 'Section 8, Aborigines Act 1905 (WA)'.
114. Auber Neville, cited in Commonwealth of Australia, 'Aboriginal Welfare: Initial Conference of Commonwealth and State Aboriginal Authorities Held at Canberra, 21st to 23rd April 1937' (Canberra: Commonwealth Government Printer, 1937), 11.
115. Rajkowski, *Linden Girl*, 23, fn. 8.
116. 'Lallie's Mob by D. J. Akbar', reproduced in Rajkowski, *Linden Girl*, 272–3.
117. Dale Kerwin, *Aboriginal Dreaming Paths and Trading Routes: The Colonisation of the Australian Economic Landscape* (Brighton: Sussex Academic Press, 2010), 102.
118. Rajkowski, *Linden Girl*, 60.
119. Anna Haebich, *For Their Own Good: Aborigines and Government in the South West of Western Australia 1900–1940* (Nedlands: University of Western Australia Press, 1992), 199–221.
120. Rajkowski, *Linden Girl*, 75.
121. Margaret Morgan, *A Drop in the Bucket: The Mount Margaret Story* (Box Hill: United Aborigines Mission, 1986), 91.
122. Ibid., 77.
123. Ibid., 133–4.
124. 'Aborigine Before Court', *News*, 11 October 1928, 21.
125. Ibid.
126. 'Walked 500 Miles to Marry', 3.
127. Rajkowski, *Linden Girl*, 191–202.
128. 'Walked 500 Miles to Marry', 3.
129. Ibid.
130. Ibid.
131. Rajkowski, *Linden Girl*, 202.
132. SABDM, 315/707, Marriage Certificate of Jack Akbar and Lali Matber, 23 May 1928. Rajkowski, *Linden Girl*, 205.
133. Mona Wilson interviewed in Daniel Browning, 'Nomads: The Aboriginal Descendants of the Afghan Camel Drivers' (Radio Broadcast), *Awaye* (Radio National, 18 July 2009).
134. 'Aborigine Before Court', 21.

135. 'Not Allowed to Love!', *Mirror* (Perth), 13 October 1928, 3.
136. 'Indian and Halfcaste', *Chronicle* (Adelaide), 17 November 1928, 57.
137. 'Walked 500 Miles to Marry', *News*, 22 November 1928, 26.
138. Whirling Dervish Media, 'Mona Akbar Interview', 30 November 2012, https://www.youtube.com/watch?v=KEgB8LxuP2g, last accessed 24 September, 2014.
139. Lallie Akbar, cited in Rajkowski, *Linden Girl*, 256.
140. Rajkowski, *Linden Girl*, 258–60.
141. Morgan, *A Drop in the Bucket*, 91.
142. Mona Wilson, cited in Stephenson, *Islam Dreaming: Indigenous Muslims in Australia*, 132.
143. Ibid., 131.
144. Rajkowski, *Linden Girl*, 264.
145. See Chapter 5: The Camel and the Prophecy.
146. Kazi Motahar Hossain, *Sritikatha* (Dhaka: Nabajuga Prokashani, 2004), 13.
147. Tayeb El-Hibri, *Reinterpreting Islamic Historiography: Hārūn Al-Rashīd and the Narrative of the 'Abbāsid Caliphate*, Cambridge Studies in Islamic Civilization (Cambridge and New York: Cambridge University Press, 1999), 53–56.
148. James Jupp, *From White Australia to Woomera: The Story of Australian Immigration* (Port Melbourne: Cambridge University Press, 2007), 33.
149. '20m Boat Brings 118', *Sydney Morning Herald*, 2 April 1990, 5. 'Navy Rescues Boat People', *Sunday Herald*, 3 June 1990.
150. Eshrat to author, October 2002. Translation by author. Original recording held by Samia Khatun.
151. Samia Khatun, 'Dreaming of Dhaka', 23 June 2011, https://www.youtube.com/watch?v=84M_-0IskiQ, last accessed 12 June 2017.
152. Eshrat to author, April 2011. Translation by author. Original recording held by Samia Khatun.
152. See excerpt from 'The Book of Marriage' reproduced in *Australianama: The South Asian Odyssey in Australia* (London: Hurst, 2018), 164.

8. TO HEAR

1. Kazi Sofiuddin, *Kasasol Ambia* (Calcutta: Hanifia Press, 1895), 150–65.
2. Wael Hallaq, 'Re-Orienting Orientalism: Toward an Epistemology of Moral Responsibility' (Lecture for the Kamel Center for the Study of Islamic Law and Civilization, 17 November 2015), https://vimeo.com/149019309, last accessed 20 June 2018.
3. 'Introduction' in Wael B. Hallaq, *Restating Orientalism: A Critique of Modern Knowledge*, (New York: Columbia University Press, 2018), 4.

4. Hallaq, 'Re-Orienting Orientalism: Toward an Epistemology of Moral Responsibility'. See 'Chapter V: Refashioning Orientalism; Refashioning the Subject' in Hallaq, *Restating Orientalism*, 229–267.
5. Deathscapes: Mapping Race and Violence in Settler States, https://www.deathscapes.org/, last accessed 7 July 2018.
6. Walter D. Mignolo, 'Preface to the 2012 Edition', *Local Histories/Global Designs: Coloniality, Subaltern Knowledges, and Border Thinking* (Princeton: Princeton University Press, 2012 [2000]), x.
7. Hallaq, *Restating Orientalism*, 232–33.
8. Ibid., 233.
9. Rajendralal Mitra, 'On the Origin of the Hindvi Language and Its Relation to the Urdu Dialect', *Journal of the Asiatic Society of Bengal* 33, no. 5 (1864), 489–518: 518.
10. Sofiuddin, *Kasasol Ambia*, 21–2.
11. C. W. Bolton, Government of Bengal, Undersecretary to the Secretary, Government of India, Home Department, 29 April 1879, cited in Tapti Roy, 'Disciplining the Printed Text: Colonial and Nationalist Surveillance of Bengali Literature', in *Texts of Power: Emerging Disciplines in Colonial Bengal* (Minneapolis: University of Minnesota Press, 1995), 30–62: 47–8.
12. For literature on Sufi listening practices see J. During and R. Sellheim, 'Samāʿ', in P. Bearman, W. P. Heinrichs, C. E. Bosworth, Th. Bianquis, and E. van Donzel, eds, *Encyclopaedia of Islam, Second Edition*, 24 April 2012.
13. Aditya Behl, 'Qutban from Mrigavati: Translated from the Hindavi', *Calque* 5 (February 2009), 75.
14. Md Mahbub Murshed, 'Husain, Qazi Motahar', in Sirajul Islam and Sajahan Miah, eds, *Banglapedia: National Encyclopedia of Bangladesh* (Dhaka: Asiatic Society of Bangladesh, 2003), http://en.banglapedia.org/index.php?title=Husain,_Qazi_Motahar, last accessed 7 July 2018.
15. Kazi Motahar Hossain, *Sritikatha* (Dhaka: Nabajuga Prokashani, 2004), 21.
16. Ibid., 15.
17. Ibid., 56–7.
18. Ibid.
19. Ibid., 57.
20. Gary P. Freeman and James Jupp, eds, *Nations of Immigrants: Australia, the United States, and International Migration* (Melbourne and New York: Oxford University Press, 1992).
21. Hossain, *Sritikatha*, 15.
22. A. K. Ramanujan, *The Collected Essays of A. K. Ramanujan* (Delhi: Oxford University Press, 1999), 158.

23. Walter Mignolo and Catherine E. Walsh, *On Decoloniality: Concepts, Analytics, Praxis*, On Decoloniality (Durham, NC: Duke University Press, 2018), 7.
24. W. E. B. Du Bois, *The Souls of Black Folk*, Oxford World's Classics (Oxford and New York: Oxford University Press, 2007), 8.
25. Ibid., 8.
26. On the 'pool of stories' in the Ramayana see A. K. Ramanujan, 'Three Hundred Ramayanas: Five Examples and Three Thoughts on Translation', in *The Collected Essays of A. K. Ramanujan* (Delhi: Oxford University Press, 1999), 158.
27. Thomas Macaulay, cited in Catherine Hall, *Macaulay and Son: Architects of Imperial Britain* (New Haven: Yale University Press, 2012), 206.
28. Hallaq, *Restating Orientalism*, 107–111.
29. Kevin Buzzacott, *Lake Eyre Is Calling* (Murray Bridge: Nyiri Publications, 1998), 7.
30. See Irene Watson, 'Walking the Land for Our Ancient Rights: Interview with Kevin Buzzacott', *Indigenous Law Bulletin* 5 (2000).
31. Ibid., 19–20.
32. 'Foreword For Leopolodo Lugones' in Jorge Luis Borges, *Collected Fictions*, trans. Andrew Hurley (New York: Penguin Books, 1999), 291.
33. Toni Morrison, *Playing in the Dark: Whiteness and the Literary Imagination* (New York: Vintage Books, 1993), xi.
34. Ibid., 17.
35. Samia Khatun, *Australianama: The South Asian Odyssey in Australia* (London: Hurst, 2018), 182–184.
36. Geert Jan H. van Gelder, 'Hearing and Deafness', in Jane Dammen McAuliffe, ed., *Encyclopaedia of the Qurʾān* (Leiden: Brill, 2001), 405–6.
37. Ishan Chakrabarti, 'Bilvamaṅgala in Bengal: Gauḍīya Hagiography and the Poetics of the Inexpressible' (Paper Presented at the 13th International Conference on Early Modern Literatures in North India, University of Warsaw, 2018). On the cultural memory of Chaitanya in nineteenth and twentieth-century Bengal, see Varuni Bhatia, *Unforgetting Chaitanya: Vaishnavism and Cultures of Devotion in Colonial Bengal* (Oxford and New York: Oxford University Press, 2017).

BIBLIOGRAPHY

Archives and Libraries

The materials consulted in this book were gathered from periodicals, newspapers, official publications, and manuscripts housed in the following collections. Please note that I have consulted National Archives of Australia holdings in Canberra, Sydney, Melbourne, Brisbane and Perth and the physical location of a record can be found by consulting www.naa.gov.au. For detailed reference to Urdu, Persian and Dhirari records cited, please see the section 'Unpublished Sources'.

National Archives of Australia
State Records of South Australia
State Records Office of Western Australia
New South Wales State Archives
Public Record Office Victoria
Noel Butlin Archives Centre, Australian National University
South Australian Registry of Births, Deaths and Marriages
Western Australian Registry of Births, Deaths and Marriages
New South Wales Registry of Births, Deaths and Marriages
Queensland Registry of Births, Deaths and Marriages
National Library of Australia
Australian Institute of Aboriginal and Torres Strait Islander Studies Library
State Library of New South Wales
State Library of Victoria
State Library of South Australia
Bourke Public Library
Broken Hill Public Library
Port Augusta Public Library
Broken Hill Historical Society Records
University of Sydney Library

University of Melbourne Library
Australian National University Library
Dhaka University Library
National Library of India
Jadavpur University Library
Centre for Studies in Social Sciences, Calcutta
Columbia University Library
University of Otago Library

Government Documents

Coghlan, T. A. 'A Statistical Account of the Seven Colonies of Australasia, 1901–02' (Sydney: Government Printer, 3 December 1902).
Commonwealth of Australia. 'Aboriginal Welfare: Initial Conference of Commonwealth and State Aboriginal Authorities Held at Canberra, 21st to 23rd April 1937' (Canberra: Commonwealth Government Printer, 1937).
Commonwealth of Australia. *Parliamentary Debates, House of Representatives: Official Hansard* 1, 24694 (12 February 2004).
Francis, William. *The Nilgiris*, Madras District Gazetteers (Madras: Government Press, 1908; repr. New Delhi: Logos Press, 1984).
Government of South Australia. 'South Australian Act or Foundation Act of 1834', 15 August 1834, http://www.foundingdocs.gov.au/resources/transcripts/sa1_doc_1834.pdf, last accessed 2 July 2015.
Government of Western Australia. 'Aborigines Act 1905 (WA)'.
Long, J. *Returns Relating to Publications in the Bengali Language, in 1857*, Selections from the Records of the Bengal Government, XXXII (Calcutta: John Gray, General Printing Department, 1859).

Published Sources

Bengali

Bhadra, Gautam. *Nyera Battalae Jae Kaubar* (Kolkata: Chatim Books, 2011).
——— 'Rashbhab Manoharini', *Robbar* (Supplement to Newspaper *Sambaad Protidin*), 12 December 2010, 12–16.
Hossain, Kazi Motahar. *Sritikatha* (Dhaka: Nabajuga Prokashani, 2004).
Khatun, Sanjida. *Atit Diner Smriti* (Dhaka: Prakash, 1993).
Sen, Sukumar. *Battalar Chappa O Chobi* (Kolkata: Ananda Publishers, 2008).
Siraj, Syed Mustafa. *Aleek Manush* (Kolkata: Sahitya Akademi, 2005).
Sofiuddin, Kazi. *Kasasol Ambia* (Calcutta: Hanifia Press, 1895).
Tagore, Rabindranath. 'Kabuliwallah', in *Galpa Guchcha* (Dhaka: Nouroj Sahitya Sangsad, 1990), 84–9.

BIBLIOGRAPHY

English

Abu-Lughod, Janet L. 'The Islamic City – Historic Myth, Islamic Essence, and Contemporary Relevance', *International Journal of Middle East Studies* 19, no. 2 (1 May 1987), 155–76.

Abu-Lughod, Lila. *Do Muslim Women Need Saving?* (Cambridge, MA: Harvard University Press, 2013).

——— 'Against Universals: The Dialectics of (Women's) Human Rights and Human Capabilities', in J. Michelle Molina, Donald Swearer and Susan McGarry, eds, *Rethinking the Human* (Cambridge, MA: Harvard University Press, 2010), 69–94.

Achyutha, Suneetha. 'Deoband Patriarchy', *Economic and Political Weekly* 46, no. 26/27 (2011), 573–4.

Agnes, Flavia. 'Economic Rights of Women in Islamic Law', *Economic and Political Weekly* 31, no. 1 (12 October 1996), 2832–38.

Ahmad, Ghulam. *Tadhkirah: English Rendering of the Divine Revelations, Dreams and Visions Vouchsafed to Hadrat Mirza Ghulam Ahmad of Qadian*, ed. Mirza Masroor Ahmad, trans. Chaudhry Muhammad Zafrullah Khan, rev. Munawar Ahmed Saeed (Tilford: Islam International Publications Ltd, 2009).

Ahmed Asif, Manan. *A Book of Conquest: The Chachnama and Muslim Origins in South Asia* (Cambridge, MA: Harvard University Press, 2016).

Ahmed, Manan. 'A New Cartography of Imperial Power', *The National* (Abu Dhabi), 17 December 2010, 4–7.

Ahuja, Ravi. 'Mobility and Containment: The Voyages of South Asian Seamen, c.1900–1960'. *International Review of Social History* 51 (2006): 111–141.

Ali, Kecia. *Marriage and Slavery in Early Islam* (Cambridge, MA: Harvard University Press, 2010).

Ali, Muhammad. *The Ahmadiyyah Movement*, trans. S. Muhammad Tufail (Lahore: Ahmadiyya Anjuman, 1973).

Allahdin, Abdullah. *Claims and Teachings of Ahmad, the Promised Messiah and Mahdi*, 4th edition (Secunderabad: The Universal Press, 1922).

Allen, Margaret. '"Innocents Abroad" and "Prohibited Immigrants"; Australians in India and Indians in Australia 1890–1910', in Ann Curthoys and Marilyn Lake, eds, *Connected Worlds: History in Transnational Perspective Canberra* (Canberra: ANU E Press, 2005).

Amin, Shahid. *Conquest and Community: The Afterlife of Warrior Saint Ghazi Miyan* (New Delhi: Orient BlackSwan, 2015).

Amos, Valerie, and Pratibha Parmar. 'Challenging Imperial Feminism', *Feminist Review* 80 (2005), 44–63.

Amrith, Sunil S. *Crossing the Bay of Bengal: The Furies of Nature and the Fortunes of Migrants* (Cambridge, MA: Harvard University Press, 2013).

BIBLIOGRAPHY

Anderson, Claire. '"Process Geographies" of Mobility and Movement in the Indian Ocean: A Review Essay', *Journal of Colonialism and Colonial History* 8 (2007).

Anzaldúa, Gloria. *Borderlands/La Frontera: The New Mestiza* (San Francisco: Aunt Lute Books, 2007).

Arnold, David. *The New Cambridge History of India*, III, 5, *Science, Technology and Medicine in Colonial India*, 1st paperback edition (Cambridge, UK and New York: Cambridge University Press, 2004).

Austin, Peter, ed. *Language and History: Essays in Honour of Luise A. Hercus* (Canberra: Dept of Linguistics, Research School of Pacific Studies, Australian National University, 1990).

Austin, Peter, Luise Hercus, and Philip Jones. 'Ben Murray (Parlku-Nguyu-Thangknyiwarna)', *Aboriginal History* 12 (1988), 115–88.

Bakhsh, K. S. Mian Rahim. *The Debt Forgotten* (Columbus: Ahmadiyya Anjuman Isha'at Islam, 1993).

Balachandran, Gopalan. 'Circulation through Seafaring: Indian Seamen, 1890–1945', in Claude Markovits, Jaques Pouchepadass and Sanjay Subrahmanyam, eds, *Society and Circulation: Mobile People and Itinerant Cultures in South Asia, 1750–1950* (Delhi: Permanent Black, 2003).

——— 'Cultures of Protest in Transnational Contexts: Indian Seamen Abroad, 1886–1945', *Transforming Cultures EJournal* 3 (2008), 45–75.

Bald, Vivek. *Bengali Harlem and the Lost Histories of South Asian America* (Cambridge, MA: Harvard University Press, 2013).

Bald, Vivek. 'American Orientalism'. *Dissent Magazine*, Spring 2015. http://www.dissentmagazine.org/article/american-orientalism, last accessed 8 April 2012.

Bald, Vivek, Miabi Chatterji, Sujani Reddy, and Manu Vimalassery, eds. *The Sun Never Sets: South Asian Migrants in an Age of U.S. Power* (New York: New York University Press, 2013).

Ballantyne, Tony. *Orientalism and Race: Aryanism in the British Empire*, Cambridge Imperial and Post-Colonial Studies Series (Basingstoke: Palgrave, 2002).

——— 'Remaking the Empire from Newgate: Wakefield's A Letter from Sydney', in Antoinette M. Burton and Isabel Hofmeyr, eds, *Ten Books That Shaped the British Empire: Creating an Imperial Commons* (Durham, NC: Duke University Press, 2014).

——— 'Te Anu's Story: A Fragmentary History of Difference and Racialisation in Southern New Zealand', in Alison Holland and Barbara Brooks, eds, *Rethinking the Racial Moment: Essays on the Colonial Encounter* (Newcastle: Cambridge Scholars Publishing, 2011), 49–74.

Banivanua-Mar, Tracy, and Penelope Edmonds, eds. *Making Settler Colonial Space: Perspectives on Race, Place and Identity* (New York: Palgrave Macmillan, 2010).

BIBLIOGRAPHY

Banks, Joseph, and J. C. Beaglehole. *The Endeavour Journal of Joseph Banks: 1768–1771*, vol. 2 (Sydney: The Trustees of the Public Library of New South Wales in association with Angus and Robertson, 1962).

Basu, Shrabani. *For King and Another Country: Indian Soldiers on the Western Front 1914–18* (New Delhi: Bloomsbury, 2015).

Basu, Srimati, ed. *Dowry and Inheritance* (London: Zed Books, 2006).

Baxi, Pratiksha. *Public Secrets of Law: Rape Trials in India* (New Delhi: Oxford University Press, 2014).

Bayly, C. A. *Empire and Information: Intelligence Gathering and Social Communication in India, 1780–1870* (Cambridge, UK: Cambridge University Press, 2000).

Beaglehole, J. C., ed. *The Voyage of the Endeavour, 1768–1771* (Cambridge, UK: Cambridge University Press, 1955).

Behl, Aditya. *Love's Subtle Magic: An Indian Islamic Literary Tradition, 1379–1545*, ed. Wendy Doniger (New York: Oxford University Press, 2012).

——— 'Qutban from Mrigavati: Translated from the Hindavi', *Calque* 5 (February 2009), 68–113.

———' The Magic Doe: Desire and Narrative in a Hindavi Sufi Romance, circa 1503', in Richard Maxwell Eaton, ed., *India's Islamic Traditions, 711–1750*, Oxford in India Readings (New Delhi and New York: Oxford University Press, 2003).

Bhatia, Varuni. *Unforgetting Chaitanya: Vaishnavism and Cultures of Devotion in Colonial Bengal* (Oxford and New York: Oxford University Press, 2017).

Borges, Jorge Luis. *Collected Fictions*, trans. Andrew Hurley (New York: Penguin Books, 1999).

Bose, Neilesh. 'Purba Pakistan Zindabad: Bengali Visions of Pakistan, 1940–1947'. *Modern Asian Studies* 48, no. 1 (January 2014), 1–36.

Bose, Sugata. *A Hundred Horizons: The Indian Ocean in the Age of Global Empire* (Cambridge, MA: Harvard University Press, 2006).

Briscoe, Gordon. *Racial Folly: A Twentieth-Century Aboriginal Family* (Canberra: ANU E Press, 2010).

Brock, Peggy. *Outback Ghettos: Aborigines, Institutionalisation and Survival* (Cambridge, UK and Melbourne: Cambridge University Press, 1993).

——— *Yura and Udnyu: A History of the Adnyamathanha of the North Flinders Ranges* (Adelaide: Wakefield Press, 1985).

Budhasvāmin. *The Emperor of the Sorcerers*, trans. James Mallinson, 1st edition, Clay Sanskrit Library (New York: New York University Press: JJC Foundation, 2005).

Burton, Antoinette. 'Some Trajectories of "Feminism" and "Imperialism"', *Gender & History* 10, no. 3 (1 November 1998), 558–68.

Burton, Richard Francis. *Personal Narrative of a Pilgrimage to El-Medinah and Meccah* (London: Longman, Brown, Green, and Longmans, 1855).

Buzzacott, Kevin. *Lake Eyre Is Calling* (Murray Bridge: Nyiri Publications, 1998).

Casson, Lionel. *The Periplus Maris Erythraei: Text with Introduction, Translation, and Commentary* (Princeton: Princeton University Press, 1989).

Chakrabarty, Dipesh. 'Aboriginal and Subaltern Histories', in Bain Attwood and Tom Griffith, eds, *Frontier, Race, Nation: Henry Reynolds and Australian History* (Melbourne: Australian Scholarly Publishing, 2009).

——— *Provincializing Europe: Postcolonial Thought and Historical Difference* (Princeton: Princeton University Press, 2000).

Chant, Barry. 'The Australian Career of John Alexander Dowie', *Centre for the Study of Australian Christianity Working Papers* 1, no. 10 (10 August 1992), 1–26.

Chatterjee, Indrani. *Forgotten Friends: Monks, Marriages, and Memories of Northeast India* (New Delhi: Oxford University Press, 2013).

Chatterjee, Kumkum. *The Cultures of History in Early Modern India: Persianization and Mughal Culture in Bengal* (New Delhi: Oxford University Press, 2009).

——— 'The Persianization of "Itihasa": Performance Narratives and Mughal Political Culture in Eighteenth-Century Bengal', *The Journal of Asian Studies* 67, no. 2 (1 May 2008), 513–43.

Chatterjee, Partha. *The Nation and Its Fragments: Colonial and Postcolonial Histories*, Princeton Studies in Culture/Power/History (Princeton: Princeton University Press, 1993).

Clarsen, Georgine. 'Gender and Mobility: Historicising the Terms', in Gijs Mom, Gordon Pirie and Laurent Tissot, eds, *Mobility in History* (Neuchâtel: Alphil, 2009), 235–41.

Cohn, Bernard. *Colonialism and Its Forms of Knowledge: The British in India* (Princeton: Princeton University Press, 1996).

——— 'The Census, Social Structure and Objectification in South Asia', in Bernard Cohn, ed., *An Anthropologist Among the Historians and Other Essays* (Delhi: Oxford University Press, 1987), 224–54.

——— 'Representing Authority in Victorian India', in E. J. Hobsbawm and T. O. Ranger, eds, *The Invention of Tradition*, Past and Present Publications (Cambridge, UK and New York: Cambridge University Press, 1983).

Conrad, Joseph. *Heart of Darkness* (London: HarperCollins, 2013 [1899]).

Cook, James, and W. J. L. Wharton. *Captain Cook's Journal During His First Voyage Round the World Made in H.M. Bark Endeavour, 1768–71* (London: Elliot Stock, 1893).

Couture, Andre. 'From Viṣṇu's Deeds to Viṣṇu's Play, or Observations on the Word Avatāra as a Designation for the Manifestations of Viṣṇu', *Journal of Indian Philosophy* 29, no. 3 (2001), 313–26.

Crooke, William. *The North-Western Provinces of India* (London: Methuen & Co., 1897).

Curthoys, Ann. *Freedom Ride: A Freedom Rider Remembers* (Crows Nest: Allen & Unwin, 2002).

D'Hubert, Thibaut. *In the Shade of the Golden Palace: Ālāol and Middle Bengali Poetics in Arakan*, South Asia Research (New York: Oxford University Press, 2018).

Dirks, Nicholas B. *Castes of Mind: Colonialism and the Making of Modern India* (Princeton: Princeton University Press, 2001).

Dodd, Reg, and Jen Gibson. 'Learning Times: An Experience of Arabana Life and Mission Education', *Aboriginal History* 13 (1989), 81–93.

Dodd, Reg, and Tom Jenkin. 'Aboriginal Tourism and Land Management in the Lake Eyre Basin: Arabunna Aboriginal Tours', in *Lake Eyre Basin – Today And Tomorrow: Place, People, Possibilities* (Renmark: Lake Eyre Conference Steering Committee, 2006), 126–45.

Doniger, Wendy, ed., *The Magic Doe: Qutban Suhravardī's Mirigāvatī, A New Translation*, trans. Aditya Behl (New York: Oxford University Press, 2012).

Drewery, Roberta J. *Treks, Camps, & Camels: Afghan Cameleers Their Contribution to Australia* (Broken Hill: Published by Author, 2008).

Du Bois, W. E. B. *The Souls of Black Folk*, Oxford World's Classics (Oxford and New York: Oxford University Press, 2007).

During, J., and R. Sellheim. 'Samāʿ', in P. Bearman, W. P. Heinrichs, C. E. Bosworth, Th. Bianquis, and E. van Donzel, eds, *Encyclopaedia of Islam, Second Edition*, 24 April 2012.

Eckermann, Ali Cobby. *Inside My Mother* (Artamon: Giramondo Publishing, 2015).

——— *Kami* (Sydney: Vagabond Press, 2010).

——— *Too Afraid to Cry* (Elsternwick: Ilura Press, 2012).

El-Hibri, Tayeb. *Reinterpreting Islamic Historiography: Hārūn Al-Rashīd and the Narrative of the Abbāsid Caliphate*, Cambridge Studies in Islamic Civilization (Cambridge, UK and New York: Cambridge University Press, 1999).

Elphinstone, Mountstuart. *An Account of the Kingdom of Caubul* (London: Longman, Hurst, Rees, Orme & Brown, 1815).

Ewald, Janet J. 'Crossers of the Sea: Slaves, Freedmen, and Other Migrants in the Northwestern Indian Ocean, c. 1750–1914', *The American Historical Review* 105, no. 1 (2000), 69–91.

Eyre, Edward John. *Journals of Expeditions of Discovery into Central Australia and Overland from Adelaide to King George's Sound, In the Years 1840–1*, vol. 1, 25 June 1840 (Project Gutenberg, 2004), http://www.gutenberg.org/ebooks/5344

Fitzmaurice, Andrew. *Sovereignty, Property and Empire 1500–2000* (New York: Cambridge University Press, 2014).

Foster, Robert. 'Coexistence and Colonisation on Pastoral Leaseholds in South Australia, 1851–99', in John McLaren, A. Buck, and Nancy Wright, eds, *Despotic Dominion: Property Rights in British Settler Societies* (Vancouver: University of British Columbia Press, 2005), 248–65.

———'Feasts of the Full-Moon: The Distribution of Rations to Aborigines in South Australia: 1836–1861', *Aboriginal History* 13 (1989), 63–78.

Foucault, Michel. *The Order of Things: Archaeology of the Human Sciences*, 2nd edition (London and New York: Routledge, 2001).

——— *Power/Knowledge: Selected Interviews and Other Writings, 1972–1977* (Brighton, Sussex: Harvester Press, 1980).

Freeman, Gary P., and James Jupp, eds. *Nations of Immigrants: Australia, the United States, and International Migration* (Melbourne and New York: Oxford University Press, 1992).

Friedmann, Yohanan. *Prophecy Continuous: Aspects of Ahmadi Religious Thought and Its Medieval Background*, Comparative Studies on Muslim Societies 3 (Berkeley: University of California Press, 1989).

Fuller, Basil. *The Ghan: The Story of the Alice Springs Railway* (Adelaide: Rigby, 1975).

Ghose, Indira. 'Imperial Player: Richard Burton in Sindh', in Tim Youngs, ed., *Travel Writing in the Nineteenth Century: Filling the Blank Spaces* (London and New York: Anthem Press, 2006), 71–86.

Ghosh, Anindita. *Power in Print: Popular Publishing and the Politics of Language and Culture in a Colonial Society* (Delhi: Oxford University Press, 2006).

Ghosh, Devleena, and Stephen Muecke, eds. *Cultures of Trade: Indian Ocean Exchanges* (Newcastle: Cambridge Scholars Publishing, 2007).

Ghosh, Devleena. 'Under the Radar of Empire: Unregulated Travel in the Indian Ocean', *Journal of Social History* 45 (2011), 497–514.

Gibbs, Leah. 'Just Add Water: Colonisation, Water Governance, and the Australian Inland', *Environment and Planning* 41 (2009), 2964–83.

——— 'Valuing Water: Variability and the Lake Eyre Basin, Central Australia', *Australian Geographer* 37 (2006), 73–85.

Ginibi, Ruby Langford. *Real Deadly* (North Ryde: Angus & Robertson, 1992).

Ginzburg, Carlo. 'Morelli, Freud and Sherlock Holmes: Clues and Scientific Method', trans. Anna Davin, *History Workshop* 9 (1 April 1980), 5–36.

Goodall, Heather. 'Landscapes of Meaning: Views from Within the Indian Archipelago', *Transforming Cultures EJournal* 3 (2008), i–xiii.

——— 'Port Politics: Indian Seamen, Australian Unions and Indonesian Independence', *Labour History* 94 (2008), 43–68.

Goodall, Heather, and Allison Cadzow. *Rivers and Resilience: Aboriginal People on Sydney's Georges River* (Sydney: UNSW Press, 2009).

Goodall, Heather, and Kevin Cook. *Making Change Happen* (Canberra: ANU Press, 2013).

Goodall, Heather, Devleena Ghosh, and Lindi Todd. 'Jumping Ship – Skirting Empire: Indians, Aborigines and Australians Across the Indian Ocean', *Transforming Cultures EJournal* 3 (2008), 44–74.

Gothard, Jan. 'Assisted Female Immigration, 1860–1920', in James Jupp, ed., *The Australian People: An Encyclopedia of the Nation, Its People and Their Origins*, 2nd edition (Cambridge, UK and Oakleigh, Victoria: Cambridge University Press, 2001), 53–7.

Green, Nile. *Bombay Islam: The Religious Economy of the West Indian Ocean, 1840–1915* (New York: Cambridge University Press, 2011).

Guilliard, Joachim, Lühr Henken, Knut Mellenthin, and Jens Wagner. *Body Count: Casualty Figures after 10 Years of the 'War on Terror'* (Washington, DC: International Physicians for the Prevention of Nuclear War, 2015), http://www.psr.org/assets/pdfs/body-count.pdf, last accessed 12 September 2016.

Gupta, Pamila, Isabel Hofmeyr, and Michael Pearson. *Eyes Across the Water: Navigating the Indian Ocean* (Pretoria: Unisa Press; Delhi: Penguin India, 2010).

H. van Gelder, Geert Jan. 'Hearing and Deafness', in Jane Dammen McAuliffe, ed., *Encyclopaedia of the Qur'ān* (Leiden: Brill, 2001).

Haddawy, Husain, trans., *Sindbad And Other Stories from the Arabian Nights* (New York: W. W. Norton and Company, 2008).

Haebich, Anna. *Broken Circles: Fragmenting Indigenous Families 1800–2000* (Fremantle: Fremantle Arts Centre Press, 2000).

——— *For Their Own Good: Aborigines and Government in the South West of Western Australia 1900–1940* (Nedlands: University of Western Australia Press, 1992).

Hall, Catherine. *Macaulay and Son: Architects of Imperial Britain* (New Haven: Yale University Press, 2012).

Hallaq, Wael. *Restating Orientalism: A Critique of Modern Knowledge* (New York: Columbia University Press, 2018).

——— 'Re-Orienting Orientalism: Toward an Epistemology of Moral Responsibility' (Lecture for the Kamel Center for the Study of Islamic Law and Civilization, 17 November 2015), https://vimeo.com/149019309, last accessed 20 June 2018.

——— *Sharī'a: Theory, Practice, Transformations* (Delhi: Cambridge University Press, 2009).

——— 'What Is Shari'a', *Yearbook of Islamic and Middle Eastern Law* 12 (2005–6), 151–80.

——— *The Origins and Evolution of Islamic Law* (Cambridge, UK: Cambridge University Press, 2005).

——— 'From Fatwās To Furū: Growth and Change in Islamic Substantive Law', *Islamic Law and Society* 1 (1994), 29–65.

Hanifi, Shah Mahmoud. *Connecting Histories in Afghanistan: Market Relations and State Formation on a Colonial Frontier* (Stanford: Stanford University Press, 2011).

——— 'Quandaries of the Afghan Nation', in Shahzad Bashir and Robert Crews, eds, *Under the Drones: Modern Lives in the Afghanistan-Pakistan Borderlands* (Cambridge, MA: Harvard University Press, 2012), 83–101.

Hazarah, Fayz Muhammad Katib. *The History of Afghanistan*, trans. R. D. McChesney, annotated edition, vol. 3 (Leiden and Boston: Brill Academic Publishers, 2012).

Hercus, L. A. *A Grammar of the Arabana-Wangkangurru Language Lake Eyre Basin, South Australia* (Canberra: Dept of Linguistics, Research School of Pacific and Asian Studies, Australian National University, 1994).

Hercus, Luise. 'Leaving the Simpson Desert', *Aboriginal History* 9 (1985), 22–43.

——— 'Afghan Stories from the Northeast of South Australia', *Aboriginal History* 5 (1981), 39–70.

Hercus, Luise, Flavia Hodges, and Jane Simpson, *The Land Is a Map* (Canberra: Pandanus Books, 2002).

Hilali, Shaikh Ghulam Maqsud. *Perso-Arabic Elements in Bengali*, ed. Muhammad Enamul Huq (Rajshahi: Hilali Foundation, 2005).

Ho, Engseng. *The Graves of Tarim: Genealogy and Mobility Across the Indian Ocean* (Berkeley and London: University of California Press, 2006).

Hokari, Minoru. *Gurindji Journey: A Japanese Historian in the Outback* (Sydney: UNSW Press, 2011).

Hopkins, Benjamin. *The Making of Modern Afghanistan* (Basingstoke: Palgrave Macmillan, 2008).

Horne, George, and George Aiston. *Savage Life in Central Australia* (London: Macmillan, 1924).

Hossein, Rokeya Sakhawat. 'Sultana's Dream', in Firdous Azim and Niaz Zaman, eds, *Galpa: Short Stories by Women from Bangladesh* (London: Stanza, 1905).

Howitt, A. W. *Native Tribes of South-East Australia* (London: Macmillan and Co., 1904).

Hussein, Shakira. *From Victims to Suspects: Muslim Women Since 9/11* (Sydney: Newsouth Books, 2016).

Inden, Ronald. 'Orientalist Constructions of India', *Modern Asian Studies* 20, no. 3 (1986), 401–46.

——— *Imagining India* (Oxford and Cambridge, MA: Basil Blackwell, 1990).

Islam, Muhammad Wohidul. 'Al-Mal: The Concept of Property in Islamic Legal Thought', *Arab Law Quarterly* 14 (1 January 1999), 361–8.

Islam, Zafarul. 'The Fatawa Firuz Shahi as a Source for the Socio-Economic History of the Sultanate Period', *Islamic Culture* 60, no. 2 (1986), 97–117.

Jaggard, E. 'Vosper, Frederick Charles Burleigh (1869–1901)', in *Australian Dictionary of Biography* (Canberra: National Centre of Biography, Australian

National University, 1990), http://adb.anu.edu.au/biography/vosper-frederick-charles-burleigh-8933, last accessed 29 May 2017.

James, C. L. R. *The Black Jacobins; Toussaint L'Ouverture and the San Domingo Revolution*, 2nd edition, rev. (New York: Vintage Books, 1963).

Jamison, Stephanie W., and Joel P. Brereton, eds. *The Rigveda: The Earliest Religious Poetry of India*, South Asia Research (Oxford: Oxford University Press, 2014).

John, Graham St. 'Off Road Show: Techno, Protest and Feral Theatre', *Continuum: Journal of Media and Cultural Studies* 19, no. 1 (2005), 5–20.

Jones, Philip. *Ochre and Rust* (Adelaide: Wakefield Press, 2007).

Jones, Philip, and Anna Kenny. *Australia's Muslim Cameleers: Pioneers of the Inland, 1860s–1930s* (Adelaide: South Australian Museum, 2007).

Jones, William. *A Grammar of the Persian Language*, 5th edition (London: Printed for J. Murray, 1801).

Jupp, James. *From White Australia to Woomera: The Story of Australian Immigration* (Port Melbourne: Cambridge University Press, 2007).

Kabir, Nahid. 'A History of Muslims in Australia', *Star Weekend Magazine* (Supplement to Bangladeshi newspaper *Daily Star*), 7 September 2007.

Kamali, Mohammad Hashim. *Law in Afghanistan: A Study of the Constitutions, Matrimonial Law and the Judiciary* (Leiden: Brill, 1985).

Kasaba, Reşat, ed. *Turkey in the Modern World*, The Cambridge History of Turkey, vol. 4 (Cambridge, UK: Cambridge University Press, 2010).

Kerwin, Dale. *Aboriginal Dreaming Paths and Trading Routes: The Colonisation of the Australian Economic Landscape* (Brighton: Sussex Academic Press, 2010).

Khan, Adil Hussain. *From Sufism to Ahmadiyya: A Muslim Minority Movement in South Asia* (Bloomington and Indianapolis: Indiana University Press, 2015).

Kinra, Rajeev. *Writing Self, Writing Empire: Chandar Bhan Brahman and the Cultural World of the Indo-Persian State Secretary*, South Asia Across the Disciplines (Oakland, CA: University of California Press, 2015).

Kolsky, Elizabeth. 'Maneuvering the Personal Law System in Colonial India', *Law and History Review* 28, no. 4 (1 November 2010), 973–8.

——— '"The Body Evidencing the Crime": Rape on Trial in Colonial India, 1860–1947', *Gender & History* 22, no. 1 (April 2010), 109–30.

Korvin, Gábor. 'Adventures of a Kashmiri Merchant in Australia – An Unknown Urdu Travelogue', *Journal of the Pakistan Historical Society* 52 (2004), 21–39.

——— 'The Memoirs of Khawajah Muhammad Bux, (Australian Businessman): Part I', *Journal of the Pakistan Historical Society (Historicus)* 64, no. 1 (2016), 67–91.

Koselleck, Reinhart. *Futures Past: On the Semantics of Historical Time*, Studies in Contemporary German Social Thought (Cambridge, MA: MIT Press, 1985).

——— '"Progress" and "Decline"', in *The Practice of Conceptual History*, trans. Todd Presner (Stanford: Stanford University Press, 2002), 218–36.

Kresse, Kai, and Edward Simpson. *Struggling With History: Islam and Cosmopolitanism in the Western Indian Ocean* (New York: Columbia University Press, 2008).

Lake, Marilyn, and Henry Reynolds. *Drawing the Global Colour Line: White Men's Countries and the International Challenge of Racial Equality* (Cambridge, UK: Cambridge University Press, 2008).

Langton, Marcia. 'Out From the Shadows: The Development of the Aboriginal Tracker Figure in Australian Film', *Meanjin* 65, no. 1 (2006), 54–64.

Lewis, I. M. *A Modern History of the Somali: Nation and State in the Horn of Africa*, 4th edition, Eastern African Studies (Oxford: James Currey and Athens, OH: Ohio University Press, 2002).

Locke, John. *Two Treatises of Government: A Critical Edition with an Introduction and Apparatus Criticus by Peter Laslett* (Cambridge, UK: Cambridge University Press, 1960), 288–90.

Low, Michael Christopher. '"The Infidel Piloting the True Believer": Thomas Cook and the Business of the Colonial Hajj', 5 October 2016, 47–80.

Loy-Wilson, Sophie. *Australians in Shanghai: Race, Rights and Nation in Treaty Port China* (Abingdon and New York: Routledge, 2017).

M. Bostdorff, Denise. 'George W. Bush's Post-September 11 Rhetoric of Covenant Renewal: Upholding the Faith of the Greatest Generation', *Quarterly Journal of Speech* 89, no. 4 (November 2003), 293–319.

Macfarlane, Ingereth. 'A Water History of the Western Simpson Desert, South Australia', in M. A. Smith and P. Hesse, eds, *23°S: Archaeology and Environmental History of Southern Deserts* (Canberra: National Museum of Australia, 2005).

Macgregor, Christine. *A History of the Beltana Pastoral Company Limited* (Adelaide: Gillingham Printers, 1965).

Macintyre, Stuart. *The Oxford History of Australia: Volume 4, 1901–1942* (Melbourne: Oxford University Press, 1986).

Macknight, C. C. 'Journal of a Voyage Around Arnhem Land in 1875'. *Aboriginal History* 5 (1981), 135–46.

Maclean, Kama. 'Examinations, Access, and Inequity Within the Empire: Britain, Australia and India, 1890–1910', *Postcolonial Studies* 18, no. 2 (3 April 2015), 115–32.

Maine, Henry Sumner. *Lectures on the Early History of Institutions* (London: J. Murray, 1875).

Manne, Robert. 'Little America', *The Monthly*, 8 March 2006, https://www.themonthly.com.au/monthly-essays-robert-manne-little-america-how-john-howard-has-changed-australia-184, last accessed 8 May 2017.

——— 'In Denial: The Stolen Generations and the Right', *Quarterly Essay*, no. 1 (2001).

Mantena, Karuna. *Alibis of Empire: Henry Maine and the Ends of Liberal Imperialism* (Princeton: Princeton University Press, 2010).

Marsden, Magnus, and Benjamin Hopkins, eds. *Beyond Swat: History, Society and Economy Along the Afghanistan-Pakistan Frontier* (London: Hurst, 2013).

Martineau, John. *The Life and Correspondence of Sir Bartle Frere* (London: Murray, 1895).

Martínez, Julia, and Adrian Vickers. *The Pearl Frontier: Indonesian Labor and Indigenous Encounters in Australia's Northern Trading Network* (Honolulu: University of Hawaii Press, 2015).

Marx, Karl. *Capital*, vol. 1 (London: Penguin Books, 1990).

Maynard, John. '"In the Interests of Our People": The Influence of Garveyism on the Rise of Australian Aboriginal Political Activism', *Aboriginal History* 29 (2005), 1–29.

McAuliffe, Jane Dammen, ed. *Encyclopaedia of the Qurʾān* (Leiden: Brill, 2001).

McGetchin, Douglas T. *Indology, Indomania, and Orientalism: Ancient India's Rebirth in Modern Germany* (Madison: Fairleigh Dickinson University Press, 2009).

McKenna, Mark. *From the Edge: Australia's Lost Histories* (Carlton, Victoria: Melbourne University Publishing, 2016).

McKinnon, Crystal. 'Indigenous Music as a Space of Resistance', in Tracy Banivanua-Mar and Penelope Edmonds, eds, *Making Settler Colonial Space: Perspectives on Race, Place and Identity* (New York: Palgrave Macmillan, 2010).

McLaren, John, A. Buck, and Nancy Wright, eds. *Despotic Dominion: Property Rights in British Settler Societies* (Vancouver: University of British Columbia Press, 2005).

McLean, Mick, and Luise Hercus. 'The End of the Mindiri People', in Peter Sutton and Luise Hercus, eds, *This Is What Happened*, trans. Luise Hercus (Canberra: Australian Institute of Aboriginal Studies, 1971).

Meisami, Julie Scott. *Structure and Meaning in Medieval Arabic and Persian Poetry: Orient Pearls* (London: RoutledgeCurzon, 2003).

Melville, Herman. *Redburn, His First Voyage, A Novel* (New York: Anchor Books, 1957).

Mernissi, Fatima. *Dreams of Trespass: Tales of a Harem Girlhood* (New York: Addison-Wesley Publishing Company, 1994).

——— *Women and Islam: An Historical and Theological Enquiry*, trans. Mary Jo Lakeland (Oxford: Basil Blackwell, 1991).

Metcalfe, Barbara. 'The Pilgrimage Remembered: South Asian Accounts of the Hajj', in *Muslim Travellers: Pilgrimage, Migration, and the Religious Imagination* (Berkeley: University of California Press, 1990).

Mignolo, Walter D. *Local Histories/Global Designs: Coloniality, Subaltern Knowledges, and Border Thinking* (Princeton: Princeton University Press, 2012 [2000]).

Mignolo, Walter, and Catherine E. Walsh. *On Decoloniality: Concepts, Analytics, Praxis*, On Decoloniality (Durham, NC: Duke University Press, 2018).

Miller, Kei. 'Imaging Nations', *Moving Worlds: A Journal of Transcultural Writings* 11, no. 1 (2011).

——— 'The Texture of Fiction', *The Edinburgh Review*, no. 123 (2008).

Mir, Farina. *The Social Space of Language: Vernacular Culture in British Colonial Punjab*, South Asia Across the Disciplines 2 (Berkeley: University of California Press, 2010).

Mitra, Rajendralal. 'On the Origin of the Hindvi Language and Its Relation to the Urdu Dialect', *Journal of the Asiatic Society of Bengal* 33, no. 5 (1864), 489–518.

Mohanty, Chandra Talpade. 'Under Western Eyes: Feminist Scholarship and Colonial Discourses'. *Boundary* 2 12, no. 3 (1984), 333–58.

Moin, A. Azfar. *The Millennial Sovereign: Sacred Kingship and Sainthood in Islam*, South Asia Across the Disciplines (New York: Columbia University Press, 2012).

Moin, Azfar. 'Akbar's "Jesus" and Marlowe's "Tamburlaine": Strange Parallels of Early Modern Sacredness', *Fragments: Interdisciplinary Approaches to the Study of Ancient and Medieval Pasts* 3 (2013–14).

Moir, Martin, and Lynn Zastoupil, eds. *The Great Indian Education Debate: Documents Relating To the Orientalist-Anglicist Controversy, 1781–1843* (Richmond, Surrey: Curzon, 1999).

Mongia, Radhika Viyas. 'Race, Nationality, Mobility: A History of the Passport', *Public Culture* 11, no. 3 (1999), 527–56.

Moorthy, Shanty, and Ashraf Jamal, eds. *Indian Ocean Studies: Cultural, Social and Political Perspectives* (New York and London: Routledge, 2010).

Morgan, Margaret. *A Drop in the Bucket: The Mount Margaret Story* (Box Hill: United Aborigines Mission, 1986).

Morrison, Toni. *Playing in the Dark: Whiteness and the Literary Imagination* (New York: Vintage Books, 1993).

Mudd, G. M. 'Mound Springs of the Great Artesian Basin in South Australia: A Case Study from Olympic Dam', *Environmental Geology* 39, no. 5 (2000), 463–76.

Muller, Craig. 'The "Allurements of the European Presence": Examining Explanations of Wongatha Behaviour in the Northern Goldfields of Western Australia', *Aboriginal History* 38 (December 2014), 59–87.

Murshed, Md Mahbub. 'Husain, Qazi Motahar', in Sirajul Islam and Sajahan Miah, eds, *Banglapedia: National Encyclopedia of Bangladesh* (Dhaka: Asiatic

Society of Bangladesh, 2003), http://en.banglapedia.org/index.php?title=Husain,_Qazi_Motahar, last accessed 7 July 2018.

Musakhan, Mohamed Hasan. *Islam in Australia: 1862–1932* (Adelaide: Mahomet Allum, 1932).

Naim, C. M. '"Prophecies" in South Asian Muslim Political Discourse: The Poems of Shah Ni'matullah Wali', *Economic and Political Weekly*, 9 July 2011.

Narayana Rao, Velcheru, David Dean Shulman, and Sanjay Subrahmanyam. *Textures of Time: Writing History in South India* (New York: Other Press, 2003).

Organ, Michael. 'Australian Aboriginal Dreaming Stories: A Chronological Bibliography of Published Works 1789–1991', *Aboriginal History* 18 (1994), 123–44.

Özcan, Azmi. *Pan-Islamism: Indian Muslims, the Ottomans and Britain, 1877–1924*, The Ottoman Empire and Its Heritage, vol. 12 (Leiden and New York: Brill, 1997).

Pathak, Zakia, Saswati Sengupta, and Sharmila Purkayastha. 'The Prisonhouse of Orientalism', *Textual Practice* 5, no. 2 (1 June 1991), 195–218.

Pati, Biswamoy, ed. *The Great Rebellion of 1857 in India: Exploring Transgressions, Contests and Diversities* (London: Routledge, 2012).

Peacock, Andrew. *Mediaeval Islamic Historiography and Political Legitimacy Bal'ami's Tarikhnamah* (Hoboken: Taylor and Francis, 2013).

Pollock, Sheldon. 'Forum: Textures of Time', *History and Theory* 46 (October 2007), 364–81.

——— *The Language of the Gods in the World of Men: Sanskrit, Culture, and Power in Premodern India* (Berkeley: University of California Press, 2006).

Pope, Andrew. 'Precious Metals Flow in the Indian Ocean in the Colonial Period: Australian Gold to India, 1866–1914', in John McGuire, Patrick Bertola and Peter Reeves, eds, *Evolution of the World Economy, Precious Metals and India* (Oxford: Oxford University Press, 2001).

——— 'The P&O and the Asian Specie Network, 1850–1920', *Modern Asian Studies* 30 (1996), 145–72.

Potts, Annette. '"I Am a British Subject, and I Can Go Wherever the British Flag Flies": Indians on the Northern Rivers of New South Wales during the Federation Years', *Journal of the Royal Australian Historical Society* 83, no. 2 (1997), 97–117.

Pratt, Mary Louise. *Imperial Eyes: Travel Writing and Transculturation*, 2nd edition (London and New York: Routledge, 2008).

Rademaker, Laura. *Found in Translation: Many Meanings on a North Australian Mission* (Honolulu: University of Hawaii Press, 2018).

Rajan, Balachandra. *Under Western Eyes: India from Milton to Macaulay, Post-Contemporary Interventions* (Durham, NC: Duke University Press, 1999).

Rajkowski, Pamela. *In the Tracks of the Camelmen: Outback Australia's Most Exotic Pioneers* (Sydney: Angus and Robertson, 1987).

——— *Linden Girl: A Story of Outlawed Lives* (Perth: University of Western Australia Press, 1995).

Ramanujan, A. K. *The Collected Essays of A. K. Ramanujan* (Delhi: Oxford University Press, 1999).

Rana, Junaid Akram. *Terrifying Muslims: Race and Labor in the South Asian Diaspora* (Durham, NC: Duke University Press, 2011).

Rangan, Haripriya, and Christian Kull. 'The Indian Ocean and the Making of Outback Australia: An Ecocultural Odyssey', in *Indian Ocean Studies: Cultural, Social, and Political Perspectives* (New York and London: Routledge, 2010), 45–72.

Rashid, Amjad. 'Industrial Concentration and Economic Power in Pakistan', *Pakistan Economic and Social Review* 14, no. 1/4 (1976), 211–61.

Ray, Rajat Kanta. 'Asian Capital in the Age of European Domination: The Rise of the Bazaar, 1800–1914', *Modern Asian Studies* 29 (1995): 449–554.

Reynolds, Dwight. 'A Thousand and One Nights: A History of the Text and Its Reception', in Roger M. A. Allen and D. S. Richards, eds, *Arabic Literature in the Post-Classical Period*, 1st edition, The Cambridge History of Arabic Literature (Cambridge, UK: Cambridge University Press, 2006), 270–91.

Rhook, Nadia. '"Turban-Clad" British Subjects: Tracking the Circuits of Mobility, Visibility, and Sexuality in Settler Nation-Making', *Transfers* 5, no. 3 (1 December 2015), 104–22.

Rose, Deborah Bird. *Nourishing Terrains: Australian Aboriginal Views of Landscape and Wilderness* (Canberra: Australian Heritage Commission, 1996).

——— 'Writing Place', in Ann Curthoys and Ann McGrath, eds, *Writing Histories: Imagination and Narration* (Clayton: Monash University ePress, 2009).

Rosenthal, Franz. *The History of Al-Tabari, Vol. 1: General Introduction and From the Creation to the Flood* (Albany: SUNY Press, 1989).

——— *A History of Muslim Historiography*, 2nd edition (Leiden: Brill, 1968).

Roy, Tapti. 'Disciplining the Printed Text: Colonial and Nationalist Surveillance of Bengali Literature', in *Texts of Power: Emerging Disciplines in Colonial Bengal* (Minneapolis: University of Minnesota Press, 1995), 30–62.

Rubin, Gayle. 'The Traffic in Women: Notes on the "Political Economy" of Sex', in Rayna Reiter, ed., *Toward an Anthropology of Women* (New York: Monthly Review Press, 1975), 157–210.

Said, Edward. *Orientalism* (London: Penguin, 2003 [1979]).

Sattar, Arshia. *The Mouse Merchant: Money in Ancient India* (New Delhi: Penguin, 2013).

Schebeck, Bernhard. 'Some Remarks on Placenames in the Flinders', in Luise Hercus, Flavia Hodges and Jane Simpson, *The Land Is a Map* (Canberra: Pandanus Books, 2002).

Scott, David. *Conscripts of Modernity: The Tragedy of Colonial Enlightenment* (Durham, NC: Duke University Press, 2004).

Shahriyār, Buzurg ibn. *The Book of the Wonders of India: Mainland, Sea, and Islands*, ed. and trans. G. S. P. Freeman-Grenville (London and The Hague: East-West Publications, 1981).

Shain, Farzana. 'Uneasy Alliances: British Muslims and Socialists since the 1950s', *Journal of Communist Studies and Transition Politics* 25, no. 1 (1 March 2009), 95–109.

Sharafi, Mitra. 'The Marital Patchwork of Colonial South Asia: Forum Shopping from Britain to Baroda', *Law and History Review* 28, no. 4 (November 2010), 979–1009.

Silverstein, Jordana. *Anxious Histories: Narrating the Holocaust in Jewish Communities at the Beginning of the Twenty-First Century*, 1st edition (New York: Berghahn Books, 2015).

Simpson, Jane. 'Camels as Pidgin-Carriers: Afghan Cameleers as a Vector for the Spread of Features of Australian Aboriginal Pidgins and Creoles', in Jeff Siegel, ed., *Processes of Language Contact: Studies from Australia and the South Pacific* (Fides: Champs Linguistiques, 2000).

Slight, John. 'British Colonial Knowledge and the Hajj in the Age of Empire', in Umar Ryad, ed., *The Hajj and Europe in the Age of Empire* (Leiden and Boston: Brill, 2016), 81–111.

Smith, Linda Tuhiwai. *Decolonizing Methodologies: Research and Indigenous Peoples* (Dunedin: University of Otago Press, 1999).

Stephenson, Peta. *Islam Dreaming: Indigenous Muslims in Australia* (Sydney: UNSW Press, 2010).

Stevens, Christine. *Tin Mosques & Ghantowns: A History of Afghan Cameldrivers in Australia* (Melbourne: Oxford University Press, 1989).

Strawson, John. 'Islamic Law and English Texts', *Law and Critique* 6, no. 1 (1 March 1995), 21–38.

Taneja, Anand Vivek. *Jinnealogy: Time, Islam, and Ecological Thought in the Medieval Ruins of Delhi*, 1st edition (Stanford: Stanford University Press, 2017).

Tanter, Richard. 'The "Joint Facilities" Revisited: Desmond Ball, Democratic Debate on Security, and the Human Interest', NAPSNet Special Reports (Nautilus Institute for Security and Sustainability Special Report, 11 December 2012).

Teo, Hsu-Ming. 'Multiculturalism and the Problem of Multicultural Histories: An Overview of Ethnic Historiography', in Richard White and Hsu-Ming Teo, eds, *Cultural History in Australia* (Sydney: UNSW Press, 2003), 142–156.

Thānvī, 'Ashraf 'Alī. *Perfecting Women: Maulana Ashraf 'Ali Thanawi's Bihishtizewar: A Partial Translation with Commentary*, trans. Barbara Daly Metcalf (Berkeley: University of California Press, 1990).

Toorawa, Shawkat M. 'Wâq Al-Wâq: Fabulous, Fabular, Indian Ocean (?) Island(s) …', *Emergences: Journal for the Study of Media & Composite Cultures* 10 (2000), 387–402.

Truschke, Audrey. *Culture of Encounters: Sanskrit at the Mughal Court*, South Asia Across the Disciplines (New York: Columbia University Press, 2016).

Tunbridge, Dorothy. 'Aboriginal Place Names', *Australian Aboriginal Studies* 2 (1987), 2–13.

——— *Flinders Ranges Dreaming* (Canberra: Aboriginal Studies Press, 1988).

Turner, Violet. *Pearls from the Deep: The Story of Colebrook Home for Aboriginal Children* (Adelaide: United Aborigines Mission, 1936).

Valentine, Simon Ross. *Islam and the Ahmadiyya Jama'at: History, Belief, Practice* (London: Hurst, 2008).

Vasudeva, Somadeva. *The Ocean of the Rivers of Story*, trans. James Mallinson, 1st edition, Clay Sanskrit Library (New York: New York University Press: JJC Foundation, 2007).

Veracini, Lorenzo. 'The Imagined Geographies of Settler Colonialism', in Tracy Banivanua-Mar and Penelope Edmonds, eds, *Making Settler Colonial Space: Perspectives on Race, Place and Identity* (New York: Palgrave Macmillan, 2010).

Ville, Simon. *The Rural Entrepreneurs: A History of the Stock and Station Agent Industry in Australia and New Zealand* (Oakleigh: Cambridge University Press, 2000).

Viswanathan, Gauri. *Masks of Conquest: Literary Study and British Rule in India*, Social Foundations of Aesthetic Forms Series (New York: Columbia University Press, 1989).

Waheed, Sarah. 'Women of "Ill Repute": Ethics and Urdu Literature in Colonial India', *Modern Asian Studies* 48, no. 4 (July 2014), 986–1023.

Wake, Charles Staniland. *The Development of Marriage and Kinship* (London: George Redway, 1889).

Walker, Alan and R. David Zorc. 'Austronesian Loanwords in Yolngu-Matha of Northeast Arnhem Land', *Aboriginal History* 5 (1981), 109–34.

Walsh, Michael. 'Languages and their Status in Aboriginal Australia', in Colin Yallop and Michael Walsh, eds, *Language and Culture in Aboriginal Australia* (Canberra: Aboriginal Studies Press, 1993).

Watkins-Thomas, M. 'Our Asian Crews', *About Ourselves: (P & O Staff Journal)* (September 1955), no page.

Watson, Irene. 'Walking the Land for Our Ancient Rights: Interview with Kevin Buzzacott', *Indigenous Law Bulletin* 5 (2000).

Wilson, Kathleen. 'Empire, Gender, and Modernity in the Eighteenth Century', in Philippa Levine, ed., *Gender and Empire* (New York: Oxford University Press, 2004).

Wilson, Ronald. *Bringing Them Home: Report of the National Inquiry into the Separation of Aboriginal and Torres Strait Islander Children from Their Families* (Sydney: Human Rights and Equal Opportunity Commission, 1997).

Wolfe, Michael. *One Thousand Roads to Mecca: Ten Centuries of Travelers Writing About the Muslim Pilgrimage*, 1st edition (New York: Grove Press, 1997).

Woods, J., George Taplin, William Wyatt, H. A. E. Meyer, C. W. Schürmann, Samuel Gason, and John William Ogilvie Bennett. *The Native Tribes of South Australia* (Adelaide: E. S. Wigg and Son, 1879).

Yasmeen, Samina. 'The Bux Family', *History West* 51, no. 3 (April 2012), 1.

Ziad, Homayra. 'The Return of Gog: Politics and Pan-Islamism in the Hajj Travelogue of Abd Al-Majid Daryabadi', in *Global Muslims in the Age of Steam and Print*, 1st edition (Berkeley: University of California Press, 2014), 227–48.

Unpublished Sources

Urdu

Bux, Khawajah Muhammad. 'Sawanih-E-Umri' (Unpublished Manuscript), c. 1944. Personal Collection of Author.

Persian

Musakhan, Abraham Khan. 'An Open Letter On a Literary Subject in the Persian Language' (Unpublished Manuscript), c. 1917. Held at State Library of Western Australia, Perth.

Dhirari

Australian Institute of Aboriginal and Torres Strait Islander Studies, Audiovisual Archives; Austin P07, Sound recordings collected by Peter Kenneth Austin, 1975–1976; Recording 004002A, timecode 00:52.00–01.00.00, Oral history elicitation in Dhirari with Ben Murray at Farina, 28 November 1975.

English

Ahmed Asif, Manan. 'Prophetic Pakistan' (Unpublished Paper, Columbia University, 2013).

Bux, Khawajah Muhammad. 'Memoirs of Khawajah Muhammad Bux, Australian Businessman' (Unpublished Manuscript), ed. Gábor Kovin, trans. Syed Haider Hassan (Rawalpindi, Pakistan, 2006).

Chakrabarti, Ishan. 'Bilvamaṅgala in Bengal: Gauḍīya Hagiography and the Poetics of the Inexpressible' (Paper Presented at the 13th International Conference on Early Modern Literatures in North India, University of Warsaw, 2018).

Hercus, Luise. 'Singing and Talking about Red Ochre' (Unpublished Manuscript, Australian National University, 2009).

Irani, Ayesha A. 'Sacred Biography, Translation, and Conversion: The "Nabivamsa" of Saiyad Sultan and the Making of Bengali Islam, 1600–Present' (PhD Thesis, University of Pennsylvania, 2011).

Jackomos, Alick. 'Genealogies of Gippsland & Wimmera (Victoria) Families, Includes Lake Tyers, Ebonezer Mission and Former Coranderrk Families That Moved to Lake Tyers and Descendants Now Living in Melbourne' (Unpublished Manuscript), 1987.

Kaladelfos, Amanda. 'Crime and Outrage: Sexual Villains and Sexual Violence in New South Wales, 1870–1930' (PhD Thesis, University of Sydney, 2010).

MacFarlane, Ingereth. 'Entangled Places: Interactive Histories in the Western Simpson Desert, Central Australia' (PhD Thesis, Australian National University, 2010).

Mir, Farina. 'The Social Space of Language: Punjabi Popular Narrative in Colonial India, c. 1850–1900' (PhD Thesis, Columbia University, 2002).

Mudd, Gavin. 'The Sustainability of Mound Springs in South Australia: Implications for Olympic Dam', Commission on Mineral and Thermal Waters Meeting (Paper Presented at the International Association of Hydrogeologists (IAH), Ballarat, Australia, 1998).

Obrock, Luther. 'Translation and History: The Development of a Kashmiri Textual Tradition from ca. 1000–1500' (PhD Thesis, University of California, Berkeley, 2015).

Shir, Jawan. 'Nationalism in Afghanistan: Colonial Knowledge, Education, Symbols, and the Junket Tour of Amanullah Khan, 1901–1929' (Master's Thesis, James Madison University, 2012).

Uddin, Layli. 'In The Land of Eternal Eid: Maulana Bhashani and the Political Mobilisation of Peasants and Lower-Class Urban Workers in East Pakistan, c.1930s–1971' (PhD Thesis, Royal Holloway, University of London, 2015).

Yasmeen, Samina. 'Muslim Australian Contributions: Bux Family as a Case Study' (Unpublished Paper, Centre for Muslim States and Societies, The University of Western Australia, 2009).

Audio-visual Materials, Online Sources and Databases

Browning, Daniel. 'Nomads: The Aboriginal Descendants of the Afghan Camel Drivers' (Radio Broadcast), *Awaye* (Radio National, 18 July 2009).

Central Australian Aboriginal Media Association (CAAMA). *The Last Camel Train* (CD) (Alice Springs: CAAMA Music, 2002).

Deathscapes: Mapping Race and Violence in Settler States, https://www.deathscapes.org/, last accessed 7 July 2018.

Dry, Joel. 'Imagine Having Your Whole History Erased: Indigenous Rights Activists Burn Australian Flag During G20 Protests' (Television Broadcast), *Nine News* (Channel Nine, 16 November 2014).

Hallaq, Wael. 'Re-Orienting Orientalism: Toward an Epistemology of Moral Responsibility' (Lecture for the Kamel Center for the Study of Islamic Law and Civilization, 17 November 2015), https://vimeo.com/149019309, last accessed 20 June 2018.

Khatun, Samia. 'Dreaming of Dhaka', 23 June 2011, https://www.youtube.com/watch?v=84M_-0IskiQ, last accessed 12 June 2017.
Lawrance, Oliver, and Melissa Abraham. *Freedom Rides: 40 Years On* (DVD) (Sydney: Australians for Native Title and Reconciliation, 2012), 50 mins.
Lindstrom, Esther. 'Sculptures in the Outback' (Television Broadcast), *Stateline* (Australian Broadcasting Corporation, 2004), https://www.youtube.com/watch?v=l53qID5AB0E, last accessed 15 September 2018.
'Snowden Digital Surveillance Archive', https://snowdenarchive.cjfe.org/, last accessed 4 March 2015.
Staight, Kerry. 'Creek Dries Up' (Television Broadcast), *Landline* (Australian Broadcasting Corporation, 7 June 2008).
Whirling Dervish Media. 'Mona Akbar Interview', 30 November 2012, https://www.youtube.com/watch?v=KEgB8LxuP2g, last accessed 24 September 2014.

ACKNOWLEDGEMENTS

This book was hard to write and I am indebted to an embarrassingly long list of people. It began as a doctoral thesis in the Australian history program at the University of Sydney under the guidance of Penny Russell, supervisor extraordinaire. Penny not only encouraged the new questions that I started asking as I took on heavier caring responsibilities, but somehow also created spaces in which I could write as life became increasingly chaotic, all while not letting me cut any corners. I thank Penny for setting an example of teaching excellence that I can only ever hope to emulate.

The postgraduate cohort that clustered around the University of Sydney was incredible. I thank Jemima Mowbray, Sophie Loy-Wilson, Andy Kaladelfos, Hannah Forsyth, Noah Pleshet, Altin Gavranovic and Alecia Prudence Simmonds for endless life-giving discussions about our respective projects, and I am indebted to Robbie Mason for his assistance with proofreading the final manuscript. I thank Devleena Ghosh for first directing my gaze across the Indian Ocean and Heather Goodall for her continued, generous advice about every difficult aspect of historical storytelling. Zeena Elton and Ben Spies-Butcher taught me all I know about how to move between research and activism and they continued to shape this book long after we all stopped working at the Edmund Rice Centre for Justice and Community Education.

I thank Jenny Camilleri from the Broken Hill Historical Society, Tina Dunemann from the Port Augusta Public Library and the librarians and archivists at the various collections I visited over the years.

ACKNOWLEDGEMENTS

Discussions with Reg Dodd changed the questions I asked in this book, radically transforming how I saw the past. I thank him for his generous, ongoing teaching. I thank Lil Khan, Donna Cook, the late Aysha Zada, Bobby Shamrose, Janet Shamrose, Toni Bauer and Aliah Bauer for inviting me into their homes and sharing family archives with me. I am indebted to wonderful Larl Zada and Christine Daley from Port Augusta for taking me repeatedly to the Camel Cup and I thank the Marree community and in particular Fred Dodd, Kevin Buzzacott, Paolo and Jan Whyte. Richard Wilson, co-traveller through Arabunna lands, became something like an older brother during that trip and I thank him for allowing me to use his photograph on the cover of this book. I am also indebted to Phil, Immy and Ariane Cox for taking me to Marree when all my money had run out and all deadlines had passed.

At Jadavpur University, Supriya Chaudhuri, Abhijit Gupta, Epsita Halder and Nilanjana Deb made Kolkata a perfect port of entry into the Indian humanities landscape. Conversations with both Lakshmi Subramanian and Bodhisattva Kar from the Centre for Studies in Social Sciences, Calcutta found a place in this book and I thank them. My world and this book expanded in dialogue with Ammel Sharon, Kena Wani, Jason Fernandes, Yagna Nag Chowdhuri, Moumita Sen, Subham Chowdhury, Titas Chakraborty and, of course, Gautam Bhadra. Kolkata could not have been home without the love of Sutanuka Bhattacharya.

The reports by my thesis examiners Dipesh Chakrabarty, Isabel Hofmeyr and Ann McGrath offered a valuable map for plotting revisions. I am deeply grateful to all of them for their ongoing support over the years since. I thank Kai Kresse for hosting me at the Zentrum Moderner Orient in Germany after I first took flight from the student nest. In Berlin, friendships with Ali Raza, Franzisca Roy, Mana Kia, Rajkamal Kahlon, Fatemeh Masjedi and Luzi Yang signposted the way forward to intellectual expansion, and I thank Nate McCarthy, Huon Curtis, Geordie Williamson, Ben Wilson and Steve Enright-Ward – the inner-city Sydney diaspora living in Germany at the time – for their grounding friendship during that exhilarating period. Continuing conversations that began in Berlin, in a writing group in New York I workshopped the manuscript with Sahar Romani, Manan Ahmed Asif and the late Kavita Datla. They undertook the difficult work of gently posing provocative challenges. I thank them for significantly shaping the scope of this book. I thank the Asian American Writers' Workshop for hosting me during my stay in New York.

I lived in six different countries over the course of writing this book and I thank Antoinette Burton for the ongoing correspondence that has long operated as a vital thread in making sense of widely diverging historical consciousness in different nation-spaces. In New Zealand, Tony Ballantyne generously gave me writing space as a visitor to the Centre for Research on Colonial Culture at the University of Otago. Vanessa Ward, Barbara Brooks, Angela Wanhalla and Michael Stevens made Dunedin an ideal point of re-entry into the antipodes, and I thank the South Island for producing the gentle, fierce Jane McCabe, who has now become a permanent inhabitant in my imaginative landscape.

The bulk of the work of revising the thesis was undertaken during my years as a McKenzie Postdoctoral Research Fellow. I thank Andrew May for hosting me at the History Department at the University of Melbourne. Many conversations strengthened this book as I rewrote. For these I thank Jordana Silverstein, Crystal McKinnon, Mary Tomsic, Kat Ellinghaus, the late Tracey Banivanua-Mar, Anthony Garnaut, Shahla Jabeen, Hafsa Khan, Kirsten McKenzie, Nur Shkembi, Richard White, Luise Hercus, Jane Simpson, Philip Jones, Ann Curthoys, Andrew Fitzmaurice, Michael McDonnell, Jackie Flecknoe-Brown, Rochelle Pinto, Oishik Sircar, Debolina Dutta, Fatima Mawas, Nicolas Low, Jerome Small, Nadia Faragaab, Shakira Hussein, Leigh Hopkinson, Léuli Eshrāghi, Beth Sometimes, Stephen Mushin, Shona Russell, Esme Holmes, Dominic Kirchner and Minoru Hokari, who kept appearing in my dreams even though I never met him. Gábor Korvin generously shared research findings and answered many questions over the years. I thank Helen Gill, Noel Turner, Dave Gregurke and Lady for their life-giving company between the bursts of intense solitude in my Brunswick studio.

In Melbourne I was privileged to pick up an earlier conversation about history writing and race with Marilyn Lake, whose generosity was extraordinary. I thank Marilyn for not only mentoring me through some miserable moments of postdoctoral precarity but also setting up an extended encounter with Catherine Hall that profoundly shaped this book. In 2015, Catherine and I co-taught a postgraduate intensive course titled 'Race Gender Empire' at the University of Melbourne and the debates that we began in those classrooms were crucial to crystallising my arguments about historical storytelling and modernity. I thank Catherine for the thrilling conversations that have continued in the Sydney Botanical Gardens, in her kitchen in London, on Hampstead Heath, and on the pages of this book.

I presented draft chapters at lectures at the South Asia Institute at the University of Texas in Austin, the New Zealand India Research Institute at the Victoria University of Wellington, the Brick Lane Circle in London, the Department of History at the University of New South Wales in Sydney, BRAC University and Jahangirnagar University in Bangladesh, the South Asia Series at Harvard University, the Middle Bengali Reading Workshop in Transylvania and the Conference on South Asia in Madison. These occasions were invaluable chances to sound out my arguments with audiences with South Asianist expertise. For their feedback I thank Rebecca Manring, Indrani Chatterjee, Azfar Moin, Pamela Ballinger, Jason Cons, David Curley, Sydney Shep, Firdous Azim, Syed Akbar Hyder, Samia Huq, Frank Korom, Farina Mir, Will Glover, Vivek Bald, Ovee Chowdhury, Muhammad Ahmedullah, Sekhar Bandyopadhyay, Kama Maclean and Layli Uddin. I am particularly indebted to Ishan Chakrabarti for ongoing exquisite discussions about non-modern South Asian texts and to Salman Hussain for inviting me to present at the Anthro-History workshop at the University of Michigan.

I thank the various funding bodies that supported my research. These included an Australian Postgraduate Award and the Endeavour Asia Research Fellowship awarded by the Australian government, the John Merewether Fellowship awarded by the State Library of NSW, a Mentorship Grant from the Copyright Agency Limited, Australia, the McKenzie Fellowship Scheme awarded by the University of Melbourne, and a grant from the American Institute of Bangladesh Studies. Earlier drafts of chapters in this book were published in *Gender & History* and *Transfers: Interdisciplinary Journal of Mobility Studies*. I thank the editors and readers of these journals and in particular M. J. Maynes and Georgine Clarsen for their detailed feedback. I also thank the three anonymous peer reviewers of the draft manuscript whose comments made clear precisely what was illegible about Australia for audiences in North America and the UK.

ACKNOWLEDGEMENTS

The last round of revisions to this book was undertaken after I began the exhilarating work of teaching history at the University of Liberal Arts Bangladesh (ULAB). For their keen interest in my research I thank the Bangladeshi scholarly community and particularly Azfar Hussain, Ahmed Kamal, Nurul Kabir, Salimullah Khan and Mahruba Mowtushi for reading parts of the manuscript. To my uncle Neaz Morshed Quaderi and cousin Shayantani Twisha, I offer my deepest gratitude for sharing their home with me. Given the exhausting demands of re-entry to Dhaka combined with teaching and curriculum design, I simply would not have been able to find the time for book rewrites and copyedits if it weren't for the work of Mehenika Nurjahan, Baby Begum and Giyas Uddin, employed as a cook, cleaner and driver respectively in my family home. I thank them for their domestic labour in a strange new reality in which I suddenly do almost none. I thank my family scattered across the world for their enthusiasm for this book and I am especially indebted to my great-aunt Sanjida Khatun, without whom I would not have had any point of re-entry to Bangladesh.

The friendship of many people sustained me during the unusually tumultuous decade that I was writing this book. I thank Seuty Sabur, the glorious Sarah Waheed, Sayam Ghosh, Mahfuz Sadique, Tariq Omar Ali, Nader Ruhayel, Ned Bertz, Rachel Seoighe, Piers Gooding, Samiya Selim, Pushpita Alam, Tabassum Zaman, Shoumik Hassin, and Daisy Rockwell for her spot on forecasting about 'where to next'. I am indebted to the love of Paulina Fusitu'a, John DeSatge, Shona Russell, Willie Leslie, Naomi Cook, Kirsten Gray, Naveed Ahmed Nadvi and Afrin Sumaya. I also thank the Coogee Women's Baths in addition to every single ocean, river and waterhole I jumped into with these friends. I thank Ali Cobby Eckermann for her extraordinary friendship. It was while sitting with Ali that I began to remember and articulate some of the events I share in this book. No words are adequate to thank Emma Torzillo for being there at every important moment over years and years of friendship. I thank the Goodall-Torzillos for inviting me into their family, feeding my mind, shaping my politics and also for constantly lending me money!

It was hard to finish this book. When I last visited Kolkata, my dear friend Sutanuka Bhattacharya astutely observed that the lonely process of book writing seemed akin to sitting in a dark room alone with mum's *navi* (navel), where the umbilical cord begins. As Sutanaka explained, when her own mother died too early, the only part of her that didn't burn when she was cremated was the *navi*. Not even fire can destroy your connection to your mother, goes the story. Along with ashes Sutanuka and her sister had to put their mother's *navi* in a little earthen vessel and set it afloat on the river. But as a child, Sutanaka found it too hard to let go of the last remaining part of her mother. It was her uncle who had to push it out of her hands and into the water, she explained.

At a juncture in Melbourne where I felt terribly trapped in this book, when I shared this *navi* story with author and friend Helen Garner, she stepped in immediately. She ordered me to let go of the manuscript in a fierce email that I did not dare disobey. Submitting to her commands led me into the experienced hands of the legendary editor and retired Australian publisher, Hilary McPhee. I was terrified of Hilary for a long time and she deftly harnessed my fear for the purposes of manuscript completion. Under her direction the chapters actually became a book. I am greatly indebted to Hilary and Helen for their care and perhaps can only thank them adequately by one day passing it on.

It was in dialogue with Farhaana Arefin, editor at Hurst in London, that the final chapter of this book came together in Dhaka. The universe somehow conspired to set in place exactly the right person with whom to bring the writing to completion and I thank Farhaana for all her patient, hard work in getting this book to press.

Finally, I am indebted to Aviva Tuffield for believing in this book and the team at University of Queensland Press for facilitating the continued circulation of these stories through that beautiful, infuriating place known today as Australia.

INDEX

INDEX